BEST ROAD TRIPS
CALIFORNIA

ESCAPES ON THE OPEN ROAD

ANDREW BENDER, BRETT ATKINSON, AMY BALFOUR, ALISON BING,
CRISTIAN BONETTO, CELESTE BRASH, JADE BREMNER, BAILEY FREEMAN,
MICHAEL GROSBERG, ASHLEY HARRELL, MARK JOHANSON,
ANDREA SCHULTE-PEEVERS, WENDY YANAGIHARA

Contents

PLAN YOUR TRIP
Welcome to California 4
Our Picks 6
When to Go 12
Get Prepared for
California 14

BY REGION
California's Greatest Hits
& Las Vegas 18
Mission Trail 26
Pacific Coast Highways 30

NORTHERN
CALIFORNIA 39
Marin County 42
Bay Area Culinary Tour 48
Napa Valley 52
Sonoma Valley 58
Healdsburg & Around 62
Russian River
& Bohemian Highway 66
Mendocino
& Anderson Valley 70
Lost Coast
& Southern Redwoods 74
Northern Redwood Coast 78
Trinity Scenic Byway 82
Volcanic Legacy Byway 86

CENTRAL
CALIFORNIA 91
Big Sur 94
Along Highway 1
to Santa Cruz 98
Around Monterey & Carmel 102
Around San Luis Obispo 106
Santa Barbara Wine Country 110
Lake Tahoe Loop 114
Yosemite, Sequoia
& Kings Canyon 118
Eastern Sierra Scenic Byway 124
Highway 49
Through Gold Country 130
Ebbetts Pass Scenic Byway 136
Feather River Scenic Byway 140
Sacramento Delta & Lodi 144

SOUTHERN
CALIFORNIA 149
Disneyland &
Orange County Beaches 152
Fun on the
San Diego Coast 156
SoCal Pop Culture 162
Route 66 166
Life in Death Valley 172
Palm Springs
& Joshua Tree Oases 178
Temecula, Julian
& Anza-Borrego 182

BACK MATTER
Arriving 188
Getting Around 189
Accommodations 190
Cars 191
Health & Safe Travel 192
Responsible Travel 193
Nuts & Bolts 194

NORTHERN CALIFORNIA p39

CENTRAL CALIFORNIA p91

SOUTHERN CALIFORNIA p149

Welcome to California

California dreamin'? The reality's even better. Grab your keys, slip on your sunglasses and put the pedal to the metal. Incredible landscapes, sensational food and glimpses of the future all await on the USA's creative coast.

Already live in California? Rest assured there are plenty more scenic routes, swimming holes and a goldmine of mom-and-pop restaurants to discover.

California's road trips swoop from the breezy, wildlife-rich Pacific coast, to the towering redwoods of Big Sur and the north, to off-the-beaten-track deserts and gold-rush towns, to big-name national parks including Yosemite, Death Valley and Joshua Tree, and through the vine-strewn valleys of celebrated wine countries from Sonoma to Santa Barbara. From backcountry lanes to beachside byways, the Golden State's got something for you.

Pacific Coast Highway, Big Sur (p94)
DOUG MEEK/SHUTTERSTOCK ©

Our Picks

BEST NATURE ROUTES

In California, Mother Nature has been as prolific as Picasso in his prime. Blissful beaches, unspoiled wilderness, big-shouldered mountains, high-country meadows, desert sand dunes and trees as tall as the Statue of Liberty – this land is an intoxicating mosaic that has inspired visionaries, artists and wanderers for centuries.

ZERO EMMISSIONS

California is an environmental regulation leader. By 2035, all new cars and light trucks sold statewide must be zero-emission.

Pacific Coast Highway

Cruise the broad, blissful beaches of Hwy 1 from San Diego to Big Sur and beyond.

P.30

Avenue of the Giants

Find your inspiration winding your way past the world's biggest redwood trees in Humboldt County.

P.74

Kings Canyon Scenic Byway

Descend into California's deepest river canyon, an eye-popping, twisting drive full of giant sequoias.

P.118

Ebbetts Pass Scenic Byway

Climb over the rooftop of the Sierra Nevada from Gold Country to Lake Tahoe.

P.134

Eastern Sierra Scenic Byway

Trace the rugged backside of the Sierra Nevada mountains, for high-altitude vistas and ghost towns.

P.124

California coastal redwood forest (p74)

BEST ROAD TRIPS: CALIFORNIA   Bixby Creek Bridge, Hwy 1 (p98)

PLASTIC BANS
A number of California municipalities have banned plastic straws and Styrofoam in food service. Single-use items like ketchup packets are on request only.

Our Picks

BEST SMALL TOWNS

Los Angeles, San Francisco and San Diego may grab the spotlight, but outside the big cities you can still find the charm of old California. From miner towns to hippie haunts, amble through farm towns, don dude-ranch chic, sip wine, soak in hot springs, scarf apple pie and relive the past that continues to make the Golden State, well, golden.

FREE ENTRY

Some of California's nearly 300 state parks have free admission; others charge $10-plus to park; many residents park outside and walk in.

Arcata
Bohemian, college-town counterculture behind the Redwood Curtain, in the heart of the North Coast.
P.85

Calistoga
The place for Napa Valley's blue-jeans-and-boots crowd and hot-springs lovers.
P.54

Nevada City
Relive history in this atmospheric, Old West mining town with a quaint main drag.
P.135

Los Olivos
Early California charm rules amid the vineyards and horse ranches of Santa Barbara Wine Country.
P.112

Julian
Pine-covered mountains, tree-shaded valleys and apple pie for days, in northern San Diego County.
P.184

Calistoga, Napa Valley (p54)

DRAGAN JOVANOVIC/SHUTTERSTOCK ©

BEST ROAD TRIPS: CALIFORNIA

Our Picks

BEST FOODIE FAVOURITES

California cuisine is a team effort that changes with every season – and it has changed the way the world eats. Fusion here is not a fad but second nature. It starts with seasonal, local ingredients courtesy of the Mediterranean climate and soil. Then, foodways from across Mexico, Latin America and Asia – even the Caribbean and Africa – bring extra spice. No matter your palate, there's a way to satisfy it.

KIDS' MENUS

When traveling with littles ones, call restaurants ahead to make sure they can accommodate food and seating needs.

Grand Central Market, Los Angeles (p23)

 1

Ferry Building
Duck inside SF's landmark featuring local, sustainable food producers and a legendary farmers market.

P.19

 2

Napa & Sonoma Wine Country
Taste your way through this idyllic, epicurean paradise which put California wines on the culinary map.

P.52

 3

Bay Area
Wander the aisles of farmers markets and drop in on artisanal food and drink producers.

P.48

 4

Grand Central Market
For smashburgers to vegan ramen, roam Downtown LA's gourmet food hall, going strong since 1917.

P.23

 5

Highway 49 & Gold Country
Sip Zinfandel in the Sierra Nevada foothills and explore the farms of Apple Hill.

P.130

Our Picks

BEST ROADSIDE ATTRACTIONS

Life's a beach in California, and so much more as well. When the fog lifts, the state's 840 miles of shoreline truly give its 'golden' moniker justice. Warm, wide beaches fill the south; rock crags, mists and drama define the north. Find family fun in La Jolla, ogle world-class surfers in Huntington Beach, mingle with eccentrics in Venice Beach, cuddle at sunset in Big Sur, or find yourself on the stunning Lost Coast. And alongside the classics, you'll find quirky, roadside oddities.

SAFETY FIRST
If outdoors during an earthquake, stay in an open space. If indoors, get under a desk or table.

Trees of Mystery
Animatronic Paul Bunyan in the redwoods, a shameless but lovable tourist trap in Klamath.
P.81

Solvang
Where windmills collide with Danish village kitsch, a great base for Santa Barbara Wine Country.
P.111

Elmer's Place
Folk-art 'bottle trees' in a desolate stretch of desert on the iconic Route 66.
P.166

World's Biggest Dinosaurs
These concrete behemoths outside Palm Springs are no desert apparition, but they sure are fun.
P.25

Mirage Volcano
Erupting nightly on the Las Vegas Strip. Then cool off watching the Bellagio's dancing fountains.
P.25

Solvang (p111)

Our Picks

BEST MOVIE MAGIC

To Shakespeare all the world may have been a stage, but in California, it is actually more of a film set. For a century, 'the industry' has made audiences laugh, cry and come back for more. To witness the magic, join a live studio audience or go on a tour of a movie studio in LA. Then stand in the celebrities' footprints and take in some famous filming locations.

LOG IN
Download theme-park apps so you can streamline your visit: check out hours, last-minute closings, dining, maps and more.

Alabama Hills (p124)

1

Hollywood
Stand in a star's footprints at TCL Chinese Theatre, next to the Dolby Theatre, home of the Oscars.
P.165

2

San Francisco
Relive film-noir classics like John Huston's *The Maltese Falcon* and Alfred Hitchcock's *Vertigo*.
P.29

3

Santa Cruz
Play like a *Lost Boy* at the horror-flick locations on the Boardwalk.
P.35

4

Eastern Sierra
Get misty-eyed over old-fashioned Westerns filmed in Lone Pine and the Alabama Hills.
P.124

5

San Diego
Stay classy in filming locations from *Some Like It Hot* to *Top Gun* and *Anchorman*.
P.30

When to Go

California is truly a destination for all seasons, but keep these tips in mind to stay ahead of the weather.

Despite California's 'endless summer' reputation, the climate can differ dramatically across the year and from region to region. That said, it's high season almost everywhere from June through August with kids' school holidays and tourists arriving from around the state, nation and world. Spring in California is brilliant after winter rains, with bright-green meadows and blooming wildflowers. While temperatures are equally comfortable and it can be sunny and cloudless in the fall, increasingly those dry months from September to November have become known as fire season. It's vital to be vigilant about the fire danger – do not light open flames, ever, and keep an eye on the news.

AN LA TRAFFIC REPORTER DRIVES CALIFORNIA

'KFI in the Sky' reporter
Will Kohlschreiber
@WILLonKFI

There are two Californias. The first is the congested tangle of freeways and pothole-scarred streets in densely populated urban centers. The other begins on the 'outskirts' – Interstate 5, just north of State Rte 126. Or I-10 east of Cabazon. Or I-15 at the summit of Cajon Pass.

Here we penetrate an invisible barrier, from city madness to serenity.

Beautiful, open roadways, the scent of ozone and freshly moistened creosote after a thunderstorm, or hundreds of miles of Central Valley farmland.

Then there's that drive along any slice of coastline… Heaven.

Tournament of Roses parade, Pasadena

Weather Watch (San Francisco)

JANUARY	FEBRUARY	MARCH	APRIL	MAY	JUNE
Avg. daytime max: **58°F.**	Avg. daytime max: **61°F.**	Avg. daytime max: **62°F.**	Avg. daytime max: **63°F.**	Avg. daytime max: **64°F.**	Avg. daytime max: **67°F.**
Days of rainfall: **8**	Days of rainfall: **8**	Days of rainfall: **8**	Days of rainfall: **4**	Days of rainfall: **2**	Days of rainfall: **0**

Santa Barbara and the Santa Ynez mountains (p110)

TOP TIP

Time your travel to avoid high season (and the coast most weekends). Accommodations prices are 50% to 100% higher on average than the rest of the year.

Coastal Fog Up North...

Especially in Northern California, summer is marked by coastal fog that doesn't always burn off. San Francisco can be blanketed with fog and chilly, when just inland in Oakland it's a sunny 75°F (24°C). September is the best month for the North Coast.

'May Gray' & 'June Gloom' Down South

Late spring is the foggy season on the Southern California coast. From Santa Barbara through to Los Angeles and San Diego, expect morning fog – and wear layers. Usually the fog burns off by late morning. To avoid fog altogether, stay inland.

MOUNTAIN DRIVING

In California, snowfall is generally linked to elevation (the higher the mountain, the greater the snowfall), and winter storms can require the use of snow tires or chains for your vehicle. Keep an eye on the Caltrans website (dot.ca.gov) whenever snowy weather is forecasted during your travels.

I LIVE HERE

YOSEMITE FILLS THE SOUL

Yosemite-lover, marketing consultant, climber, hiker and skier
Theresa Ho
@sosimplytheresa

For me as a climber, the heart-stopping moment is when you drive into Yosemite Valley and come around the corner, and there's El Capitan right in front of you.

It fills the windshield, from the dashboard to out of sight, and you have to lean forward to see all of it. But my deep-down, soul-filling experience of Yosemite-as-home starts long before that, on the winding roads leading into the mountains.

That's where the emotional sense of belonging, that sense of being in the perfect place for me, really begins.

JULY	AUGUST	SEPTEMBER	OCTOBER	NOVEMBER	DECEMBER
Avg. daytime max: **67°F.**	Avg. daytime max: **68°F.**	Avg. daytime max: **71°F.**	Avg. daytime max: **70°F.**	Avg. daytime max: **64°C.**	Avg. daytime max: **58°F.**
Days of rainfall: **0**	Days of rainfall: **0**	Days of rainfall: **0**	Days of rainfall: **2**	Days of rainfall: **6**	Days of rainfall: **8**

Get Prepared for California

Useful things to load in your bag, your ears and your brain.

Clothing

Casual layers: California is a laid-back, anything-goes kind of place, especially when it comes to fashion. The prevailing style is more 'dress down' than dress up. Even in the business world or for a big night on the town, 'smart casual' will usually be enough.

Weather-conscious gear: Travelers who have only ever seen California on TV are in for a shock along the coast. Here marine fog reprimands anyone who wears shorts all morning, then rolls back in the afternoon to make you wish that you'd worn some sweat-proof sunscreen, and returns by evening to mock any skimpy date-night outfits.

The mountains can be cold and the deserts can be blazing hot. It's best to layer up with sweaters, wraps or light jackets over your underlayers.

Shoes: Walking shoes are essential for both cities and trails alike. Even on a night out, stilettos or natty oxfords are not necessary – just dress however you like.

Sun protection: Sunscreen is essential wherever you go in this state of Endless Summer. It's always a good idea to have a wide-brimmed hat for sun protection, and Californians are famous for wearing sunglasses even when it isn't particularly sunny.

WATCH

Vertigo
(Alfred Hitchcock; 1958)
This famous noir thriller is set in San Francisco, starring James Stewart and Kim Novak.

LA Confidential
(Curtis Hanson; 1997)
A neo-noir tale of corruption and murder in 1950s LA replete with beaucoup glam.

Boyz n the Hood
(John Singleton; 1991)
This groundbreaking coming-of-age story is set in Los Angeles' South Central neighborhood.

Santa Monica Pier

Words

Freeway: Elsewhere in the US, they're called highways, expressways or interstates. According to the US Department of Transportation, they were named 'for the uninterrupted passage of vast numbers of vehicles.' That was in the 1930s and seems quaint now, as anyone who's been in California traffic can attest.

Bay Area: San Francisco Bay and surrounding counties.

Southern California (aka SoCal): Los Angeles and surrounding counties to the Mexican border.

HOV: High occupancy vehicle, as in 'HOV Lane' on the freeway. Don't drive in one if you have fewer than the minimum number of passengers.

CHP: California Highway Patrol, or the state traffic cops.

DUI: Driving under the influence (of alcohol, cannabis etc). Sometimes called DWI (driving while intoxicated). Either way, a big no-no.

SigAlert: SoCal speak for massive traffic jam.

Looky-loos: Drivers who slow down to look at an accident.

LISTEN

American Beauty
(Grateful Dead; 1970)
A peak for these San Francisco rockers, because no song says road trip like 'Truckin'.

Straight Outta Compton
(NWA; 1988)
This pioneering gangsta rap album remains as relevant as when it was released.

Teenage Dream
(Katy Perry; 2010)
An album full of feel-good hits from 'California Gurls' to 'Firework' and the titlular song.

READ

Where I Was From
(Joan Didion; 2003)
California-born essayist shatters the state's palm-fringed fantasies, unsparingly examining everything from individualism to water use.

If They Come in the Morning
(Angela Davis; 1971)
Chronicles of the Black Power movement collected by one of its leading figures.

The Big Sleep
(Raymond Chandler; 1939) This iconic Phillip Marlow mystery based in Los Angeles sets the bar for gumshoes.

ROAD TRIPS

Torrey Pines State Natural Reserve (p160)

Contents

California's Greatest Hits & Las Vegas 18

Mission Trail 26

Pacific Coast Highways 30

NORTHERN CALIFORNIA 39

CENTRAL CALIFORNIA 91

SOUTHERN CALIFORNIA 149

01

California's Greatest Hits & Las Vegas

BEST FOR FOOD & DRINK

Visit Napa Valley wineries and star chefs' tables.

Golden Gate Park, San Francisco

DURATION	DISTANCE	GREAT FOR
12–15 DAYS	1600 miles / 2575km	Wine, Books, Nature

BEST TIME TO GO	June to September for sunny days and snow-free mountain roads.

This epic road trip hits the all-time greats of the Golden State plus a slew of fascinating spots along the way, ultimately stopping in glitzy Las Vegas, Nevada.

Link Your Trip

03 Pacific Coast Highways
California's most famous driving route hugs the Pacific Ocean from Mexico to Oregon. Join up in San Francisco, Big Sur or LA.

31 Life in Death Valley
California's biggest, wildest and most road-trip-worthy national park is just over two hours' drive west of Las Vegas, Nevada.

01 SAN FRANCISCO

In two action-packed days, explore **Golden Gate Park** (sfrecpark.org/770/Golden-Gate-Park), spy on sea lions lolling around **Pier 39** (pier39.com) at Fisherman's Wharf and saunter through the streets of busy **Chinatown** to the Italian sidewalk cafes of **North Beach**. Feast on an overstuffed burrito in the **Mission District** after wandering its mural-splashed alleys.

Queue up at Powell and Market Sts for a ride on a bell-clanging cable car and then cruise to the infamous prison island of **Alcatraz** (alcatraz cruises.com) out in the bay. Book Alcatraz tickets

online at least two weeks ahead. At the foot of Market St, indulge your inner epicurean at the food stalls of the **Ferry Building** (ferrybuildingmarketplace.com), and stop by its **farmers market** (cuesa.org) year-round to wallow in the bounty of California-grown produce and gourmet prepared foods.

Inside the historic **Castro Theatre** (castrotheatre.com), the crowd goes wild when the great organ rises from the floor and pumps out show tunes until the movie starts, and the sumptuous chandelier complements a repertory of silver-screen classics.

THE DRIVE
Without traffic jams, it's an hour's drive from San Francisco to Napa, the nexus of Wine Country. Take Hwy 101 north over the soaring Golden Gate Bridge, stopping at the Vista Point on the far side of the bridge, and into Marin County. Zigzag northeast on Hwys 37, 121, 12 and 29 to reach downtown Napa.

02 NAPA VALLEY
The Napa Valley is famous for regal cabernet sauvignon, château-like wineries and fabulous food. The city of Napa anchors the valley, but the real work happens up-valley. Scenic towns along Hwy 29 include St Helena, Yountville and

Hiking Half Dome
Just hold on, don't forget to breathe and – whatever you do – don't look down. A pinnacle so popular that hikers need a permit to scale it, Half Dome lives on as Yosemite Valley's must-reach-it obsession for millions. Reaching the top can only be done when the fixed cables are up, usually from late May until mid-October. Permits go on sale by lottery in March, with a limited number via another daily lottery two days in advance during hiking season. See **nps.gov/yose/planyourvisit/hdpermits.htm** for details.

BEST ROAD TRIPS: CALIFORNIA 19

Calistoga – the last more famous for its natural hot-springs water than its wine.

Start by the river in downtown Napa, where the **Oxbow Public Market** (xbowpublicmarket.com) showcases all things culinary – produce stalls, kitchen shops, and everywhere something to taste – with emphasis on seasonal eating and sustainability. Come hungry.

A dozen miles north of Napa, tour buses flock to the corporate-owned **Robert Mondavi Winery** (robertmondaviwinery.com); if you know nothing about wine and can cope with crowds, the worthwhile tours provide excellent insight into winemaking.

Driving back down-valley, follow the bucolic **Silverado Trail**, which passes several other landmark, over-the-top wineries, including **Robert Sinskey Vineyards** (robertsinskey.com), where a dramatic hilltop tasting room resembles a small cathedral.

THE DRIVE
From Napa, it's a four-hour drive of nearly 200 miles to the dramatic Big Sur coast. Head south over the Carquinez Bridge to Berkeley, then sail over the Bay Bridge into San Francisco, taking Hwy 101 south toward Silicon Valley. Detour on Hwy 17 over the mountains to Santa Cruz, then join Hwy 1 south past Monterey and Carmel-by-the-Sea.

03 BIG SUR

Highway 1 along Big Sur coast may be the most famous stretch of highway in the entire state. The road twists and turns a thousand feet above the vast blue Pacific, hugging the skirts of mile-high sea cliffs, above which California condors fly. In the 1950s and '60s, Big Sur – so named by Spanish settlers who referred to the wilderness as *el país grande del sur* (the big country to the south) – became a bohemian retreat for artists and writers, including Henry Miller and the Beat Generation. Today it attracts new-age mystics, hippies and city slickers seeking to unplug on this emerald-green edge of the continent.

All along Hwy 1 in Big Sur's **state parks** (parks.ca.gov), you'll find hiking trails through forests of redwoods (incidentally, the tallest trees on earth) and to magical waterfalls – don't miss **McWay Falls**, which tumbles onto an ocean beach.

THE DRIVE

It's a five-hour, 220-mile trip from Big Sur to Yosemite Valley. Backtrack north on coastal Hwy 1 past Monterey, then veer inland through California's agricultural valleys, taking Hwy 152 east past San Luis Reservoir and crossing I-5, then continuing east toward Hwy 99. Outside Merced, join Hwy 140 – an all-weather highway normally open year-round – to Yosemite National Park.

04 YOSEMITE NATIONAL PARK
With wild rock formations, astonishing waterfalls, vast swaths of granite and humbling Sierra Nevada peaks, **Yosemite National Park** (nps.gov/yose) is no less than perfect. On your way in, stop at **Tunnel View** to drink in views of the Yosemite Valley, with iconic Half Dome and plunging Bridalveil Fall in the distance. Go deeper into the valley to see triple-decker **Yosemite Falls** up close, or to hike the Mist Trail, which climbs a rocky staircase beside mighty Vernal and Nevada Falls. Drive up to **Glacier Point** to catch a brilliant sunset. The next day, detour along high-elevation Tioga Rd (closed in winter and spring) to wildflower-strewn **Tuolumne Meadows**, encircled by skyscraping peaks and granite domes. Picnic beside sparkling **Tenaya Lake** and pull over at roadside Olmsted Point for panoramic views over the rooftop of the Sierra Nevada. Then backtrack down to the valley and take Hwy 41 south, exiting the park near the **Mariposa Grove** of giant sequoia trees.

THE DRIVE

It's a straight shot south on Hwy 41 from Yosemite's south entrance to Fresno, then head east on Hwy 180, which eventually

Sequoia National Park (p22)

TOP TIP:

Driving in All Weather

If you plan on driving this route in winter, be prepared for snow in the Sierra Nevada; carry tire chains in your car. During summer, the deserts can be dangerously hot; avoid overheating your car by not running the air-conditioning and by traveling in the cooler morning and late-afternoon hours.

winds uphill and gains over 6000ft in elevation to enter Kings Canyon National Park. The 120-mile trip to Grant Grove Village takes about 2½ hours, without traffic.

05 KINGS CANYON NATIONAL PARK

From **giant sequoia** crowns down into one of the USA's deepest canyons, the twisting scenic drive in **Kings Canyon National Park** (nps.gov/seki) is an eye-popping, jaw-dropping revelation.

At the northern end of the Generals Hwy, take a walk in **General Grant Grove**, encompassing the world's second-largest living tree, then wash off all that sweat with a dip down the road at **Hume Lake**.

Get back on the **Kings Canyon Scenic Byway** (Hwy 180; closed in winter and spring), which makes a precipitous descent, and make sure you pull over to survey the canyon depths and lofty Sierra Nevada peaks from Junction View. At the bottom of the canyon, cruise past Cedar Grove Village. Admire striking canyon views from verdant **Zumwalt Meadow**, a wildlife-watching hot spot with a boardwalk nature trail. At truthfully named **Road's End**, cool off by the sandy Kings River beach or make an 8-mile round-trip hike to **Mist Falls**, which roars in late spring and early summer.

Photo Opportunity

Stop at Tunnel View to drink in views of Yosemite Valley.

 THE DRIVE
It's only a 60-mile drive from Cedar Grove to the Giant Forest in Sequoia National Park, but it can take nearly two hours, thanks to hairpin turns and gawking drivers. Backtrack along the Kings Canyon Scenic Byway (Hwy 180) to Grant Grove, then wind south on the Generals Hwy through the sun-dappled forests of the Giant Sequoia National Monument.

06 SEQUOIA NATIONAL PARK

Big trees, deep caves and high granite domes are all on the agenda for this day-long tour of Sequoia National Park. Arriving in the Giant Forest, let yourself be

Hume Lake, King's Canyon National Park

dwarfed by the majestic **General Sherman Tree**. Learn more about giant sequoias at the **Giant Forest Museum** (nps.gov/seki). Snap a photo of your car driving through the **Tunnel Log**, or better yet, leave your car behind and hop on the park shuttle for a wildflower walk around Crescent Meadow and to climb the puff-and-pant stairway up **Moro Rock**, granting bird's-eye canyon and peak views.

Picnic by the river at the **Lodgepole Market Center**, then get back in the car and make your way to the chilly underground wonderland of **Crystal Cave** (recreation.gov) where you can marvel at delicate marble formations while easing through eerie passageways. You must book tour tickets online in advance. Before sunset, take the dizzyingly steep drive down the Generals Hwy into the **Foothills** area, stopping at riverside swimming holes.

 THE DRIVE
After a few days in the wilderness, get ready to zoom down to California's biggest city. The fastest route to Los Angeles takes at least 3½ hours to cover 200 miles. Follow Hwy 198 west of Three Rivers to Hwy 65 south through the valley. In Bakersfield, join Hwy 99 south to I-5, which streams south toward LA.

07 LOS ANGELES
Make a pilgrimage to **Hollywood**, with its pink-starred sidewalks, blingy nightclubs and restored movie palaces. Long ago, the TV and movie biz (locals just call it 'the Industry') decamped over the hills to the **San Fernando Valley**. Peek behind the scenes on a **Warner Bros Studio Tour**

WHY I LOVE THIS TRIP
Amy C Balfour, writer

This jam-packed journey sweeps in the best of California – beaches, mountains, deserts, wineries, big trees and even bigger cities. It even includes the glitzy charms of Las Vegas, a casino-loving city a short hop away in Nevada and a favorite weekend getaway for Californians. The Sierra Nevada mountains are best visited in summer; spring brings wildflower blooms to the deserts.

(wbstudiotour.com), or get a thrill along with screaming tweens at **Universal Studios Hollywood** (universalstudioshollywood.com).

Downtown LA is a historical, multilayered and fascinating city within a city, known for its landmark architecture. Wander through the old town of **El Pueblo** (elpueblo.lacity.org), then be awed by the museum of art **Broad** (thebroad.org), which is free but requires reservation, before partying at the entertainment complex **LA Live** (lalive.com) and worshipping at the star-spangled altar of the **Grammy Museum** (grammymuseum.org).

Grab a bite at the gourmet food market **Grand Central Market** (grandcentralmarket.com) before hitting LA's sunny beaches. This is a must-do – and pretty darn fun. In laid-back **Santa Monica** and hipper **Venice**, you can mix with the surf rats, skate punks, muscled bodybuilders, yogis and street performers along a stretch of sublime coastline cradling the city.

THE DRIVE
It's a tedious 25-mile trip south on I-5 between Downtown LA and Anaheim. The drive can take well over an hour, especially in rush-hour traffic. As you approach Anaheim, follow the freeway signs and take exit 110b for Disneyland.

08 DISNEYLAND
When Walt Disney opened **Disneyland** (disneyland.com) on July 17, 1955, he declared it the 'Happiest Place on Earth.' More than 65 years later, it's hard to argue with the ear-to-ear grins on the faces of kiddos, grandparents, honeymooners and everyone else here in Anaheim.

If you've only got one day to spend at Disneyland, buy tickets online in advance and arrive early. Stroll **Main Street USA** toward Sleeping Beauty Castle. Enter Tomorrowland to ride Space Mountain. In Fantasyland don't miss the classic 'It's a Small World' ride or racing downhill on the Matterhorn Bobsleds.

Grab a FASTPASS for the Indiana Jones Adventure or the Pirates of the Caribbean before lunching in New Orleans Square. Plummet down Splash Mountain, then visit the Haunted Mansion before the Fantasmic! show and fireworks begin.

In the **Galaxy's Edge** area, which celebrates the best of the *Star Wars* movie franchise, the thrilling Millennium Falcon: Smugglers Run hurtles you into hyperspace.

 THE DRIVE
A few different routes from Anaheim to Palm Springs all eventually funnel onto I-10 eastbound from Los Angeles. It's a trip of almost 100 miles, which should take less than three hours without traffic jams.

Watch for the towering wind turbines on the hillsides as you shoot through San Gorgonio Pass. Take Hwy 111 south to downtown Palm Springs.

 PALM SPRINGS
In the 1950s and '60s, Palm Springs was the swinging getaway of Sinatra, Elvis and dozens of other stars. Now a new generation has fallen for the city's mid-century modern charms: steel-and-glass bungalows designed by famous architects, boutique hotels with vintage decor and kidney-shaped pools, and hip bars serving perfect martinis.

North of downtown 'PS,' ride the revolving **Palm Springs Aerial Tramway** (pstramway.com) which climbs 6000ft vertically in under 15 minutes. It's 30°F to 40°F (up to 22°C) cooler as you step out into pine forest at the top, so bring warm clothing – the ride up from the desert floor is said to be the equivalent (in temperature) of driving from Mexico to Canada.

Down-valley in Rancho Mirage, **Sunnylands** (sunnylands.org) was the glamorous modern estate of the Annenberg family. Explore the magnificent desert gardens or book ahead for tours of the stunning house with its art collection.

THE DRIVE
North of Palm Springs, take I-10 west to Hwy 62, which winds northeast to the high desert around Joshua Tree. The 35-mile trip goes by quickly; it should take you less than an hour to reach the park's west entrance. Fuel up first in the town of Joshua Tree – there's no gas, food or water inside the park.

DETOUR
World's Biggest Dinosaurs
Start: **Palm Springs**

West of Palm Springs, you may do a double take when you see the **World's Biggest Dinosaurs** (cabazondinosaurs.com). Claude K Bell, a sculptor for Knott's Berry Farm, spent over a decade crafting these concrete behemoths, now owned by Christian creationists who contend that God created the original dinosaurs in one day, along with the other animals, as part of his 'intelligent design.' In the gift shop you'll find the sort of dino-swag you might find at science museums.

10 JOSHUA TREE NATIONAL PARK
Taking a page from a Dr Seuss book, whimsical-looking Joshua trees (actually tree-sized yuccas) symbolize this **national park** (nps.gov/jotr) at the convergence of the Colorado and Mojave Deserts. Allegedly, it was Mormon settlers who named the trees because the branches stretching toward heaven reminded them of the biblical prophet pointing the way to the promised land.

Rock climbers know 'JTree' as the best place to climb in California, but kids and the young at heart also welcome the chance to scramble up, down and around the giant boulders. Hikers seek hidden, shady, desert-fan-palm oases fed by natural springs and small streams. Book ahead for fascinating guided tours of **Keys Ranch** (nps.gov/jotr), built by a 20th-century desert homesteader. Scenic drives worth taking inside the park include the side road to panoramic **Keys View** and the Pinto Basin Rd, which winds down to Cottonwood Spring, letting you watch nature transition from the high Mojave Desert to the low Colorado Desert. A bird's-eye view of the park is your reward at the end of the steep **Ryan Mountain Trail**.

THE DRIVE
It's a gloriously scenic back-road adventure to Las Vegas, three hours and nearly 200 miles away. From Twentynine Palms, Amboy Rd barrels east then north, opening up desert panoramas. At Amboy, head east on Route 66 and north on Kelbaker Rd across I-40 into the Mojave National Preserve. North of the preserve, join I-15 northbound to Las Vegas.

 LAS VEGAS, NEVADA
Vegas is the ultimate escape. It's the only place in the world where you can spend the night partying in ancient Rome, wake up in Egypt, brunch under the Eiffel Tower, watch an erupting volcano at sunset and get married in a pink Cadillac at midnight.

Double down with the high rollers, pick up some tacky souvenirs and sip a neon 3ft-high margarita as you stroll along the Strip. Traipse through mini versions of New York, Paris and Venice before riding the **High Roller**, the world's tallest Ferris wheel (for now). After dark, go glam at ultra-modern casino resorts Cosmopolitan and Wynn.

Do you like old-school casinos, vintage neon signs and dive bars? No problem. Head downtown to historic 'Glitter Gulch' along the **Fremont Street Experience**, a pedestrian-only zone with the **Slotzilla** zip-line canopy (vegasexperience.com), near the **Mob Museum** (themobmuseum.org). Afterward, mingle with locals at hip hangouts in the **Fremont East** district.

02

Mission Trail

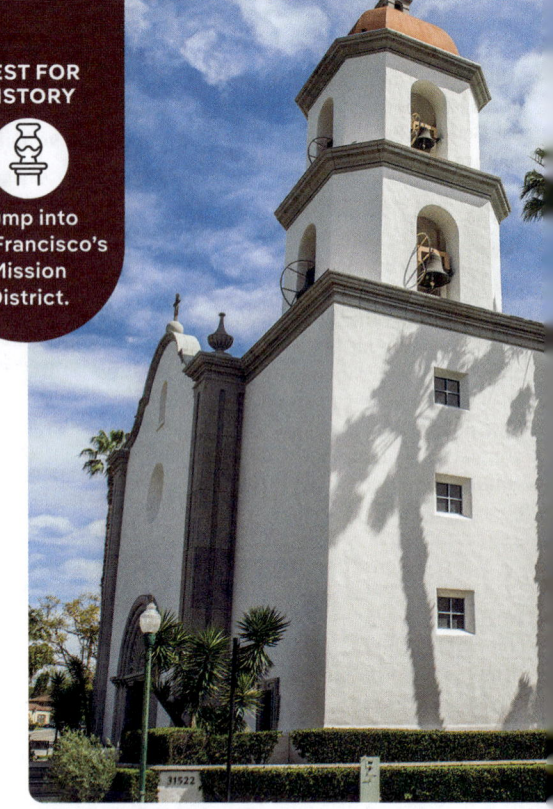

BEST FOR HISTORY

Jump into San Francisco's Mission District.

DURATION	DISTANCE	GREAT FOR
5 days	620 miles / 998km	Books, Food, History

BEST TIME TO GO	April to October for sunny skies.

Mission San Juan Capistrano

Established over the course of more than 50 years, a chain of 21 missions stretches along El Camino Real (the Royal Road), first forged by Spanish conquistador Gaspar de Portolá and Franciscan priest Junípero Serra in the late 18th century. Each mission was a day's ride on horseback from the next, but today you can drive the entire route in less than a week.

Link Your Trip

03 Pacific Coast Highways
California's mission trail intersects with the classic coastal route at San Diego, Los Angeles, Santa Barbara and San Francisco.

07 Sonoma Valley
Where this trip ends at Sonoma Plaza, you can start exploring Northern California's rustic-chic Wine Country.

01 SAN DIEGO

In the spring of 1769, a forlorn lot of about 100 Spanish soldiers and missionaries straggled ashore at San Diego Bay. After sailing for weeks up the coast from Baja California, many were sick and over half had died. They were soon joined by Padre Junípero Serra, who had traveled from Baja California by land. Serra spearheaded the establishment that year of **Mission Basilica San Diego de Alcalá** (missionsandiego.org), the oldest in California's chain of missions. West atop Presidio Hill, the **Junípero Serra Museum** (sandiegohistory.

org) recounts Native American struggles with mission life. Where the colonists' original military fort and church once stood, this 1920s Spanish Colonial Revival building echoes early mission architecture.

Nearby, **Old Town San Diego State Historic Park** (parks.ca.gov) preserves buildings from the Spanish, Mexican and early American periods, with an old-fashioned plaza surrounded by shops and cafes.

THE DRIVE
El Camino Real, which is marked throughout California by freestanding bronze mission bells erected in the 1920s, follows I-5 north from San Diego. After more than 60 miles, exit onto Hwy 74 (Ortega Hwy), turn left and drive west to Mission San Juan Capistrano.

 SAN JUAN CAPISTRANO
Archaeologists, engineers and restoration artists have done an exquisite job of keeping alive **Mission San Juan Capistrano** (missionsjc.com). Built around a series of 18th-century arcades, the mission complex encloses bubbling fountains and flowery gardens. The **Serra Chapel**, where the padre first celebrated mass in 1783, is considered California's oldest building, and even the mighty San Andreas Fault hasn't been able to topple it yet. Every year on March 19, the **Festival of the Swallows** celebrates the birds' return from their Argentine sojourn to make their nests in the mission's walls. One block west, by the train depot, the tree-shaded **Los Rios Historic District** comprises quaint cottages and adobes housing cafes and gift shops.

THE DRIVE
Get back on I-5 north for the often traffic-jammed 50-mile drive to downtown Los Angeles. Take the Alameda St/Union Station exit, turn right onto Main St and look for metered street parking or pay-parking lots.

 LOS ANGELES
A few dozen Spanish colonists founded the 'City of Angels' in 1781, near the

site of today's **El Pueblo de Los Ángeles Historical Monument** (elpueblo.lacity.org). Peek inside 19th-century historical buildings like the Avila Adobe and 'La Placita' plaza church and jostle down crowded block-long Olvera St, an open-air marketplace lined with Mexican food vendors and *folklorico* shops, then unwind in front of the wrought-iron bandstand, where mariachis often play on sunny weekend afternoons. Nearby, **LA Plaza** (lapca.org) vibrantly chronicles the Mexican American experience in LA.

 THE DRIVE
Follow Hwy 101 north of Downtown LA past Hollywood and west through the suburban San Fernando Valley all the way to the Pacific coast. Northwest of Ventura, another SoCal mission town with beautiful beaches, lies Santa Barbara, about 100 miles from LA.

04 SANTA BARBARA
After a magnitude 6.3 earthquake hit Santa Barbara in 1925, downtown's State St was entirely rebuilt in Spanish Colonial Revival style, with whitewashed adobe walls and red-tile roofs. Head north to hillside **Old Mission Santa Barbara** (santabarbaramission.org), another victim of historical quakes. From the front of its imposing Doric facade, itself a homage to an ancient Roman chapel, you can look up at the unique twin bell towers.

Founded in 1786 on the feast day of St Barbara, the mission has been continuously occupied by Franciscan priests, having escaped Mexico's enforced policy of secularization that destroyed most of California's other missions. Artwork by Chumash

WHY I LOVE THIS TRIP
Amy C Balfour, writer

California's original road trip connects a string of Spanish colonial missions, beautified by sunny cloisters, adobe buildings and pleasingly frescoed chapels. Striking in their reverent simplicity, the missions are direct links to the earliest days of the modern state. The most moving of them thoughtfully spotlight the glories as well as the tragedies stemming from their creation. Serene San Juan Capistrano should not be missed.

tribespeople adorns the chapel. Look for a centuries-old cemetery out back.

 THE DRIVE
El Camino Real follows Hwy 101 north. For a more scenic route, take winding Hwy 154 up into the mountains and Wine Country. Turn left onto Hwy 246 (Mission Dr) toward the Danish village of Solvang, which has a pretty little mission, then keep driving west along Hwy 246 almost to Lompoc. It's a 50-mile trip from Mission Santa Barbara.

05 LA PURÍSIMA MISSION
Drive through the hills outside Lompoc, past vineyards and commercial flower fields, to **La Purísima Mission State Historic Park** (lapurisimamission.org). Resurrected by the Civilian Conservation Corps (CCC) during the Depression era, almost a dozen buildings have been restored to their original 1820s appearance. Amble past Spanish soldiers' living quarters, a weaving room and a blacksmith's shop, all beside grassy fields where cows, horses and goats graze.

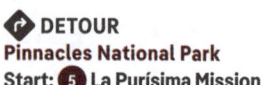 **THE DRIVE**
Follow scenic, rural Hwy 1 north to Pismo Beach, then rejoin Hwy 101 north to San Luis Obispo, a peaceful mission town that's a convenient place to break your journey. The next day, follow Hwy 101 north for 140 miles past Salinas to Hwy 156, connecting east to San Juan Bautista.

↱ **DETOUR**
Pinnacles National Park
Start: **5** La Purísima Mission

Named for the towering spires that rise abruptly out of the chaparral-covered hills, this **park** (nps.gov/pinn) is a study in geological drama, with its craggy monoliths, sheer-walled canyons and ancient volcanic remnants. Besides hiking and rock climbing, the park's biggest attractions are its endangered California condors and talus caves where bats live. It's best visited during spring or fall; summer's heat is too extreme. Camping is available near the east entrance off Hwy 25 between San Juan Bautista and King City, accessed via Hwy 101 north of San Luis Obispo.

06 SAN JUAN BAUTISTA
Unknowingly built atop the San Andreas Fault, **Old Mission San Juan Bautista** (oldmissionsjb.org) has the largest church among California's historical missions. The original chapel was toppled by the 1906 San Francisco earthquake. Scenes from Alfred Hitchcock's 1960s film *Vertigo* were shot here, although the climactic bell tower was just a special-effects prop. The old Spanish plaza opposite the mission anchors **San Juan Bautista State Historic Park** (parks.ca.gov). A short walk away, dusty San Juan Bautista is crowded with restaurants and shops.

San Juan Bautista State Historic Park

 THE DRIVE
Backtrack west on Hwy 156 to Hwy 101, which speeds north past Gilroy's garlic farms to San Jose, then curves alongside San Francisco Bay and Silicon Valley. After almost 90 miles, you'll arrive in San Francisco: exit at Duboce Ave, turn left on Guerrero St, then right on 16th St to arrive at Mission San Francisco de Asís.

07 SAN FRANCISCO
Time seems to stand still at **Mission San Francisco de Asís** (missiondolores.org), also known as Mission Dolores. With its gold-leafed altar and redwood beams decorated with Native American artwork, this is the only intact original mission chapel in California, its adobe walls having stood firm in the 1906 earthquake. Today it's overshadowed by the ornate 1913 basilica, where stained-glass windows commemorate the 21 original California missions.

The graveyard out back, where Kim Novak wandered in a daze in Hitchcock's Vertigo, is where 5000 Ohlone and Miwok who died in measles epidemics are memorialized, surrounded by the graves of early Mexican and European settlers.

 THE DRIVE
Hwy 101 rolls up and down San Francisco's famous hills, from the Mission District to the Marina and the Presidio, finally exiting the city via the Golden Gate Bridge. North of the mission town of San Rafael, follow Hwy 37 east to Hwy 121 north, then take Hwy 12 north into downtown Sonoma, over a 40-mile drive from San Francisco.

08 SONOMA
The Wine Country town of Sonoma is not only the site of the last Spanish mission established in California. It also happens to be the place where American settlers attempted to declare independence from Mexico in 1846. Mission San Francisco Solano is now part of **Sonoma State Historic Park** (parks.ca.gov), which preserves military barracks and a mid-19th-century Mexican general's home. Its petite adobe chapel, dating from 1841, is also the finish line for El Camino Real.

03

Pacific Coast Highways

DURATION	DISTANCE	GREAT FOR
7–10 days	1030 miles / 1660km	Families, Drink, Outdoors

BEST TIME TO GO	November to April, but try to avoid school holidays, Christmas and Easter.

Escape from California's tangled, traffic-jammed freeways for a breezy cruise in the slow lane. Once you get rolling, you'll never want to leave those ocean views behind. Officially, only the short, sun-loving stretch of Hwy 1 through Orange and Los Angeles Counties can legally call itself Pacific Coast Highway (PCH). But never mind those technicalities, because equally bewitching ribbons of Hwy 1 and Hwy 101 await all along this route.

Link your trip

15 Big Sur
Get lost on the rugged Big Sur coast, stretched between Hearst Castle and the painterly scenery of Carmel-by-the-Sea on the Monterey Peninsula.

28 Fun on the San Diego Coast
Continue south from Waihi Beach to Tauranga (55km) and around the east coast.

01 SAN DIEGO
At the bottom of the state map, the pretty peninsular beach town of Coronado is connected to the San Diego mainland via the white-sand beaches of the Silver Strand. If you've seen Marilyn Monroe cavort in *Some Like It Hot*, you'll recognize the dapper **Hotel del Coronado** (hoteldel.com), which has hosted US presidents, celebrities and royalty, including the Prince of Wales who gave up his throne to marry a Coronado *divorcée*. Wander the turreted palace's labyrinthine corridors, then quaff tropical cocktails at ocean-view **Babcock & Story Bar**.

BEST FOR TWO DAYS

Explore Santa Barbara north to Monterey via Big Sur.

San Diego–Coronado Bridge

Hold tight driving over the 2.1-mile-long **San Diego–Coronado Bridge**. Detour inland to Balboa Park. Head west, then south to Point Loma's **Cabrillo National Monument** (nps.gov/cabr) for captivating bay panoramas from the 19th-century lighthouse and monument to the West Coast's first Spanish explorers. Roll north of Mission Beach and the old-fashioned amusement park at Pacific Beach, and suddenly you're in hoity-toity **La Jolla**, beyond which lie North County's beach towns.

THE DRIVE
It's a 70-mile trip from La Jolla north along coastal roads then I-5 into Orange County (aka the 'OC'), passing Camp Pendleton Marine Corps Base and recently shuttered – but still decommissioning – San Onofre Nuclear Generating Station. Exit at San Clemente and follow Avenida del Mar downhill to the beach.

 02 SAN CLEMENTE
In off-the-beaten-path spots such as beautiful San Clemente, sloping steeply toward the sea, the Orange County coast feels like a trip back to the beach culture of yesteryear. Home to living surfing legends and top-notch surfboard companies, this may be the last place in the OC where you can authentically live the surf lifestyle. Ride your own board or swim at the city's main beach beside **San Clemente Pier**. A fast detour inland, the community's **Surfing Heritage & Culture Center** (surfingheritage.org) exhibits surfboards ridden by the greats, from Duke Kahanamoku to Kelly Slater. Head back toward the pier for the California sunset of your dreams.

THE DRIVE
Slingshot north on I-5, exiting onto Hwy 1 near Dana Point. Speed by the wealthy artists colony of Laguna Beach, wild Crystal Cove State Park, Newport Beach's yacht harbor and 'Surf City USA', Huntington Beach. Turn west off Hwy 1 near Naples toward Long Beach, about 45 miles from San Clemente.

03 LONG BEACH

In Long Beach, the biggest stars are the **Queen Mary**, a grand (and allegedly haunted) British ocean liner permanently moored here, and the giant **Aquarium of the Pacific** (aquariumofpacific.org), a high-tech romp through an underwater world in which sharks dart and jellyfish float. Often overlooked, the **Museum of Latin American Art** (molaa.org) shows off influential, contemporary Latinx creators from south of the border and right here in California. A mile away, vintage shoppers will be in their element on **Retro Row**, several blocks of mid-century fashion and furnishings.

THE DRIVE
Wind slowly around the ruggedly scenic Palos Verdes Peninsula. Follow Hwy 1 north past the South Bay's prime-time beaches. Curving around LAX airport and Marina del Rey, Hwy 1 continues north to Venice, Santa Monica and all the way to Malibu, almost 60 miles from Long Beach.

04 MALIBU

Leaving traffic-jammed LA behind, Hwy 1 breezes northwest of Santa Monica to Malibu. You'll feel like a movie star walking around on the public beaches, fronting gated compounds owned by Hollywood celebs. One mansion you can actually explore inside – for free – is the **Getty Villa**, a hilltop showcase of Greek, Roman and Etruscan antiquities and manicured gardens.

Next to Malibu Lagoon State Beach, west of the surfers by Malibu Pier, **Adamson House** (adamsonhouse.org) is a Spanish-Moorish villa lavishly decorated with locally made hand-painted tiles. Motoring further west along the coast, where the Santa Monica Mountains plunge into the sea, take time out for a frolic on Malibu's mega-popular beaches like sandy Point Dume, Zuma or Leo Carrillo.

THE DRIVE
Hwy 1 crosses into Ventura County, winding alongside the ocean and windy Point Mugu. In Oxnard join Hwy 101 northbound. Motor past Ventura, a jumping-off point for boat trips to Channel Islands National Park, to Santa Barbara, just over 90 miles from Malibu Pier.

DETOUR
Channel Islands National Park
Start: Malibu

Imagine hiking, kayaking, scuba diving, camping and whale-watching, and doing it all amid a raw, end-of-the-world landscape. Rich in unique flora and fauna, tide pools and kelp forests, the islands of this national park are home to nearly 150 plant and animal species found nowhere else in the world, earning them the nickname 'California's Galápagos.' Anacapa and Santa Cruz, the most popular islands, are within an hour's boat ride of Ventura Harbor, off Hwy 101 almost 40 miles northwest of Malibu on the way to Santa Barbara.

Reservations are essential for weekends, holidays and summer trips. Before you shove off from the mainland, stop by the park's visitor center for educational natural history exhibits, a free 25-minute nature film and family-friendly activities.

05 SANTA BARBARA

Seaside Santa Barbara has almost perfect weather and a string of idyllic beaches, where surfers, kite flyers and dog walkers mingle. Admire the city's iconic Spanish Colonial Revival–style architecture along State St downtown or from the county courthouse, its tower rising above the red-tiled rooftops. Gaze south toward the busy harborfront and **Stearns Wharf** (stearnswharf.org) or north to the historic **Spanish Mission Santa Barbara** (santabarbaramission.org). Santa Barbara's balmy climate is also perfect for growing grapes – its wine country, made famous by the 2004 movie *Sideways*, is a 45-minute drive northwest along Hwy 154. Hit wine-tasting rooms in **Los Olivos**, then take Foxen Canyon Rd north past more wineries to rejoin Hwy 101.

THE DRIVE
Keep following fast Hwy 101 northbound or detour west onto slow Hwy 1, which squiggles along the coastline past Guadalupe, gateway to North America's largest sand dunes. Both highways meet up again in Pismo Beach, 100 miles northwest of Santa Barbara.

WHY I LOVE THIS TRIP
Amy C Balfour, writer

Rock-'em-sock-'em scenery never stops on this coastal adventure, from the gorgeous sun-kissed beaches of Southern California to soaring coastal redwoods in foggy Northern California. My travels on this route have ranged from joyous romps to reflective sojourns – and the landscape has somehow matched my mood every time. Laguna Beach, Malibu, Big Sur, north of Santa Cruz, and Jenner to Mendocino and Westport are reliable crowd-pleasers.

Trouble-Free Road-Tripping

In coastal areas, thick fog may impede driving – slow down, and if it's too soupy, get off the road. Along coastal cliffs, watch out for falling rocks and mudslides that could damage or disable your car if struck. For current highway conditions, including road closures (which aren't uncommon during the rainy winter season) and construction updates, visit dot.ca.gov.

06 PISMO BEACH

A classic California beach town, Pismo Beach has a long, lazy stretch of sand for swimming, surfing and strolling onto the pier at sunset.

After digging into bowls of clam chowder and baskets of fried seafood at surf-casual cafes, check out the retro family fun at the bowling alley, billiards halls and bars uphill from the beach, or dash 10 miles up Hwy 101 to San Luis Obispo's vintage **Sunset Drive-In**, where you can put your feet up on the dash and munch on bottomless bags of popcorn while watching some Hollywood blockbuster double-features.

Photo Opportunity
Golden Gate Bridge over San Francisco Bay.

THE DRIVE
Follow Hwy 101 north past San Luis Obispo, exiting onto Hwy 1 west to landmark Morro Rock in Morro Bay. North of Cayucos, Hwy 1 rolls through bucolic pasture lands, only swinging back to the coast at Cambria. Ten miles further north stands Hearst Castle, about 60 miles from Pismo Beach.

07 HEARST CASTLE

Hilltop Hearst Castle (hearstcastle.org) is California's most famous monument to wealth and ambition. William Randolph Hearst, the early-20th-century newspaper magnate, entertained Hollywood stars and royalty at this fantasy estate furnished with European antiques, accented by shimmering pools and surrounded by flowering gardens. Try to make tour reservations in advance, especially for living-history evening programs during the Christmas holiday season and in spring.

About 4.5 miles further north along Hwy 1, park at the sign-

Piedras Blancas Light Station

posted vista point and amble the boardwalk to view the elephant seal colony that breeds, molts, sleeps, plays and fights on the beach. Seals haul out year-round, but the winter birthing and mating season peaks on Valentine's Day. Nearby, **Piedras Blancas Light Station** (piedrasblancas.org) is outstandingly scenic.

 THE DRIVE
Fill your car's gas tank before plunging north into the redwood forests of the remote Big Sur coast, where precipitous cliffs dominate the seascape, and tourist services are few and far between. Hwy 1 keeps curving north to the Monterey Peninsula, approximately a three-hour, 95-mile trip from Hearst Castle.

08 MONTEREY

As Big Sur loosens its condor's talons on the coastal highway, Hwy 1 rolls gently downhill toward Monterey Bay. The fishing community of Monterey is the heart of Nobel Prize–winning writer John Steinbeck's country, and although Cannery Row today is touristy claptrap, it's worth strolling down to step inside the mesmerizing **Monterey Bay Aquarium** (montereybayaquarium.org), a converted sardine cannery on the shores of a national marine sanctuary. All kinds of aquatic denizens swim in the giant tanks, from sea stars to pot-bellied seahorses and comical sea otters.

THE DRIVE
It's a relatively quick 45-mile trip north to Santa Cruz. Hwy 1 traces the crescent shoreline of Monterey Bay, passing Elkhorn Slough wildlife refuge near Moss Landing boat harbor, Watsonville's strawberry and artichoke farms, and a string of tiny beach towns in Santa Cruz County.

 ### 09 SANTA CRUZ

Here, the flower power of the 1960s lives on, and bumper stickers on surfboard-laden woodies shout 'Keep Santa Cruz weird.' Next to the ocean, **Santa Cruz Beach Boardwalk** (beachboardwalk.com) has a glorious old-school Americana vibe and a 1911 Looff carousel.

Its fun-for-all atmosphere is punctuated by squeals from nervous nellies on the stomach-turning **Giant Dipper**, a 1920s wooden roller coaster that's a national historic landmark, as seen in the vampire cult-classic movie *The Lost Boys*. Visit **Santa Cruz' Museum of Art & History** (santacruzmah.org) for regular special exhibitions and excellent permanent displays on the city's history and culture.

Interesting one-off exhibitions have included the history of both skateboarding and tattooing in the city. Adjacent, there's good eating and drinking at **Abbott Square Market** (abbottsquaremarket.com).

THE DRIVE
It's a blissful 75-mile coastal run from Santa Cruz up to San Francisco past Pescadero, Half Moon Bay and Pacifica, where Hwy 1 passes through the tunnels at Devil's Slide. Merge with heavy freeway traffic in Daly City, staying on Hwy 1 north through the city into Golden Gate Park.

10 SAN FRANCISCO

Gridlock may shock your system after hundreds of miles of wide-open, rolling coast. But don't despair. Hwy 1 runs straight through the city's biggest, most breathable greenspace: **Golden Gate Park** (goldengatepark.com). You could easily spend all day in the conservatory of flowers, arboretum and botanic gardens, or perusing the **California Academy of Sciences** (calacademy.org) and the fine arts **de Young Museum**. Then follow Hwy 1 north over the **Golden Gate Bridge** (goldengatebridge.org). Guarding the entry to San Francisco Bay, this iconic bridge is named after the strait it spans, not for its 'International Orange' paint job. Park in the lots on the bridge's south or north side, then traipse out onto the pedestrian walkway for a photo.

THE DRIVE
Past Sausalito, leave Hwy 101 in Marin City for slow-moving, twisted Hwy 1 along the Marin County coast, passing nearby Point Reyes. Over the next 100 miles from Bodega Bay to Mendocino, revel in a remarkably uninterrupted stretch of coastal highway. More than halfway along, watch for the lighthouse road turnoff north of Point Arena town.

 DETOUR
Point Reyes
Start: 10 San Francisco

A rough-hewn beauty, Point Reyes National Seashore lures marine mammals and birds, as well as scores of shipwrecks. It was here that Sir Francis Drake repaired his ship the *Golden Hind* in 1579 and, while he was at it, claimed the indigenous land for England. Follow Sir Francis Drake Blvd to the point's edge-of-the-world lighthouse, whipped by ferocious winds, where you can observe migrating whales in winter. The lighthouse, which reopened in 2019 after a multi-million-dollar renovation, sits below the headlands and is reached via 300 descending steps. You'll find it about 20 miles west of Point Reyes Station off Hwy 1 along Marin County's coast.

11 AROUND POINT ARENA

The fishing fleets of **Bodega Bay** and the seal colony at Jenner's harbor are the last things you'll see before Hwy 1 dives into California's great rural northlands. The road twists and turns past the Sonoma Coast's state parks packed with hiking trails, sand dunes and beaches, as well as underwater marine reserves, rhododendron groves and a 19th-century Russian fur-trading fort. At **Sea Ranch**, don't let exclusive-looking vacation homes prevent you from following public-access trailhead signs and staircases down to empty beaches and across ocean bluffs. Further north, guarding an unbelievably windy point since 1908, **Point Arena Lighthouse** (pointarenalighthouse.com) is the only lighthouse in California you can actually climb to the top. Check in at the museum, then ascend the 115ft tower to inspect the Fresnel lens, and panoramas of the sea and the jagged San Andreas Fault below.

THE DRIVE
It's an hour-long, 35-mile drive north along Hwy 1 from the Point Arena Lighthouse turnoff to Mendocino, crossing the Navarro, Little and Big Rivers. Feel free to stop and stretch at wind-tossed state beaches, parklands crisscrossed by hiking trails and tiny coastal towns along the way.

12 MENDOCINO & FORT BRAGG

Looking more like Cape Cod than California, the quaint maritime town of **Mendocino** has white picket fences surrounding New England–style cottages with blooming gardens and redwood-built water towers.

This yesteryear timber town and shipping port with dramatic headlands jutting into the Pacific was 'discovered' by artists and bohemians in the 1950s and has served as a scenic backdrop in more than 50 movies. Once you've browsed the cute shops and art galleries selling everything from driftwood carvings to homemade fruit jams – the town is nicknamed 'Spendocino' – escape north to workaday **Fort Bragg**, with its simple fishing harbor and brewpub. Stop first for a short hike on the ecological staircase and pygmy forest trail at oceanfront **Jug Handle State Natural Reserve** (parks.ca.gov).

THE DRIVE
About 25 miles north of Mendocino, Westport is the last hamlet along this rugged stretch of Hwy 1. After 28 miles, rejoin Hwy 101 northbound at Leggett for another 90 miles to Eureka, detouring along the Avenue of the Giants and, if you have more time to spare, to the Lost Coast.

13 EUREKA

Highway 101 trundles alongside **Humboldt Bay National Wildlife Refuge**, (fws.gov/refuge/humboldt_bay) a major stopover for migratory birds on the Pacific Flyway. Next comes the sleepy railroad town of Eureka. As you wander downtown, check out the ornate **Carson Mansion**, (ingomar.org) built in the 1880s by a timber baron and adorned with dizzying Victorian turrets, towers, gables and gingerbread details.

Blue Ox Millworks & Historic Park (blueoxmill.com) still creates Victorian detailing by hand, using traditional carpentry and 19th-century equipment.

Back by Eureka's harborfront, climb aboard the blue-and-white **1910 Madake**, docked at the foot of C St. Sunset cocktail cruises are served from California's smallest licensed bar.

THE DRIVE
Follow Hwy 101 north past the Rastafarian-hippie college town of Arcata and turnoffs for Trinidad State Beach and Patrick's Point State Park. Hwy 101 drops out of the trees beside marshy Humboldt Lagoons State Park, rolling north toward Orick, just over 40 miles from Eureka.

14 REDWOOD NATIONAL & STATE PARKS

At last, you'll reach **Redwood National Park** (nps.gov/redw). Get oriented to the tallest trees on earth at the coastal **Thomas H Kuchel Visitor Center** (nps.gov/redw), just south of the tiny town of Orick. Then commune with the coastal giants on their own mossy turf inside **Lady Bird Johnson Grove** or the majestic **Tall Trees Grove** (free drive-and-hike permit required).

For more untouched redwood forests, wind along the 10-mile Newton B Drury Scenic Parkway in **Prairie Creek Redwoods State Park** (parks.ca.gov), passing grassy meadows where Roosevelt elk roam. Then follow Hwy 101 all the way north to **Crescent City**, the last pit stop before the Oregon border.

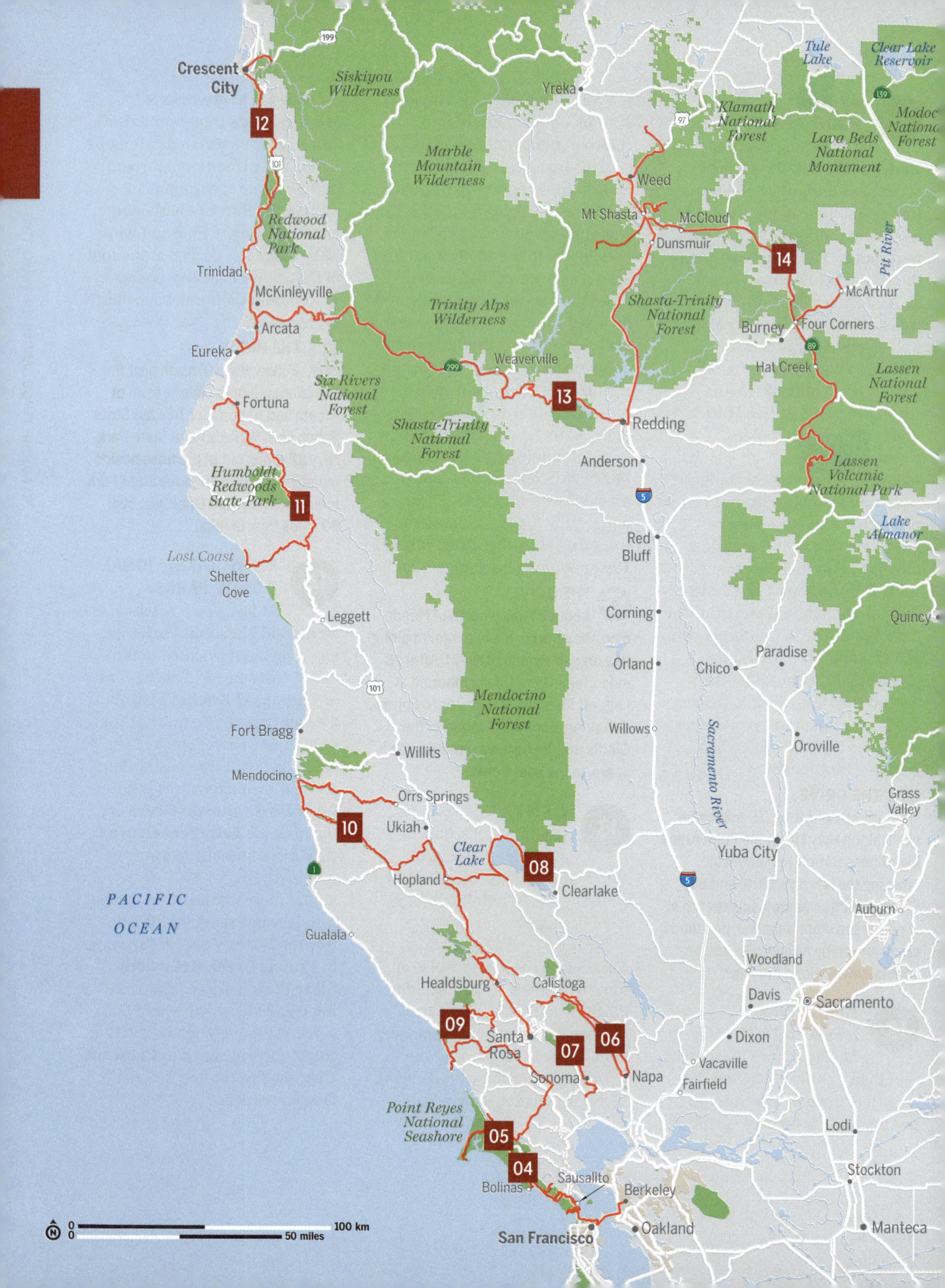
Crescent City
Siskiyou Wilderness
Yreka
Tule Lake
Clear Lake Reservoir
Klamath National Forest
Modoc National Forest
Lava Beds National Monument
Marble Mountain Wilderness
Weed
Mt Shasta
McCloud
Dunsmuir
Redwood National Park
Trinidad
McKinleyville
Arcata
Eureka
Trinity Alps Wilderness
Shasta-Trinity National Forest
Pit River
McArthur
Four Corners
Burney
Hat Creek
Weaverville
Six Rivers National Forest
Fortuna
Redding
Anderson
Lassen National Forest
Lassen Volcanic National Park
Humboldt Redwoods State Park
Lost Coast
Shelter Cove
Red Bluff
Lake Almanor
Leggett
Corning
Quincy
Orland
Chico
Paradise
Mendocino National Forest
Fort Bragg
Willows
Sacramento River
Oroville
Willits
Mendocino
Orrs Springs
Ukiah
Clear Lake
Grass Valley
Yuba City
Hopland
Clearlake
PACIFIC OCEAN
Gualala
Auburn
Woodland
Healdsburg
Calistoga
Davis
Sacramento
Santa Rosa
Dixon
Vacaville
Sonoma
Napa
Fairfield
Point Reyes National Seashore
Lodi
Stockton
Bolinas
Sausalito
Berkeley
San Francisco
Oakland
Manteca
04
05
06
07
08
09
10
11
12
13
14
0
100 km
0
50 miles

Vineyards, Napa Valley (p52)

Northern California

04 Marin County
Leave behind the heady hills of cosmopolitan San Francisco by driving north across the Golden Gate Bridge. **p42**

05 Bay Area Culinary Tour
Make a delicious loop around the Bay Area and wander through celebrated farmers markets and meet artisanal producers. **p48**

06 Napa Valley
Fabulous winery estates and the restaurants of celebrity chefs grace this grand wine-producing region. **p52**

07 Sonoma Valley
Discover historic terraced vineyards and pristine forest parklands while raising a glass to the good times. **p58**

08 Healdsburg & Around
Shake the dust off your jeans, make yourself comfortable, and let California show you what dreaming is all about. **p62**

09 Russian River & Bohemian Highway
Paddle canoes, wander orchards and country lanes in pinot noir country. **p66**

10 Mendocino & Anderson Valley
Find vineyards, redwoods and idiosyncratic villages between California's rolling hills and the jagged cliffs of the Pacific. **p70**

11 Lost Coast & Southern Redwoods
Head north from the Bay Area and follow the Avenue of the Giants to redwood trees and offbeat towns. **p74**

12 Northern Redwood Coast
Follow curving roads and misty trails to lush, spectacular natural wonders that are unlike any other place on earth. **p78**

13 Trinity Scenic Byway
An epic cruise through one of California's most distinctive mountains that leads to the Pacific shore. **p82**

14 Volcanic Legacy Byway
Volcanic peaks, hot springs and peaceful wilderness lakes dominate a naturalist's drive around majestic Mt Lassen. **p86**

Explore

Northern California

San Francisco anchors California's most diverse region. From rambling rugged Lost Coast beaches and floating down the tranquil Russian River, to poking around redwoods and surmounting volcano summits, there's no shortage of natural beauty to explore.

Then there's the wine and food. Napa Valley is world famous for top-drawer cabernet sauvignon, chardonnay and sparkling wines, but you can sip equally impressive vintages in the Sonoma Valley, the nearby Russian River, Dry Creek and Alexander Valleys. Then soak in hot springs, where conversations start with, 'Hey, dude!' and end hours later.

Hub Towns

Most international travelers to Northern California arrive via San Francisco International Airport (SFO). Nearby Oakland (OAK) and San Jose (SJC) airports serve mostly domestic flights. Other airports in Northern California are regional with limited, short-haul flights.

San Francisco

San Francisco (SF) has an outsize reputation in the American consciousness, from the myth-making gold rush to the Summer of Love, from gay liberation to tech bros. This city of some 808,500 people (the anchor of a metro area of 4.5 million) offers a heady mix of counterculture and culinary gems, dive bars and dot-coms, sailors and psychonauts, all wrapped up in the world's most beautiful urban settings.

All this is to say that you should visit San Francisco, even if you stay elsewhere – hotels can cost dearly. Try positioning yourself along the BART regional rail network and taking the train in. Or to stay in the center of the action, Union Sq makes a good base, with convenient transit connections so you can ditch the rental car (and steep parking fees).

Wine Country

Near the midpoint of the Napa Valley, Yountville is also a hub for lodgings and restaurants. If you can't take out a loan for a meal at the famed French Laundry, then take heart in local favorites such as Tacos Garcia. Then you should rest your tired caboose in a converted railcar at

WHEN TO GO

Fog is common all along the north coast, but 10 miles inland it might be blazing hot. Case in point: San Francisco summers are often foggy and cool; visit in April and May or September and October for warmer temps. Autumn is prime foliage season in the mountainous north, near Mt Shasta and Lassen Volcanic National Park.

Napa Valley Railway Inn. About 20 miles (32km) northwest, Calistoga is famed for its hot-spring resorts; Indian Springs Resort here can accommodate families in its bungalows.

Meanwhile, over in Sonoma, the Sonoma Hotel has a classic Western vibe right on Sonoma Plaza, surrounded by boutiques, restaurants and tasting rooms.

Lost Coast

Arcata and Eureka are the main towns in this remote area. As a university town (home of Cal Poly Humboldt), Arcata has arguably the funkiest vibe, but it's easy enough to stay in one town and visit the other. The Carter House Inns in Eureka have a Victorian feel and Jacuzzi suites, and you should try local oysters at Humboldt Bay Provisions. Arcata offers the renovated 1915 Hotel Arcata with great people-watching from the front rooms. Nearby, try pies from savory to sweet at Slice of Humboldt Pie, while the Samoa Cookhouse is in the dining hall of an 1893 lumber camp.

WHERE TO STAY

Northern California boasts some of the USA's most splurge-worthy lodgings, like Healdsburg's Madrona Manor and the **Philo Apple Farm and Cottages**. Don't have that kind of budget? Consider soaking in geothermal tubs at resorts like **Orr Hot Springs** or **Indian Springs Resort** in Calistoga.

In Crescent City, near the Oregon border, **Curly Redwood Lodge** is a kitschy gem whose wood paneling came from a single redwood tree. Or get close to nature at **campgrounds** near the coast, like at Mendocino Grove and Van Damme or Humboldt Redwoods State Parks.

TRANSPORT

San Francisco International Airport (SFO) is conveniently served by the BART light rail into 'the City'. Fans of longer train journeys might consider Amtrak's Coast Starlight, which starts in Seattle and makes stops including Portland, Redding (for Mt Shasta) and Sacramento en route to the Bay Area and LA (Seattle to Oakland: from $160, 23 hours).

WHAT'S ON

Chinese New Year Festival
San Francisco claims the biggest Chinese New Year parade outside Asia. January–February.

San Francisco Pride
One of the world's largest LGBTIQ+ pride celebrations, held in June.

BottleRock
Napa Valley festival of music, wine and more, with headliners from Lizzo to the Red Hot Chili Peppers. Late May.

Outside Lands
Each August, San Francisco's Golden Gate Park comes alive with music, comedy and food.

Resources

National Park Service
(nps.gov) Guides and up-to-the-minute info.

San Francisco Travel Association
(sftravel.com) San Francisco trip planning.

Visit California
(visitcalifornia.com) Official state tourism site.

Visit Napa Valley
(visitnapavalley.com) Wineries, restaurants, and events.

BEST ROAD TRIPS: CALIFORNIA

04

Marin County

BEST FOR NATURE

Take a walk under the redwood trees of Muir Woods.

Point Bonita Lighthouse, Marin Headlands

DURATION	DISTANCE	GREAT FOR
2–3 days	100 miles / 160km	Food & Drink, Outdoors

BEST TIME TO GO | April to October for dry, warmer days.

Leave behind the heady hills of cosmopolitan San Francisco by driving north across the wind-tunneling passageway of the Golden Gate Bridge. From there, the scenery turns untamed, and Marin County's undulating hills, redwood forests and crashing coastline prove a welcome respite from urban living. Finish up with exhilarating, end-of-the-world views at wild Point Reyes, jutting 10 miles out into the Pacific.

Link Your Trip

05 Bay Area Culinary Tour
From Point Reyes Station, drive meandering Point Reyes–Petaluma Rd northeast past green pastures for 19 miles to Petaluma.

16 Along Highway 1 to Santa Cruz
Wind south from San Francisco along Hwy 1 for more lighthouses, organic farms and your pick of sandy cove beaches.

01 GOLDEN GATE BRIDGE
Other suspension bridges impress with engineering, but none can touch the **Golden Gate Bridge** (goldengatebridge.org/visitors) for showmanship, with its soaring art deco design. On sunny days it transfixes crowds with its radiant glow – thanks to a couple dozen daredevil painters, who reapply about 1000 gallons of 'International Orange' paint weekly. When afternoon fog rolls in, the bridge performs its disappearing act: now you see it, now you don't and, abracadabra, it's sawn in half. There's no toll to pay when driving northbound

over the turret-topped bridge, which first opened in 1937. On the Marin side of the span, pull into the parking lot and stroll around the Vista Point area. Sashay out onto the iconic bridge to spy on cargo ships threading through its pylons. Memorize the 360-degree views of the rugged Marin Headlands, downtown skyscrapers and the speck that is Alcatraz.

🚗 THE DRIVE
Immediately north of the bridge and the Vista Point turnoff, take the Alexander Ave exit and take a left on Bunker Rd before swinging back under the highway and through the Barry-Baker Tunnel (also referred to as the Five-Minute Tunnel, because its single lane of traffic changes direction every five minutes). From there, it's 3.5 miles to Point Bonita Lighthouse.

02 MARIN HEADLANDS
Near echoey WWII battery tunnels, bird-watchers should stop to hike up **Hawk Hill** (www.nps.gov/goga/learn/nature/hawk-hill.htm). Thousands of migrating birds of prey soar here from late summer to early fall, straddling a windy ridge with views of Rodeo Lagoon all the way to Alcatraz.

Stay west on Conzelman Rd until it ends in about 2 miles, then bear left towards the bay. The third lighthouse built on the West Coast, **Point Bonita Lighthouse** (nps.gov/goga/pobo.htm) was completed in 1855, but after complaints about its ridgetop performance in fog, it was scooted down to the promontory in 1877. Two afternoons a week you can traverse a steep half-mile trail and cross through a dark rock tunnel – carved out with hand tools only – and over suspension bridges to inspect the beacon.

Continue north along the oceanview bluffs of Field Rd, joining westbound Bunker Rd after passing the **visitor center** (nps.gov/goga/marin-headlands.htm). At the end of the road, picnic-worthy **Rodeo Beach** (parksconservancy.org/visit/park-sites/rodeo-beach.html) awaits with breezy Pacific panoramas and hiking trails.

BEST ROAD TRIPS: CALIFORNIA   43

THE DRIVE

Turn around and take Bunker Rd eastbound (signed San Francisco). Pass back through the timed one-way tunnel and continue straight ahead onto Murray Circle. Down by the waterfront, turn left onto Center Rd. The 5-mile drive takes 15 minutes or less.

03 SAUSALITO

Just under the north tower of the Golden Gate Bridge, at East Fort Baker, families should stop by the **Bay Area Discovery Museum** (bayareadiscoverymuseum.org), an excellent hands-on activity museum with exhibits including an oversized kitchen sink called Wobbleland and a large playground area with a shipwreck.

Follow East Rd as it curves alongside Richardson Bay, then take three quick rights onto Alexander Ave, 2nd St and Bridgeway Blvd. Perfectly arranged on a secure little harbor on the bay, Sausalito's pretty houses tumble neatly down a green hillside into a well-heeled downtown with stunning bay views.

Northwest of downtown, you can poke around Sausalito's picturesque **houseboat docks** off Bridgeway Blvd between Gate 5 and Gate 6½ Rds. Structures range from psychedelic mural-splashed castles to dilapidated salt-sprayed shacks and three-story floating mansions.

THE DRIVE

Follow Bridgeway Blvd onto Hwy 101 north for less than a mile to the Hwy 1 exit. Ascend a mostly residential section of two-lane Hwy 1 and after 3 miles, follow signs to Muir Woods via the Panoramic Hwy. Parking must be booked online in advance.

DETOUR
Angel Island
Start: 03 Sausalito

Inland from Hwy 101, just over 8 miles northeast of Sausalito, is the well-to-do town of **Tiburon** (Spanish for 'shark'). There you can catch a ferry (angelislandferry.com) to Angel Island State Park (parks.ca.gov/AngelIsland) and its historical sites, hiking and cycling trails, campgrounds and beaches.

Angel Island's varied history – it was a hunting and fishing ground for the Miwok people, a military base, an immigration station, a WWII Japanese internment camp and a Nike missile site – has left it with evocative old forts and bunkers to explore. You can get back to nature on 13 miles of hiking trails, including up Mt Livermore (788ft), granting panoramic views when it's not foggy, or by cycling the 6-mile perimeter loop road.

Nicknamed the 'Ellis Island of the West,' the **Angel Island Immigration Station** (aiisf.org/visit) operated from 1910 to 1940. It was primarily a screening and detention center for Chinese immigrants, who were at that time restricted from entering the US. Tours of the haunting site are given three times daily. It's a 1-mile walk, bicycle ride or shuttle trip (round-trip $6) from Ayala Cove's dock.

The best times to visit Angel Island are on summer weekends, when more of the historical buildings and sites are open, and when spring wildflowers bloom. Bring your own food, or grab takeaway salads, drinks and snacks from **Angel Island Café** (angelisland.com) near the ferry dock.

04 MUIR WOODS

The old-growth redwoods at **Muir Woods National Monument** (nps.gov/muwo) are the closest redwood stand to San Francisco. Logging plans were halted when power couple William Kent (a congressman and naturalist) and Elizabeth Thatcher Kent (a women's rights activist) bought a section of Redwood Creek, and in 1907 donated 295 acres to the federal government. President Theodore Roosevelt made the site a national monument in 1908, the name honoring John Muir, naturalist and founder of environmental organization the Sierra Club.

Muir Woods can get crowded, especially on weekends. But even at busy times, a short hike will take you to quieter trails with huge trees and stunning vistas. Near the entrance, a bustling cafe serves sandwiches, soups, baked goods and hot drinks.

THE DRIVE

Head southwest on Muir Woods Rd (signed Muir Beach/Stinson Beach) and rejoin Hwy 1/Shoreline Hwy, a spectacularly scenic and curvy Pacific Ocean byway that winds north. It's about 3 miles downhill from Muir Woods to the turnoff for Muir Beach.

05 MUIR BEACH & STINSON BEACH

The turnoff from Hwy 1 for **Muir Beach** (nps.gov/goga/planyourvisit/muirbeach.htm) is marked by the north coast's longest row of mailboxes at mile marker 5.7, just before the Pelican Inn. Another mile northwest along Hwy 1, there are superb coastal views at **Muir Beach Overlook**, where WWII scouts kept watch from the surrounding concrete lookouts for invading Japanese ships.

Over the next 5 miles, Hwy 1 twists and makes hairpin turns atop ocean cliffs – both the road and the seascapes unfurling below will make you gasp.

The highway eases as it rolls gently downhill to the town of

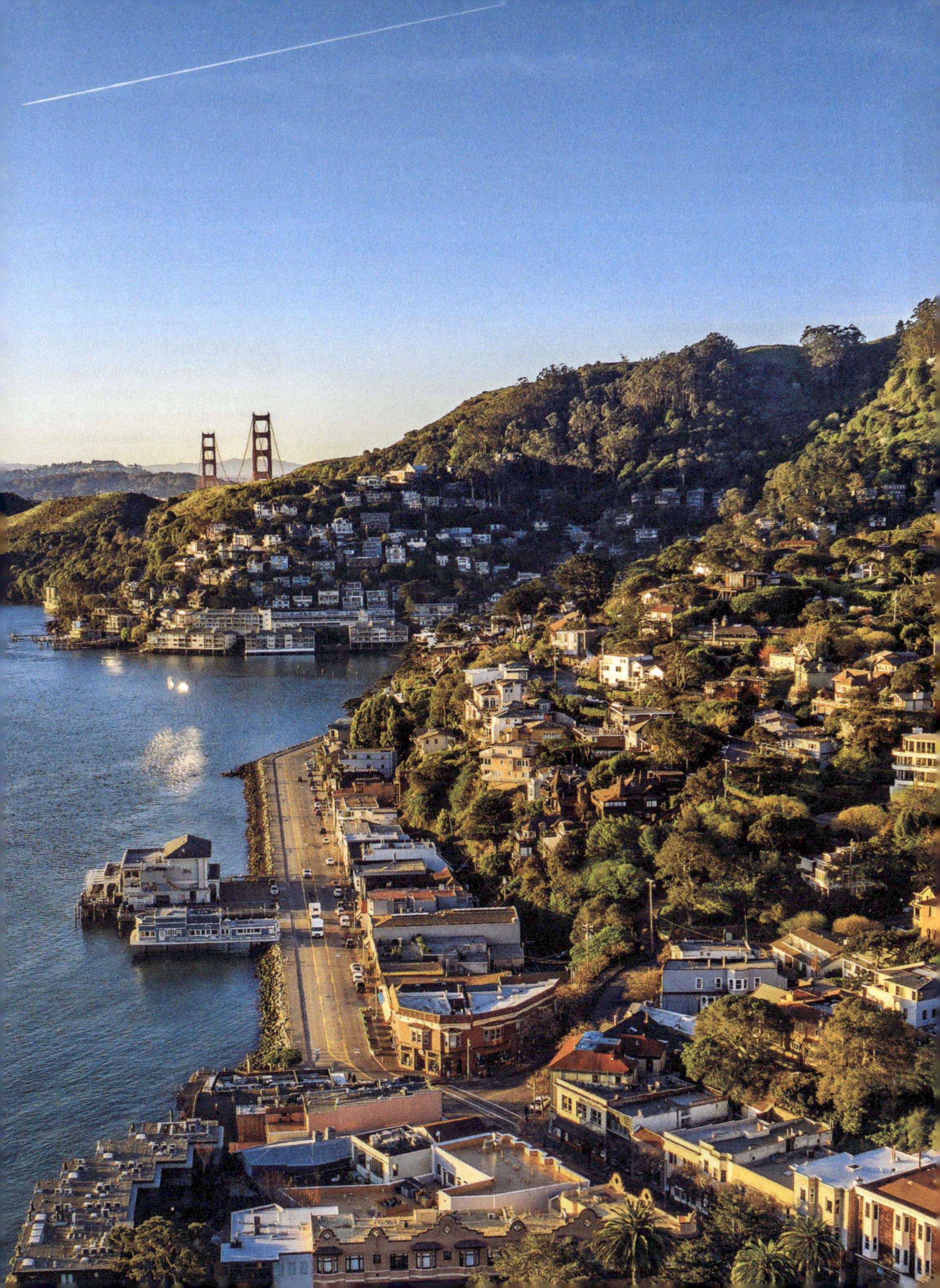

Stinson Beach, a three-block strip of densely packed art galleries, shops, eateries and inns. A block west of Hwy 1, the 3-mile long beach itself is often blanketed with fog, but when the sun is shining, it's covered with surfers, families and picnickers.

THE DRIVE
In town, turn onto the Panoramic Hwy for Mt Tamalpais. It's a curvy 3.5-mile drive uphill to the state park's headquarters at Pantoll Station.

06 MT TAMALPAIS
Standing guard over Marin County, majestic 'Mt Tam' affords breathtaking 360-degree views of ocean, bay and hills rolling into the distance. The rich, natural beauty of the mountain is inspiring – the 6300-acre **state park** (parks.ca.gov/mttamalpais) is home to deer, foxes, bobcats and many miles of hiking and cycling trails.

Mt Tam was a sacred place to the coastal Miwok people for thousands of years before the arrival of European and American settlers. By the late 19th century, San Franciscans were escaping the bustle of the city with all-day outings on the mountain, and from 1896 to 1930, the 'world's crookedest railroad' (281 turns) connected Mill Valley to the summit (2571ft).

Turn left at Pantoll Station onto Pantoll Rd, then after almost 1.5 miles, turn right onto Ridgecrest Blvd, which climbs another 3 miles to a parking lot below **East Peak** summit. Follow the short, steep hiking trail uphill to a fire lookout with commanding ocean views.

THE DRIVE
Backtrack downhill to Stinson Beach, turning right onto Hwy 1 northbound. Trace the eastern shore of Bolinas Lagoon, where waterfowl prowl during low tide and harbor seals often haul out. Take the first left after the lagoon then go left on Olema–Bolinas Rd, continuing on Wharf Rd into central Bolinas. The 15-mile drive takes just over half an hour.

Photo Opportunity
Views of Alcatraz, the Pacific Ocean and San Francisco from atop the Golden Gate Bridge.

Mt Tamalpais

07 BOLINAS

Don't look for any signs directing you here. Residents from this famously private town tore the road sign down so many times that state highway officials finally gave in and stopped replacing it years ago. Known as 'Jugville' during the gold rush days, this sleepy beachside community is home to writers, musicians and fisherfolk. Stroll along the sand from access points along Wharf Rd or Brighton Ave.

Hikers veer off Olema–Bolinas Rd onto Mesa Rd and follow it northwest nearly 5 miles to road's end at Palomarin Trailhead, the setting-off point for lovely coastal day hikes. On a sunny day, hightail it out to **Bass Lake**, a popular freshwater swimming spot reached by way of a 3-mile hike skirting the coast. Another 2.5 miles of walking brings you to majestic **Alamere Falls**, a waterfall that tumbles 50ft off a cliff to the beach below.

THE DRIVE
Return to Hwy 1 and continue 9 miles northwest through Olema Valley. Just past the stop sign in Olema, turn left onto Bear Valley Rd and follow the brown Point Reyes National Seashore signs to the Bear Valley Visitor Center.

08 POINT REYES NATIONAL SEASHORE

A national park that covers much of the peninsula, wind-blown **Point Reyes National Seashore** (nps.gov/pore) shelters free-ranging elk, scores of marine mammals and all manner of raptors and wild cats. Beginning across the street from the **Bear Valley Visitor Center** (nps.gov/pore), the short, paved **Earthquake Trail** reaches a 16ft gap between the two halves of a once-connected fence line, a testimonial to the power of the magnitude 7.8 earthquake that rocked SF in 1906.

Follow Bear Valley Rd north to Sir Francis Drake Blvd. Raptors perch on fence posts of historical cattle ranches, and the road bumps over rolling hills as it twists for 20 miles out to the lighthouse. Initially, the road parallels **Tomales Bay**, a thin channel that teems with harbor seals. In Point Reyes Station, **Blue Waters Kayaking** (bluewaterskayaking.com) offers bay tours or you can rent a kayak and paddle the secluded beaches and rocky crevices on your own.

At the very end of Sir Francis Drake Blvd, **Point Reyes Lighthouse** endures ferocious winds at the base of more than 300 stairs. This is one of the best whale-watching spots along the coast, as gray whales pass during their winter migration.

WILDLIFE WATCHING

Want to see marine wildlife in Marin County? The following are a few choice spots:

In the **Marin Headlands**, sea lions, seals and other injured, sick and orphaned marine creatures are rehabilitated at the **Marine Mammal Center** (pictured; marinemammalcenter.org) before being returned to the wild.

In **Bolinas**, stroll along Wharf Rd to spot great blue herons, great egrets and snowy egrets, who build nests on the western shore of Bolinas Lagoon in springtime. Outside town, drop by **Palomarin Field Station** (pointblue.org) to watch bird-banding demonstrations most mornings.

At **Point Reyes National Seashore**, you can spot whales from **Point Reyes Lighthouse** (nps.gov/pore/planyourvisit/lighthouse.htm), where barking sea lions laze on the shore. At nearby **Chimney Rock**, a seasonal colony of elephant seals breeds and gives birth between December and March. Hike out toward windy **Tomales Point** to observe free-ranging herds of tule elk.

05

Bay Area Culinary Tour

BEST FOR PICNICS

Briny oysters, local bread and cheeses, and sparkling mead

DURATION	DISTANCE	GREAT FOR
2–3 days	255 miles / 311km	Food & Drink, Nature

BEST TIME TO GO	Late summer or early fall, when farms deliver their tastiest bounty.

Cheese store, Petaluma

Making a delicious loop around the Bay Area, you'll wander through the aisles of celebrated farmers markets and drop in on artisanal food and drink producers, from Hog Island oyster farm to Cowgirl Creamery and more. A hike at Point Reyes National Seashore will work up a healthy appetite. You'll need it on this straight-from-the-source trip to foodie heaven.

Link Your Trip

06 Napa Valley
Cruise 26 miles east from Petaluma to Napa, the gateway to America's most famous wine region, home to several of California's best restaurants.

09 Russian River & the Bohemian Highway
Starting in Sebastopol, revel in the country charms of 'Slow-noma,' stopping at orchards, vineyards and Freestone's famous bakery.

01 SEBASTOPOL

This western Sonoma farm town was founded in the 19th century, when apples were its main cash crop. Swing by in August for the **Gravenstein Apple Fair** (gravensteinapplefair.com), a lively weekend celebration of local food, wines and brews, accompanied by live music and more. In late summer and early autumn, you can pick your own apples at orchards on the outskirts of town along **Sonoma County's Farm Trails** (farmtrails.org).

But Sebastopol is about so much more than apples these days. Just look at the **Barlow** (thebarlow.net), a former apple processing plant that has been repurposed into a 12-acre village of food producers, artists, winemakers, coffee roasters and spirits distillers who showcase West County's culinary and artistic diversity. Wander shed to shed, sample everything from microbrewed beer to nitrogen flash-frozen ice cream, and meet artisanal makers.

🚗 THE DRIVE
Follow Hwy 116 south out of town for 8 miles to Cotati. Keep going across Hwy 101 (the speedier but more boring route to Petaluma) and turn right onto Old Redwood Hwy. After 3 miles, go left on pastoral Old Adobe Rd for 6 miles, turning left just past Petaluma Adobe State Historic Park.

02 PETALUMA
'The world's egg basket' – as the agrarian town of Petaluma has long been known – is home to countless chicken farms that sell fresh eggs and dairy products. Across Hwy 101 and west of downtown, the **Petaluma Creamery** (springhillcheese.com) has been in business for more than a century. Stop by to sample organic cheeses or for a scoop of lavender or Meyer-lemon ice cream from the small specialty foods market and cafe.

More recently, Petaluma has earned a reputation for its densely foggy and wind-whipped appellation, which winegrowers have dubbed 'the Petaluma Gap.' As wineries such as **Keller Estate** (kellerestate.com) have become more prominent, the region's chardonnays, pinot noirs and syrahs have gained recognition for their elegance and complexity.

🚗 THE DRIVE
From downtown Petaluma, take D St southwest to Red Hill Rd and follow Point Reyes–Petaluma Rd toward the coast, turning left onto Hwy 1 for Point Reyes Station. It's a relaxing 19-mile country drive; stop en route for Camembert or Brie at the Marin French Cheese factory store.

03 POINT REYES STATION
Surrounded by dairies and ranches, Point Reyes Station became a hub for artists in the 1960s. Today it offers a collection of art galleries, boutique shops and excellent food. The tour of the town's edibles begins by fighting your way through the spandex-clad crowd of weekend cyclists to grab a crusty loaf of fire-baked Brickmaiden Bread at **Bovine Bakery** (bovinebakeryptreyes.com).

Next, step down the block to the restored barn that houses one of California's most sought-after cheesemakers, **Cowgirl Creamery** (cowgirlcreamery.com). In spring the must-buy is its St Pat's, a smooth, mellow round wrapped in wild nettle leaves. Otherwise, the Mt Tam (available year-round) is pretty damn good, and there's a gourmet deli for picking up picnic supplies.

Heading north out of town **Heidrun Meadery** (heidrunmeadery.com) pours tasting sips of sparkling mead, made from aromatic small-batch honey in the style of French champagne.

BEST ROAD TRIPS: CALIFORNIA   49

THE DRIVE
Follow Hwy 1 north out of the tiny village of Point Reyes Station. Cruise for 9 miles along the east side of tranquil Tomales Bay, which flows many miles out into the Pacific. Just before the turnoff for rural Marshall–Petaluma Rd, look for the sign for bayfront Hog Island Oyster Company on your left.

04 TOMALES BAY
Only 10 minutes north of Point Reyes Station, you'll find the salty turnout for the **Hog Island Oyster Company** (hogislandoysters.com). There's not much to see: just some picnic tables and BBQ grills, an outdoor cafe and a small window vending the famously silky oysters and a few other picnic provisions. While you can buy oysters to go, for a fee you can nab a picnic table, borrow shucking tools and take a lesson on how to crack open the oysters yourself. Lunch at the waterfront farm is unforgettable – and very popular, so reserve ahead for a picnic table or a seat at the communal tables.

THE DRIVE
Backtrack 10 miles south on Hwy 1 through Point Reyes Station. Turn right onto Sir Francis Drake Blvd, following the signs for Point Reyes National Seashore, just on the other side of Tomales Bay.

05 POINT REYES NATIONAL SEASHORE
For another perfect picnic spot, look down the coast to **Point Reyes National Seashore** (nps.gov/pore). The windswept peninsula's rough-hewn beauty lures marine mammals and migratory birds. The 110 sq miles of pristine ocean beaches also offer excellent hiking and camping opportunities.

Photo Opportunity
Briny oysters, local bread and cheeses, and Heidrun sparkling mead at Hog Island Oyster Company.

For an awe-inspiring view, follow Sir Francis Drake Blvd beside Tomales Bay all the way out toward the **Point Reyes Lighthouse** (nps.gov/pore/plan yourvisit/lighthouse.htm). Follow the signs and turn left before the lighthouse to find the trailhead for the 1.6-mile round-trip hike to **Chimney Rock**, where wildflowers bloom in spring.

THE DRIVE
Leaving the park, trace the eucalyptus-lined curves of Hwy 1 south toward Stinson Beach and past one stunning Pacific view after another. If you don't stop, you'll be back across the Golden Gate Bridge in about an hour and a half. From the bridge, follow Hwy 101 through the city to Broadway, then go east to the waterfront piers.

06 SAN FRANCISCO
From the center of the Golden Gate Bridge, it's possible to view the clock tower of the city's **Ferry Building** (ferrybuildingmarketplace.com), a transit hub turned gourmet emporium, where foodies happily miss their ferries slurping Hog Island oysters and bubbly. Star chefs are frequently spotted at the thrice-weekly **Ferry Plaza Farmers Market** (cuesa.org) that wraps around the building year-round. The largest market is on Saturday, when dozens of family farmers and artisanal food and flower vendors show up. From dry-farmed tomatoes to organic kimchi, the bounty may seem like an embarrassment of riches.

If your trip doesn't coincide with a market day, never fear: dozens of local purveyors await indoors at the **Ferry Building Marketplace**. Take a taste of McEvoy Ranch and Stonehouse olive oils, fresh-baked loaves from Acme Bread Company and Humphry Slocombe ice cream.

THE DRIVE
It's a straight shot over the San Francisco–Oakland Bay Bridge and into Berkeley via I-80 eastbound. Exit at University Ave and follow it east to Shattuck Ave, then go north of downtown Berkeley to the 'Gourmet Ghetto.'

07 BERKELEY
San Francisco might host a handful of banner dining rooms, but California's food revolution got started across the bay, in Berkeley. You may spot the inventor of California cuisine, famed chef Alice Waters, in her element and in raptures at the **North Berkeley Farmers Market** (ecologycenter.org), run by the Ecology Center. It's in the so-called 'Gourmet Ghetto' – a neighborhood that marries the progressive 1960s ideals of Berkeley with haute-dining sensibility.

The neighborhood's anchor, and an appropriate final stop, is **Chez Panisse**, Alice Waters' influential restaurant. It's unpretentious, and every mind-altering, soul-sanctifying bite of the food is emblematic of the chef's revolutionary food principles. The kitchen is even open so diners can peek behind the scenes.

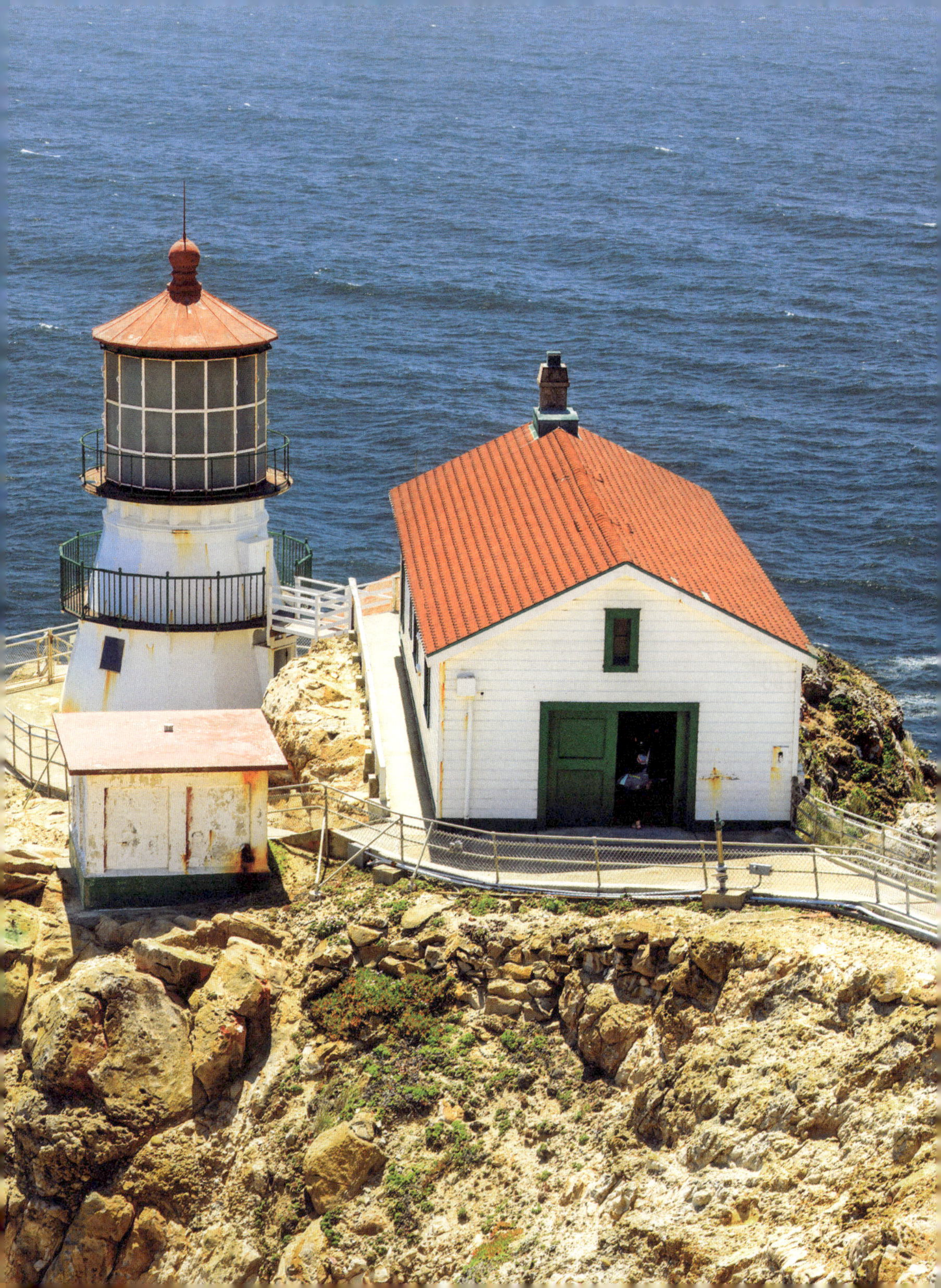

06

Napa Valley

BEST FOR FOOD & WINE

Book a star chef's table in tiny Yountville or historic St Helena.

DURATION	DISTANCE	GREAT FOR
2–3 days	90 miles / 145km	Wine

BEST TIME TO GO — May for the lull before summer; September to October to experience the 'crush'

Wining and dining is a glorious way of life in Napa today – grapes have grown here since the gold rush. Right off Hwy 29, organic family wineries are daring to make wines besides classic cabernets, and indie winemakers have opened up shop on Napa's revitalized 1st St. Traveling through this lush valley, you'll notice Napa's commitment to sustainability and local character. The signs are clear: you've arrived right on time for Napa's renaissance.

Link Your Trip

07 Sonoma Valley
For lower-key wine tasting and early California historical sites, head to Sonoma Valley via Hwy 12/121.

08 Healdsburg & Around
From Calistoga, take Hwy 128 northwest less than 20 miles to more wineries in Alexander and Dry Creek Valleys.

01 NAPA

Your first stop in Napa may be the only one you need. This is where Napans come to unwind at laid-back downtown tasting rooms, historic music halls, and local gourmet **Oxbow Public Market**. Napa's newly revitalized 1st St is lined with indie wine-tasting rooms and world-class, California-casual bistros.

The new **Napa Valley Vine Trail** (vinetrail.org) connecting downtown Napa to Yountville provides a welcome respite from Hwy 29 traffic, and Napa's riverbank parks help manage seasonal floods with sus-

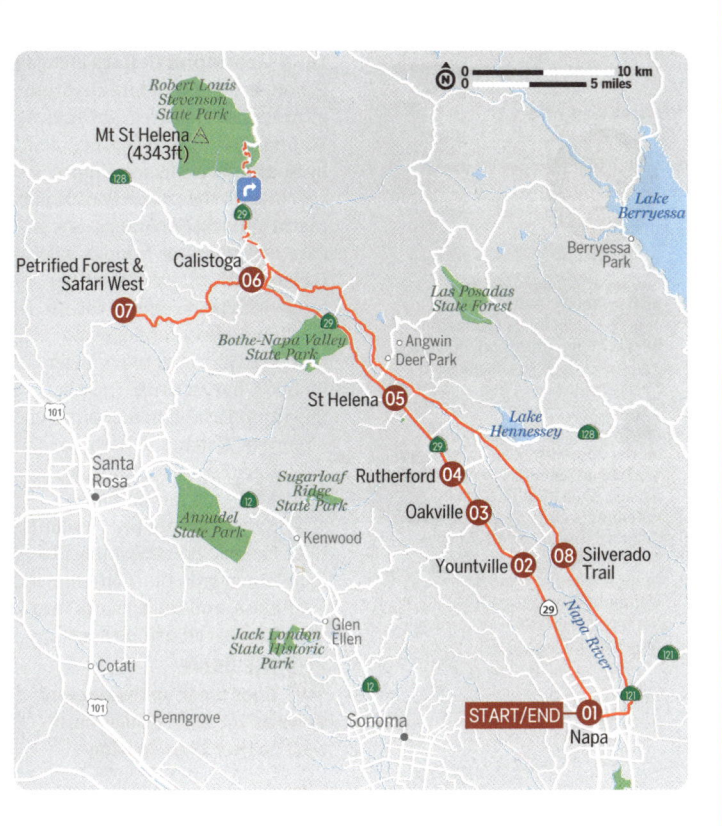

Napa Valley Wine

Cab is king in Napa. No varietal captures this sun-drenched valley like the fruit of the cabernet sauvignon vine, and no wine fetches a higher price. But with climate change, Napa Valley's floor is heating up, so even hardy cabernet grapes can develop highly concentrated, over-extracted flavors – resulting in fiery tannins, raisin flavors or syrupy notes. To take the edge off cabs and introduce more subtle notes, Napa winemakers are increasingly making Napa cab blends called Meritages.

Napa farmers tend to plant prestigious, pricey cabernet, so when they make an exception and grow another red grape, like merlot, it's because they believe it will be exceptional. California zinfandel grows extremely well in many of the same sunny Napa Valley blocks as cabernet – so it's a time-honored specialty at many Napa wineries.

Lately, more unusual varietals and blends are gracing Napa tasting-room shelves. A new crop of winemakers called 'garagistes' are buying grapes from across Northern California, and fermenting them in downtown Napa warehouse facilities. So even in the heart of Napa Valley, tasting rooms are pouring coastal chardonnay, Russian River sauvignon blanc, white picpoul from the Sierra foothills, and cool-climate Sonoma pinot noir.

---

tainable design. Lately downtown Napa has raised its profile with the star-studded **Napa Valley Film Festival** (napavalleyfilm fest.org) and breakout-hit **BottleRock Music Festival** (bottlerocknapavalley.com). Between events, Napa remains the sweet spot where wine flows and conversation meanders.

🚗 **THE DRIVE**
From Napa, Yountville is 9 miles north on Hwy 29, a divided four-lane road surrounded by vineyards and framed by low hills.

02 YOUNTVILLE
Planets and Michelin stars are aligned over Yountville, a tiny Western stagecoach stop that's been transformed into a global dining destination. Sounds like an urban legend – until you take a stroll down Yountville's quiet, tree-lined Washington St. Say hey to interns weeding **French Laundry Gardens**, chocolatiers pouring out new creations at **Kollar Chocolates** (kollarchocolates.com), and trainee sommeliers grabbing lunch at **Tacos Garcia**. You've just met the talents behind Yountville's gourmet landmarks, including the legendary (but reservation-only) **French Laundry** (thomaskeller.com/tfl).

🚗 **THE DRIVE**
Go north to Oakville via 4 miles of vineyard vistas on Hwy 29,

which narrows to two lanes just outside Yountville. Tracks for the Napa Valley Wine Train line the west side of the road.

03 OAKVILLE

Except for the famous **Oakville Grocery** (oakvillegrocery.com) and its next-door wine-history museum, you could drive through Oakville and never know you'd missed it. But when wine aficionados look at this green valley, they see red – thanks in no small part to **Robert Mondavi** (robertmondavi winery.com), the visionary vintner who knew back in the 1960s that Napa was capable of more than jug wine. His marketing savvy launched Napa's premium reds to cult status, including his own Opus One Meritage (Napa red blend).

THE DRIVE
Pass gilded signs of name-brand mega-wineries as you continue 2 miles north on Hwy 29 to Rutherford.

04 RUTHERFORD

Hard to believe it looking at these lush vineyards, but Napa Valley's most famous patch of cab country was once covered in wheat. Local farmers saw grape opportunity in this rich bottom land, and the rest is history in a bottle. Trailblazing winemaker **Mike Grgich** (grgich.com) put Napa chardonnay on the map in 1976 with his historic win in a French wine competition, dubbed the 'Judgment of Paris.'

Exit Hwy 29 onto back roads off Rutherford Rd, and you'll find idiosyncratic organic winemaking flourishing in the heart of mega-brand cab country. Meandering paths wind through fruit-bearing orchards at **Frog's Leap** (frogsleap.com) winery, where merlot and sauvignon blanc are produced in an 1884 barn.

THE DRIVE
St Helena is another 4 miles north on Hwy 29, though you may be slowing to a crawl before reaching downtown.

05 ST HELENA

Even people with places to go can't resist downtown St Helena, which looks like a Western movie set. Three blocks of Main St are a designated national historic site, covering 160 years of California history, including one of the oldest cinemas in America still in operation. Up the street, the

WHY I LOVE THIS TRIP
Alison Bing, writer

Napa Valley is America's fanciest stretch of farmland, with million-dollar steel sculptures in sun-drenched fields and marble bars in architect-designed barns. You'll recognize the scene from glossy magazines – but spend a day in Napa, and you'll also notice 150-plus years of hard work. No matter how early you rise, vineyard workers are already pruning grapes; even after fine-dining restaurants close, taqueros keep pulling carne asada off the grill. This calls for a toast: to vigilant firefighters, who protect this wondrous 30-mile stretch of dreams and dirt from increasingly regular wildfires.'

1889 Greystone Cellars château is home to the Culinary Institute of America. This area was native Wappo land until it was claimed by Spain, then Mexico – more specifically, the property of Doña María Ygnacia Soberanes. She gave her daughter Isadora Bale **Grist Mill**, still grinding flour today, and prime vineyards to her daughter Caroline, who married a German winemaker named Charles Krug. Together they founded the first commercial winery in Napa in 1858.

Today if you're thirsty, you're in luck: there's more than an acre of wine grapes per resident in St Helena. So raise a toast to the women who put that wine in your glass, and their hearts into building this charming town.

THE DRIVE
Trees break up the vineyard views as you head 8 miles northwest on Hwy 29 to Calistoga.

06 CALISTOGA

With soothing natural hot springs, bubbling volcanic mud pools and a spurting geyser, the settlement of Nilektsonoma was renowned across Talahalusi (Napa Valley) by the Wappo people for some 8000 years.

Then in 1859, legendary speculator Sam Brannan talked bankers into backing his scheme to transform Nilektsonoma into Calistoga, California's signature spa resort. But California cowboys preferred dirt, and by 1873 Sam cut his losses in Calistoga and left town. Only a few Brannan cottages remain from his original resort plan.

Some 150 years later, Brannan's dream seems to have come true. Local hills dotted with defunct silver and mercury mines

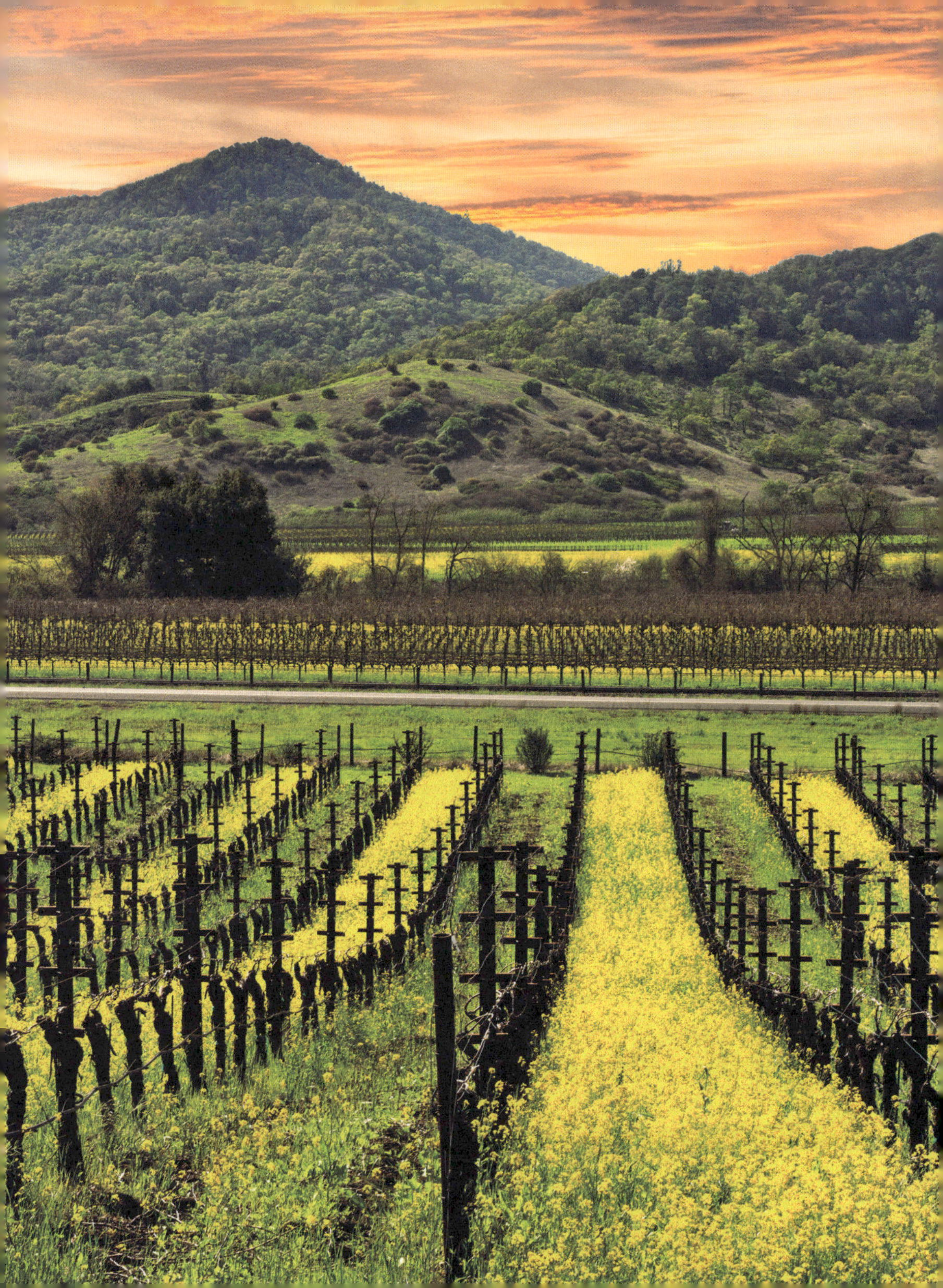

are reclaimed as parkland, including **Bothe-Napa** (parks.ca.gov) and Robert Louis Stevenson State Park. Calistoga's extraordinary geology is a featured attraction at the Petrified Forest and **Old Faithful Geyser** (oldfaithful geyser.com) and its spring water still appears on store shelves today.

Meanwhile at Calistoga's hot-springs spas, brochures still extoll the curative powers of mineral springs and bubbling mud baths. Have some wine at **Sam's Social Club** (samssocialclub.com), and go with the volcanic flow.

THE DRIVE
Backtrack southeast on Hwy 128 and go 4 miles west on forested, curvy Petrified Forest Rd.

Photo Opportunity
Three... Two... One! Get ready for an eruption at Old Faithful Geyser.

DETOUR
Robert Louis Stevenson State Park
Start: 06 Calistoga

Eight miles north of Calistoga via curving Hwy 29, the extinct volcanic cone of Mt St Helena marks a dramatic end to Napa Valley at **Robert Louis Stevenson State Park** (parks.ca.gov). It's a strenuous 5-mile climb to the park's 4343ft summit, but what a view – 200 miles on a clear day. For a shorter hike with views over valley vineyards, take Table Rock Trail (2.2 miles one-way) from the parking-area trailhead. Check conditions before setting out. The park also includes the old Silverado Mine site where writer Robert Louis Stevenson and artist Fanny Osbourne honeymooned in 1880 in an abandoned bunkhouse. Broke, sick and cold, they miraculously survived – and stayed married. He became famous as the author of *Treasure Island*, *Silverado Squatters*, and *Dr Jekyll and Mr Hyde*, with Fanny as his editor. Robert never recovered his health and died young.

07 PETRIFIED FOREST & SAFARI WEST

Three million years ago, a volcanic eruption at Mt St Helena blew down a stand of redwoods. Their trunks gradually turned to stone, and in 1914, enterprising environmentalist Ollie Bockee preserved this land as an

Old Faithful Geyser, Calistoga

educational attraction. Her vision remains remarkably intact today at the **Petrified Forest** (petrified forest.org) Wildfires struck in 2017, but the petrified redwoods were spared and the living redwoods are recovering beautifully, as you can see along two restored half-mile trails.

Four miles west, where Petrified Forest Rd curves right onto Porter Creek, you may hear some strange sounds...yes, that was a rhino. Welcome to **Safari West** (safariwest.com), a 400-acre wildlife preserve where endangered species roam free of predators and poachers.

Meet rare wildlife on a guided two-hour safari in open-sided jeeps, plus a 30-minute hike. Your guide will point out areas scorched by wildfires; the owners heroically saved all 1000 animals.

THE DRIVE
Return east via Petrified Forest Rd and drive 1 mile south on hwy 29/128, then 1 mile north on Lincoln Ave to take lovely, vineyard-lined Silverado Trail almost 30 miles southeast to downtown Napa.

08 SILVERADO TRAIL
Bountiful Silverado Trail meanders from Calistoga to Napa, with tempting pit stops at three dozen wineries. Just outside Calistoga, **Joseph Phelps** (josephphelps.com) has been making its iconic Insignia red blend sustainably since 1974. Phelps dares you to make your own version of Insignia, blending the same six components winemaker Ashley Hepworth used for the latest release – and then taste them side by side, or just lounge under California oaks with a panoramic terrace tasting.

GETTING AROUND NAPA VALLEY
Napa Valley is 30 miles long and 5 miles wide at its widest point (the city of Napa), 1 mile at its narrowest (Calistoga). Two roads run north–south: Hwy 29 (St Helena Hwy) and the more scenic Silverado Trail, a mile east. Drive up one, and down the other. Summer and fall weekend traffic crawls, especially on Hwy 29 between downtown Napa and St Helena around 5pm, when wineries close.

Cross-valley roads that link Silverado Trail with Hwy 29 (including Yountville, Oakville and Rutherford Cross Rds) are bucolic and get less traffic. Oakville Grade Rd and rural Trinity Rd (which leads southwest from Oakville on Hwy 29 to Hwy 12 near Glen Ellen in Sonoma Valley) are narrow, curvy and beautiful – but treacherous in rainstorms.

Napa Valley Vine Trail (vinetrail.org) aims to connect the entire valley via tree-lined bike trails; maps available online. The **Napa Valley Wine Train** (pictured; winetrain.com) takes you from downtown Napa to St Helena and back in a plush vintage dining car, with meal service included and optional winery stops. Trains depart from **Napa Valley Wine Train Depot** on McKinstry St near 1st St.

If you reserve ahead, a memorable multicourse brunch with sparkling wine awaits on the scenic balcony at **Auberge du Soleil** (aubergedusoleil.com). Or follow the convoy of foodies to **Robert Sinskey** (robertsinskey.com), where close collaboration with chef Maria Sinskey produces Napa's most food-friendly wines and inspired pairings. Sinskey's silky pinot noir and merlot are specifically crafted to harmonize with food. Reserve ahead to enjoy bar tastings of biodynamic, organic wines with small-bite pairings, or bountiful food and wine dining.

One of Napa's most prestigious growing areas is Stag's Leap district, east of Yountville. Turn east off Silverado and follow the signs to **Quixote** (quixotewinery.com), a gold-leafed onion dome sprouting from a grassy knoll. Reserve ahead to enter the only US building by outlandish Austrian eco-architect Friedensreich Hundertwasser between crayon-colored ceramic pillars – and taste acclaimed, organically farmed Stag's Leap estate cabs and petit syrah.

07

Sonoma Valley

BEST FOR OUTDOORS

Choose your own adventure at Jack London State Historic Park.

DURATION	DISTANCE	GREAT FOR
2 days	30 miles / 48km	Vineyards, literary

BEST TIME TO GO	Witness 'the crush' in September and October, Warm days May to October.

Autumn vineyard, Sonoma Valley

Sonoma Valley is an easy groove to fall into. Hwy 12 follows the footsteps of Miwok, Pomo and Wintun people, who called this enchanted place 'Valley of the Moon' – and its charms are undeniable. Historic terraced vineyards and pristine forest parklands survived wildfires and Prohibition amazingly intact, thanks to pioneering conservation efforts and 'communion wine' slyly sold by the trainload. Raise a toast to good times and resilient vines.

Link Your Trip

06 Napa Valley
Take Hwy 12/121 to Napa's upscale wineries, hot-springs resorts and world-renowned restaurants.

09 Russian River & Bohemian Highway
Head west on Hwy 12 from Kenwood into boho Western Sonoma for Russian River dips, redwood forest rambles, crisp chardonnays and wild woody pinot noirs.

01 CORNERSTONE GARDENS
The giant orange Adirondack chair by the roadside invites you into this Wine Country **garden and design showplace** (cornerstonesonoma.com), featuring 10 landscape-artist-designed gardens, five kid-friendly education gardens, and local design boutiques. Stop by on-site **Sonoma Valley Visitors Bureau** (sonomavalley.com) for free trip advice and handy tasting-room passes.

THE DRIVE
Go north on Hwy 121 and follow it for 3 miles as it bears east. Turn south on Burndale Rd. Ceja winery is on your right.

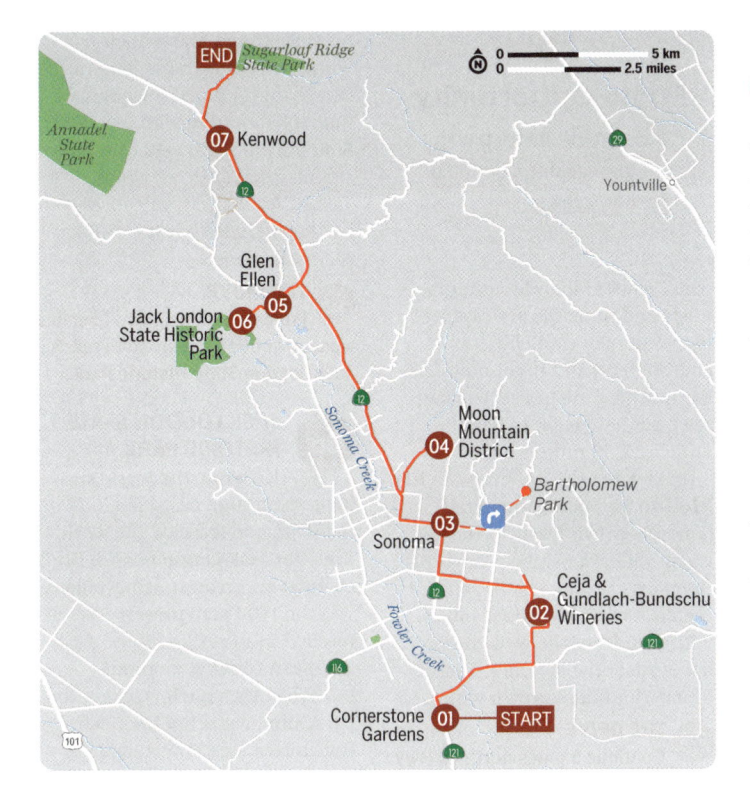

03 DOWNTOWN SONOMA

Native Americans once gathered here at the village of Huichi to trade goods and songs. Spanish missionaries conscripted them to build **adobe** (sonomaparks.org), but most died of measles and smallpox introduced by the Spanish. Under Mexican rule, land was supposed to revert to Native Californian ownership – but Sonoma's mission vineyards were claimed by ranchers instead.

Then one drunken night in 1846, a motley group of partiers took over the **Sonoma barracks**, staggered over to **Mexican General Vallejo's home** (sonomaparks.org) to confiscate his brandy, and proclaimed a breakaway Bear Flag Republic. After a month, the US military took over Sonoma, Vallejo became a US citizen and Sonoma's first state senator, and the barracks were converted into (what else?) a winery. One ticket covers same-day admission to the mission, barracks, Vallejo's home and **Toscano Hotel history museum**.

The town's pride and joy remains the **plaza** (sonomaplaza.com) – the largest town square in California, home to a legendary **farmers market** (5:30pm to 8pm Tuesdays) and ringed with fabulous family-owned bistros, indie boutiques, Victorian inns and dozens of tasting rooms.

Around the corner at **Vella Cheese** (vellacheese.com), parmesan-like Dry Jack has been making spaghetti Western for almost a century. Across the street is **The Patch**, California's oldest community-run urban farm. The pesticide-free, peak-season

02 CEJA & GUNDLACH BUNDSCHU WINERIES

Start your tour of Sonoma Valley's historic vineyards at **Ceja** (cejavineyards.com), for a taste of true vineyard romance. When Amelia Morán met Pedro Ceja in 1967, they were both picking grapes for Mondavi in Napa. Marriage, kids, and decades of trailblazing later, Amelia is the first Mexican-American female winery president – and her family pours their hearts and 50 years of winemaking savvy into Ceja's signature pinot noir, aged chardonnay and Vino de Casa, a silky blend of Italian arneis and chardonnay (bottles $25 to $60). From Ceja, go north on Burndale Rd, jog left briefly onto Napa Rd and then right onto Denmark St. That castle just ahead is California's oldest family-run winery, **Gundlach Bundschu** (gunbun.com), where everyone gets a royal welcome at the bar. Six generations of Bundschus have kept the delightful dry Gewürztraminer flowing since 1858, all while innovating sustainable winemaking practices. Follow the country lane to taste their award-winning merlot, and picnic by the water-recycling pond (bottles $20-$50).

🚗 THE DRIVE
Follow Denmark St back to Napa Rd, and go west to Hwy 12. Drive Hwy 12/Broadway north about 1 mile.

produce is yours to select, weigh and purchase on the honor system – drop your cash in the box, and enjoy your picnic with local wine on the plaza.

THE DRIVE
From downtown Sonoma, take Hwy 12 about 2 miles north, then turn onto Lomita Ave to climb Moon Mountain toward Hanzell Vineyard.

DETOUR
Bartholomew Park
Start: **03** Downtown Sonoma

These peaceful woods have seen it all: the 1857 start of California's wine industry under Hungarian count Agoston Haraszthy, devastation by phylloxera and bankruptcy, construction of an 1885 castle for millionaire philanthropist Kate Johnson and her 42 cats, and its 1919 conversion into a home for 'delinquent women' before fires destroyed it. **Bartholomew Estate** (bartholomewestate.com) rose from the ashes, and despite fires in 2017 and 2019, these certified-organic vineyards are again producing sauvignon blanc, cabernet sauvignon and zinfandel.

Picnics are allowed, and the estate's sun-dappled private park is free and open to visitors from 11am to 4:30pm, with a 3-mile trail winding through vineyards, oaks, madrones and redwoods. Pass the windmill and pond to reach an overlook with sweeping views all the way to the San Francisco Bay.

04 MOON MOUNTAIN DISTRICT
Overlooking downtown Sonoma is an ancient landmark, and the newest local AVA (American Viticultural Region). Grapes have been grown on Moon Mountain for a century, though its steep slopes and mysterious mists are notoriously tricky. Reserve ahead to visit historic **Hanzell Vineyards** (hanzell.

Photo Opportunity
Pause mid-bite for picnic photos in historic Sonoma Plaza.

com), where Moon Mountain's mists and minerals are captured in exceptional cool-climate chardonnays and pinot noirs. As the morning mists rise, you can see from here clear to San Francisco, 50 miles south.

Head down the mountain to **El Molino** for Yucatan-inspired, Sonoma-grown feasts in the warm valley sunshine. Conversation flows among visitors and regulars around outdoor tables, with help from the well-chosen list of sustainable Sonoma- and Moon Mountain–grown wines.

THE DRIVE
Continue 5 miles north on Hwy 12 to reach Glen Ellen.

05 GLEN ELLEN
You'll know you've arrived at the center of tiny Glen Ellen when you spot gargoyles made of rusted tractor parts grinning at you from the gate of **Chuck Gillet's Cyclops Iron Works** (Brazen Estates; 13623 Arnold Dr). Sonoma lawyer-turned-sculptor Chuck has completely covered his 7ft-high fence with recycled-metal art. 'Private but peek freely,' says the sign next to a garden-shear-eared bat, peering shyly from the ivy. Message received: invitation accepted, artist respected. Right across the road, that little cottage is actually a pinot noir powerhouse. **Talisman** (talismanwine.com) founder/winemaker team Scott and Marta Rich worked in major Napa wineries before they jumped the county line, collaborating with legendary Sonoma pinot growers to produce singular, sought-after wines. Tasting fee waived with three-bottle purchase (bottles $38 to $85); call ahead.

THE DRIVE
From Glen Ellen, head 1.5 miles west on London Ranch Rd to reach Jack London State Historic Park.

06 JACK LONDON STATE HISTORIC PARK
He wrote the world's longest-running bestseller, *Call of the Wild,* and traveled the world over, but Jack London (1876–1916) claimed his greatest achievement was the 1400-acre preserve he rescued from early settlers' slash-and-burn farming methods.

Today it's a **park** (jacklondonpark.com), featuring the Beauty Ranch farmstead much as Jack left it. From the farmstead, a short but rugged hiking trail leads past Jack's gravesite to Wolf House ruins, Jack's stone-and-redwood lodge that burned down days before completion in 1913.

His widow, fellow writer and free spirit Charmian Kittredge London repurposed Wolf House stones to build the **House of Happy Walls**. Today it's a **museum** – don't miss Jack's rejection letters in the downstairs bookstore, and Charmian's fabulous flapper dresses in her walk-in wardrobe upstairs. Insightful displays cover Jack's death-defying travels and controversial ideas, including socialism and Darwinism, and address Charmian's strikingly modern writing, outspoken feminism, and challenging role as Jack's editor. Influenced by his friend, trailblazing

Sugarloaf Ridge State Park

Santa Rosa botanist Luther Burbank, Jack also pioneered organic farming and built a circular piggery to collect fertilizer. Hike up to the piggery, or take the easy 2-mile loop to London Lake for a scenic picnic.

THE DRIVE
Drive 2.5 miles east back to Hwy 12 via Arnold Dr, and hang a right onto Miller Lane to reach Quarryhill Botanical Garden..

07 KENWOOD NATURE RETREATS

Take a quick detour off vineyard-lined Hwy 12 into Asian woodlands at **Quarryhill Botanical Garden**. Over 30 years, founder Jane Davenport Jansen and a dedicated team of conservationists cultivated an artful woodland of Asian magnolias, dogwood, lilies and maples. Today this 25-acre botanical garden is fragrant in spring, colorful in fall, and inspiring year-round.

Further north along Hwy 12, take Adobe Canyon Rd uphill to **Sugarloaf Ridge State Park** (sugarloafpark.org) for 25 miles of panoramic hiking and biking. The 2017 fires burned 80% of this 3300-acre park and restoring Sugarloaf has been a mammoth effort, taken on by Sonoma community nonprofits and local volunteers.

Nature is rebounding beautifully. On clear days, Bald Mountain views stretch to the Pacific, while Brushy Peaks Trail overlooks Napa Valley. The trail is moderately strenuous; plan on a three-hour round-trip. For mellower experiences, check online for ecologist-guided forest-bathing walks and weekend stargazing at on-site **Robert Ferguson Observatory**. Check current programs and hiking conditions at the volunteer-run visitor center.

08

Healdsburg & Around

DURATION	DISTANCE	GREAT FOR
2–3 days	135 miles / 215km	Vineyards, nature

BEST TIME TO GO	April, May, September and October for dry, sunny days that aren't too hot.

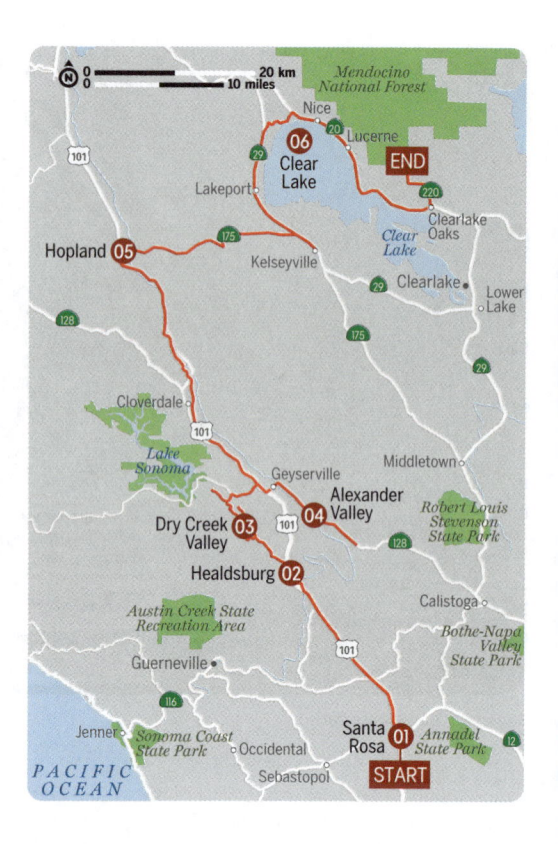

You'll never need to change out of your jeans to find a fabulous meal and inspired wine pairings in this laid-back, sun-blessed corner of Wine Country. But don't let the casual charm fool you: these farmstead wineries are organic pioneers, jaw-dropping natural wonders abound, and Western storefront bistros rack up critical accolades. Shake the dust off your jeans, make yourself comfortable, and let California show you what dreaming is all about.

Link Your Trip

06 Napa Valley

From Geyserville, head 24 miles southeast on Hwy 128 toward Calistoga, where the showcase wineries and destination restaurants of Napa Valley begin.

10 Mendocino & Anderson Valley

Hopland is the jumping-off point for a country drive through Anderson Valley's vineyards and apple orchards to the Pacific Ocean.

01 SANTA ROSA

Wine Country's biggest town is classic Americana, with neighbors waving hello from cottage rose gardens. Cheerful mid-century storefronts still beckon visitors into mom-and-pop shops around Old Courthouse Sq, and historic Railroad Sq greets commuters arriving on tracks first laid by local Chinese laborers in the 1870s.

Seems like a vintage comic-strip backdrop, because it is: *Peanuts* creator Charles Schulz lived, dreamed and doodled here. The **Charles M Schulz Museum** (schulzmuseum.org) captures his lovable legacy with original drawings of Charlie Brown and

BEST FOR FOODIES

Reserve ahead for the meal of a lifetime in one of Healdsburg's top eateries.

Luther Burbank Home & Gardens, Santa Rosa

company, plus a recreation of his home studio. Walk around the tree-shaded, mural-lined streets of **SofA**, the South of A St Art District, and you can't help but stop and smell the flowers – many are fragrant heirloom varietals developed just up the street at **Luther Burbank Home & Gardens** (lutherburbank.org). Pioneering horticulturist Luther Burbank (1849–1926) cultivated 800 hybrid plant species over 50 years, aiming for delight, usefulness and sustainability. His backyard experiments with fragrant flowers, spineless cacti and medicinal plants are still growing outside his Greek Revival home.

Today Santa Rosa is so leafy and laid-back, it's hard to believe it survived two earthquakes and wildfires. Destined to be a survivor, the city was named for the patron saint of first responders, and built on land granted in 1841 to one very determined single mom – and Doña María Ygnacia Lopez de Carrillo and her son Julio designed Santa Rosa to be enjoyed by all.

THE DRIVE
Take Hwy 101 north from downtown Santa Rosa for about 14 miles to exit 503 (Healdsburg Ave). Traffic slows to a crawl as you roll over half a mile north to Healdsburg Plaza.

02 HEALDSBURG

Healdsburg turns on the Western charm, with a sun-dappled central square ringed by Western storefronts, stately Victorian inns and gingerbread-trimmed B&Bs. Downtown stays run around $300 a night – but staying overnight is wise to fully enjoy Healdsburg's world-class restaurants and tasting rooms.

Reserve ahead for the meal of a lifetime at **SingleThread**, inspired Italian pairings at **Idlewild** (idlewildwines.com) and wild pinots at **Lioco** (liocowine.com). True to Healdsburg's origins, the best local wines taste of stubborn roots and undeniable romance, with a faint whiff of scandal.

THE DRIVE
From Healdsburg Plaza, drive 1 mile north on Healdsburg Ave. Turn west onto Dry Creek Rd, a fast-moving thoroughfare; it's 5.5 miles to Truett Hurst. To reach wineries on West Dry Creek Rd, an undulating country lane with no center stripe (ideal for cyclists), turn onto Lambert Bridge Rd by Dry Creek General Store.

03 DRY CREEK VALLEY

Cross the highway from Healdsburg and head back through time in Dry Creek Valley. The scenery here looks a lot like it did 150 years ago, when **Dry Creek General Store** (drycreekgeneralstore1881.com) first opened its Western saloon doors. Load up on cowboy picnic provisions – coffee, slow-cooked brisket, just-baked pie – before making the rounds of Dry Creek's sustainable farmstead wineries.

Picturesque **Preston Farm & Winery** (prestonvineyards.com) invites you to stay awhile, with bocce courts, fresh-baked bread and cold-pressed organic olive oil to enjoy with your organic sauvignon blanc under walnut trees. Sheep bleat welcome to **Reeve** (reevewines.com), where leisurely pinot pairings with cheese and charcuterie are held on the farmhouse patio. Your new favorite red is served in a shed at **Unti** (untivineyards.com), where signature sangiovese and radical rosé of mourvedre bring the taste of the Mediterranean to the Pacific.

THE DRIVE
Follow Dry Creek Rd north to Canyon Rd, which passes underneath Hwy 101. Hang a right on Geyserville Ave (Hwy 128) into Geyserville.

Mustard plants and vineyard, Healdsburg

HEALDSBURG'S EPIC ORIGIN STORY

Healdsburg seems to have it all, but its history is a real-life telenovela. It begins in 1829 with a forbidden romance, when rebellious teenager Joséfa Carrillo fell for Massachusetts-born sea captain Henry Fitch. California was part of Spanish-controlled Mexico – so to marry Joséfa, Harry became a citizen and converted to Catholicism. But California's governor had a crush on Joséfa, and he blocked the wedding. Joséfa convinced her brothers to help her elope.

Joséfa and Henry's star-crossed affair was California's first major scandal, and it took a lawsuit before the governor recognized the marriage. On a winning streak, Joséfa and Henry applied to homestead a 48,000-acre ranch on leased Wappo land in Sonoma. But Henry died of pneumonia in 1849, leaving Joséfa widowed at age 39, with 11 kids and a not-yet-working ranch.

Joséfa came from a long line of resilient Carillo women – her ranchera mother Doña María Ygnacia founded Santa Rosa. So Joséfa made the perilous 700-mile journey north by horse-drawn wagon, only to discover that her mom had died and US prospectors were contesting their land rights. Under US law at the time, women could not own property.

While Joséfa battled in the courts for her property rights, a squatter named George Heald settled on her property refusing to leave for seven years. Turf battles among settlers broke out, dubbed the Healdsburg Wars. When the dust finally settled in the 1870s, the town turned to fighting fires and growing grapes. The pioneering fire department has saved the town many times over, and grapes keep making visitors fall in love with Healdsburg.

04 ALEXANDER VALLEY

Welcome to Geyserville, population 862 – but where are the geysers? Wander the town's old wooden boardwalk, and you'll find genuine Wild West character, plus **Diavola Pizza** and wine made by Alexander Valley neighbors, but no sign of the geothermal wonders that initially attracted visitors here in 1847.

The hot springs are underground, making Geyserville an early adopter of geothermal power generation. Harnessing 350 fumaroles just uphill from Geyserville, the local power-generating operation now produces 20% of California's renewable energy. The power station is off-limits; to get into hot water, reserve a spot at the vast hilltop swimming pools at **Francis Ford Coppola Winery** (francisfordcoppolawinery.com).

Geyserville also invested in a state-of-the-art fire station that has saved the town and rescued the historic vineyards of Alexander Valley. Follow Hwy 128 to **Soda Rock** (sodarockwinery.com) winery's tasting room in the old fire-singed barn, and raise a toast to firefighters with signature California zinfandel.

Follow Hwy 128 and turn onto Chalk Hill Rd, where you'll find resilient Chalk Hill AVA vineyards flourishing at **Sutro** (sutrowine.com) and **Carpenter** (carpenter wine.com), two indie wineries run by women. Reserve ahead to try velvety Carpenter pinots and mineral-rich Sutro sauvignon blanc, amid glorious rolling hills.

THE DRIVE
Follow Hwy 128 back north through Geyserville and join Hwy 101 northbound. It's a 23-mile trip via Cloverdale to the tiny town of Hopland.

Photo Opportunity
Shimmering Clear Lake from atop Hopland Grade.

05 HOPLAND

You're not out of Wine Country yet: Hopland is the gateway to Mendocino County's wine region.

Back in 1866, local fields mostly grew hops for beer – hence the town's name. But after Prohibition decimated their beer business, savvy farmers switched to more profitable crops, including grapes and cannabis. Just south of downtown is the 12-acre **Solar Living Center**, a green landmark where solar energy panels were pioneered in 1978, exhibits promote sustainable permaculture farming, and a legal cannabis dispensary showcases locally farmed weed.

Drive up Main St to find a dozen tasting rooms where you can pick up a free map to local wineries. **Brutocao Cellars** (brutocaocellars.com) has bocce courts, bold red wines and chocolate – a dream combo. Three blocks north, **Graziano Family of Wines** (grazianofamilyof-wines.com) specializes in 'Cal-Ital' wines, including primitivo, barbera, dolcetto and sangiovese. Bet you won't miss the hops in Hopland.

THE DRIVE
Get ready for a stunning yet gut-wrenchingly twisted trip on Hwy 175 east of Hopland. After ascending unnervingly steep Hopland Grade, panoramic views of Clear Lake and Mt Konocti open up below. Eighteen miles from Hopland, turn right to stay on Hwy 175, which joins Hwy 29 south for an easy 5-mile coast into Kelseyville.

06 CLEAR LAKE

With over 100 miles of shoreline, Clear Lake is the largest naturally occurring freshwater lake entirely in California. In summer its warm water blooms with green algae, preventing swimming but creating fabulous habitat for fish and tens of thousands of birds. The 4300ft-tall dormant volcano Mt Konocti is reflected in the waters.

What looks like a Western movie set is real-life **Kelseyville**, where family-owned winery tasting rooms bustle alongside vintage soda fountains, general stores and cafes. Four miles northeast of town, **Clear Lake State Park** (clearlake estatepark.org) offers hiking trails, fishing, boating and camping on the lake's south shore. Check current conditions at the park; some trails may be closed due to recent wildfires.

Follow Soda Bay Rd back west to Hwy 29, which heads north to Lakeport. Take the Nice-Lucerne Cutoff Rd for a scenic drive on Hwy 20 along the lake's north shore, passing the vintage white-cottage resorts of California's 'Little Switzerland.'

About 10 miles east of Lucerne, turn off for a steep climb up High Valley Rd to panoramic **Brassfield Estate** (brassfieldestate.com), where the estate-grown Eruption red is blended from grapes grown on volcanic slopes.

NORTHERN CALIFORNIA 08 HEALDSBURG & AROUND

09

Russian River & Bohemian Highway

BEST FOR WILDLIFE
Gray whales breach at Bodega Head in winter and spring.

DURATION	DISTANCE	GREAT FOR
2 days	75 miles / 120km	Nature, Wine

BEST TIME TO GO | June to September, for toasty days and refreshing river dips.

Redwood forest, Russian River

Sonoma's wild western side has been the place to let loose for over a century. Easy living along the Russian River was first fueled by hard cider, then bubbly wine. Heirloom apple orchards line rolling vineyards producing California's finest cult pinot noir. Come as you are and do your thing – paddle canoes, wander winding country lanes and dream the days away in redwood forests.

Link Your Trip

08 Healdsburg & Around

East of Guerneville, follow River Rd (which becomes Eastside Rd) or scenic Westside Rd for 18 country miles to Healdsburg.

07 Sonoma Valley

From Sebastopol, head east on Hwy 12 for less than 20 miles, passing through Santa Rosa and into the Sonoma Valley for more wine tasting.

01 SEBASTOPOL

No amount of fermented grapes can explain free-spirited Sebastopol. In the 19th century, independent Pomo villagers and immigrant apple farmers formed a US township in the Pomo homeland of Bitakomtara. According to legend, an epic local bar brawl was jokingly compared to the famous Crimean War battlefront, and the nickname Sebastopol stuck.

While the rest of Wine Country started growing grapes, Sebastopol kept growing heirloom apples and wildflowers developed by local horticulture hero Luther Burbank at his **Gold Ridge Experiment Farm** (wschs. org). When the apple-canning factory closed, the old

02 BOHEMIAN HIGHWAY

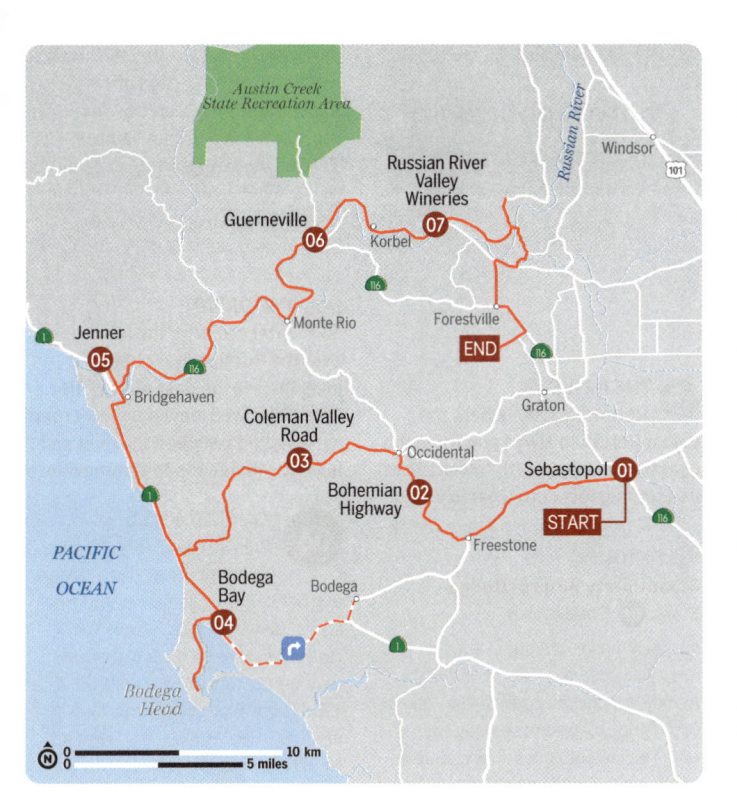

Follow your bliss north of Freestone along the aptly named Bohemian Hwy, passing shaggy barns in Occidental, winding through dense redwoods and emerging at the vintage Russian River resort of Monte Rio.

Pull over in **Freestone** for organic, nutty buns at **Wild Flour Bread**, or for the full Freestone immersion experience, take a warm bath in soft, fermenting cedar chips at **Osmosis** (osmosis.com). Three miles north in **Occidental**, you can meet local artists at **Hinterland & Neon Raspberry** (hinterlandempire.com), and browse recycled, organic and female-made goods sporting Hinterland's motto: 'The future is feral.' On Fridays during summer and fall, everyone emerges from the woods for Occidental's **farmers market** (occidentalcommunityfarmersmarket.com), a free-form street party featuring local musicians, crafts and homemade food. Meanwhile in **Monte Rio**, everyone's at the **beach** (mrrpd.org/monteriobeach.html).

THE DRIVE
In the center of Occidental, turn west onto well-signed Coleman Valley Rd.

03 COLEMAN VALLEY ROAD

Sonoma County's most scenic drive isn't through the grapes, but along these 10 miles of winding byway from Occidental to the sea. It's best in the late morning, when the fog has lifted and the sun's filtering through the tree canopy. Once you reach the ridgeline on Coleman Valley Rd, jog left onto Joy Rd and right onto Fitzpatrick Lane to find a

sheds were creatively repurposed into **The Barlow** (thebarlow.net), an indie maker collective where creatives converge for local food and drink.

Back-to-the-land hippies brought fresh ideas to western Sonoma, including organic farming, home beekeeping and marijuana cultivation. You can visit many trailblazing local farms using the **Sonoma County Farm Trails Guide** (farmtrails.org), and admire the fruits of local labor at Sebastopol's organic **Farmers Market** (sebastopolfarmmarket.org), **BeeKind** (beekind.com) beekeeping boutique, and **Solful** (solful.com) farm-to-spliff cannabis dispensary.

To meet more local characters, check out jam sessions at **People's Music** (peoplesmusic.com), where you might meet Grateful Dead drummer Mickey Hart.

Or take a walk down Florence Ave, lined with recycled-art creatures **Patrick Amiot** (patrickamiot.com) made for his neighbors: a milk-jug cow rides a tractor, tin-can firefighters leap from a refrigerator-sized fire truck, and an auto-parts dinosaur grabs a red convertible for lunch.

THE DRIVE
From the central intersection of Hwys 116 and 12, head west on Bodega Ave (signed Bodega Bay) for 6 miles, passing apple orchards en route to tiny Freestone.

hidden glory: the **Grove of the Old Trees** (landpaths.org). This peaceful, 48-acre redwood forest was once owned by local lumberjacks, yet they couldn't bear to cut down these ancient giants. Environmental activists rallied to save the trees, and conservation nonprofits purchased the entire grove.

On the easy 1-mile loop trail, you'll spot faint blue marks on towering trees once destined for lumberyards. Today they're thriving in this designated 'Forever Wild' conservation site.

Back on Coleman Valley Rd, you'll dip into lush valleys where Douglas firs are cloaked in sphagnum moss – an eerie sight in the fog. Pass gnarled oaks and craggy rock formations as you ascend 1000ft, until finally you see the vast blue Pacific, unfurling at your feet.

THE DRIVE
The road ends at coastal Hwy 1 in the midst of Sonoma Coast State Park, which stretches 17 miles from Bodega Head to just north of Jenner. From Hwy 1, head 2.5 miles south, then west onto Eastshore Rd. Go right at the stop sign onto Bay Flat Rd and along the harbor until road's end.

04 BODEGA BAY
The town of Bodega Bay signals your approach to **Sonoma Coast State Park**, where rocky headlands lean into the horizon over hidden beach coves, and coastal hiking trails wind along wildflower-carpeted bluffs. Go all the way to the tip of the peninsula to reach **Bodega Head**, rising 265ft above sea level for sweeping ocean views, exciting close-up **whale-watching**, kite-flying and hiking as seals bark approval from the rocks below.

Photo Opportunity
Hug a giant redwood in Armstrong Woods.

THE DRIVE
Return to SH47, where the volcanReturn to Hwy 1 and trace the coastline 8 miles north toward Jenner, turning left onto Goat Rock Rd.

DETOUR
Bloodthirsty Birds of Bodge
Start: 04 Bodega Bay

As pretty much everyone in Bodega Bay will tell you, this was the setting for Alfred Hitchcock's classic thriller *The Birds* (1963). It's easy to see why, with all the boisterous gulls flapping around windswept coastal farmsteads. Venture 5 miles inland (south on Hwy 1) to the tiny town of Bodega and you'll find two icons from the film: the schoolhouse (now a private home) and St Teresa of Avila Church. Both look just as they did in the movie – and a crow overhead may make the hairs rise on your neck.

05 JENNER
The charming fishing village of Jenner marks the spot where the Russian River flows into the ocean. At the end of Goat Rock Rd, bear left for **Blind Beach**, where the views are dominated by looming Goat Rock overhead and Arched Rock on the ocean's horizon. Double back and turn left (north) to **Goat Rock Beach**, where your arrival is greeted by the raucous barks of a harbor seal colony – pups are born here from March to August. Get to know your new marine mammal friends better by renting a kayak from **Water Treks EcoTours** (watertreks.com), where you can get tips on river routes and navigating harbor seal habitats.

THE DRIVE
After crossing the last bridge over the Russian River before it joins the sea, go east on Hwy 116/River Rd, a well-paved country road sandwiched between the river and hillsides that leads to Guerneville.

06 GUERNEVILLE
The Russian River's biggest vacation destination almost doubles in size some hot summer weekends, when vacationers arrive to hike redwoods, canoe and hammer cocktails. This town is a good time had by all since the 1870s – it's been an LGBTIQ-plus resort destination for over a century, and a biker pit stop since the '50s.

Downtown Guerneville is lined with cafes, indie maker boutiques, straight-friendly gay bars, down-home dining, and wine tasting for a cause at **Equality Vines** (equalityvines.com).

During summer and fall, the absolute best thing to do on the Russian River is to float down it, on an inner tube, raft or inflatable flamingo, with some friends and a flask in hand. If you're feeling ambitious, rent kayaks and canoes on **Johnson's Beach** (johnsonsbeach.com).

THE DRIVE
Follow Main St east of central Guerneville onto River Rd and drive almost 3 miles to Korbel which will be on your left.

Vineyards, Russian River Valley

07 RUSSIAN RIVER VALLEY WINERIES

There are 50 wineries within a 20-minute drive of Guerneville. The **Russian River AVA** (American Viticulture Area) produces California's cult-favorite pinot noir and chardonnay, thanks to nighttime coastal fog that swirls through the redwoods, then burns off midday in dramatic silvery haloes of mist.

The highest concentration of wineries is along Westside Rd, between Guerneville and Healdsburg. Where Westside Rd turns northeast, 5 miles from Guerneville, you'll find low-key **Porter Creek** (portercreekvineyards.com), where pioneering biodynamic wines are served in a 1930s tool shed. From family vineyards Demeter-certified in 2003, Alex Davis crafts sensational, sustainable pinot noir, syrah, viognier and chardonnay – step up to the tasting bar to try his latest creations.

Backtrack south just over a mile on Westside Rd, then jog left onto Wohler Rd and right back onto River Rd, then follow Mirabel Rd south toward the hamlet of **Forestville**. Turn right onto Hwy 116, and drive just over 4 miles west to the turnoff to Mays Canyon Rd to enter the hidden valley home of **Porter-Bass** (porterbass.com).

Mists swirl around redwoods above, with sunny vineyards below – and under a walnut tree, farmer Sue Bass pours wine that captures this splendid scenery in organic, biodynamic sauvignon blanc, chardonnay, pinot noir and zinfandel.

Head back onto Hwy 116 east, and after a mile, turn right onto sun-dappled, winding Green Valley Rd. Continue 8 miles to Thomas Rd, which bends three times before reaching the entry to **Iron Horse Vineyards** (ironhorsevineyards.com).

Drive to the hilltop barn for drop-dead views over the county, and toast with bubbly pinot noir – including special cuvées celebrating LGBTIQ+Pride and climate resilience.

10

Mendocino & Anderson Valley

BEST FOR DAY HIKES

Hike pygmy forests in Van Damme State Park and canoe the Big River.

DURATION	DISTANCE	GREAT FOR
3-4 days	105 miles / 170km	Food & Drink, Outdoors

BEST TIME TO GO: In fall, when skies are clear and apples harvested.

Vineyard near Philo

This trip is about family-operated vineyards, hushed stands of redwoods and a string of idiosyncratic villages perched in the border area between California's rolling coastal hills and the jagged cliffs of the Pacific. Just far enough out of the Bay Area orbit to move to its own relaxed rhythm, this makes an unforgettable trip filled with low-key pampering, specialty pinot noir, sun-drenched days and romantic, foggy nights.

Link Your Trip

03 Pacific Coast Highways
Can't get enough beachcombing and breathtaking cliffs? Join California's most epic drive along Hwy 1.

12 Lost Coast & Southern Redwoods
The northern edge of this trip nears California's wildest shores. Continue up Hwy 101 to connect with this trip.

01 HOPLAND

Tired of treading over the same ground in Napa and Sonoma? Make for adorable little Hopland, the wine hub of the Mendocino County. Just 100 miles north of San Francisco, this unsung winemaking region offers a lighter, more delicate style of pinot noir and chardonnay. You can taste the wines from many of the family farms you'll see en route at the downtown wine shop **Sip Mendocino** (sipmendocino.com). Its expert staff pour hand-picked flights that include rare vintages you might not even taste at the wineries themselves.

THE DRIVE
Head north on Hwy 101 about 10 miles before exiting on Hwy 253, a beautiful serpentine route southwest through the hills. Hwy 253 ends at Hwy 128, just south of Boonville by the brewery.

02 BOONVILLE
Descending from the hills, visitors spill out into the sun-washed village of Boonville, a short main street with historical buildings, boutiques and artisanal ice cream. The town's most famous taste is just a mile down the road at the **Anderson Valley Brewing Company** (avbc.com). The Bavarian-style brewhouse sits on a big corner lot overlooking the valley, and the grounds are complete with a sparsely furnished tasting room, copper-clad brewing vats and beefy, grazing draft horses. The place also includes a disc-golf course, and players can buy beer inside the tasting room to drink as they play. The brewery's long-standing green credentials include a solar array that generates much of its power.

THE DRIVE
Drive just north out of town on Hwy 128, passing a number of family wineries and fruit stands. The best fruit is ahead, in Philo, only 6 miles north of Boonville.

03 PHILO
The gorgeous **Philo Apple Farm** (philoapplefarm.com) is a bit like something out of a storybook: a dreamy patch of green run by warm-hearted staff and scented with apple blossoms. It's worth trying this (and the other farm stands on the way here) for its organic preserves, chutneys and heirloom apples and pears. If you get here after hours, you're likely to be able to leave a few dollars in a jar and take some goodies along for the ride.

Those who linger can take cooking classes with some of the Wine Country's best chefs. For a swim, the rocky shallow waters of the Navarro River are just a short stroll up the road.

🚗 THE DRIVE
Take the twisting drive west along Hwy 128 through majestic fog-shrouded stands of redwood and you'll eventually emerge at Hwy 1. Go north on Hwy 1 through the seaside town of Albion and on toward Van Damme State Park.

04 VAN DAMME STATE PARK

After emerging on one of California's most serene stretches of Hwy 1, a stroll by the waves seems mandatory. Three miles south of Mendocino, this sprawling 1831-acre **park** (mendoparks.org/parks/van-damme-state-park) draws beachcombers, divers and kayakers to its easy-access beach, and hikers to its pygmy forest. The latter is a unique and precious place, where acidic soil and an impenetrable layer of hardpan have created a miniature forest of decades-old trees.

You can reach the forest on the moderate 2.5-mile **Fern Canyon Scenic Trail**, which crosses back and forth over Little River and past the Cabbage Patch, a bog of skunk cabbage that's rich with wildlife. The **visitor center** has nature exhibits and programs.

🚗 THE DRIVE
A short 2-mile drive north along Hwy 1 brings you to the bridge over the Big River. Just before the bridge, take a right on Comptche Ukiah Rd.

05 BIG RIVER

A lazy paddle up the Big River is a chance to get an intimate look at the border between land and sea – a place where otters, sea lions and majestic blue herons keep you company as you drift silently

Vineyard, Anderson Valley

TOP ANDERSON VALLEY WINERIES

The valley's cool nights yield high-acid, fruit-forward, food-friendly wines. Pinot noir, chardonnay and gewürztraminer grapes flourish. Most **Anderson Valley wineries** (avwines.com) sit outside Philo. Many are family-owned and offer tastings, and some give tours. The following are particularly noteworthy:

Toulouse Vineyards (toulousevineyards.com) Sample standout (and organic!) pinot gris, valdiguié and pinot noir from a stunning hilltop tasting room tucked into the forest.

Navarro Vineyards (navarrowine.com) One of the most visitor-friendly options around, with award-winning pinot noir and dry gewürztraminer; has twice-daily free tours (10:30am and 2pm).

Pennyroyal Farm (pennyroyalfarm.com) You'll get the highlights reel of Anderson Valley at this sustainable farm, creamery and vineyard where you can pair small-batch cheeses with Alsatian-style wines.

by. Although the area near the mouth of the river is an excellent place to watch the waves or catch the sunset, more adventurous travelers can check in at **Catch A Canoe & Bicycles, Too!** (catchacanoe.com), a friendly riverside outfit that rents bikes, kayaks and canoes (including redwood outriggers) for trips up the 8-mile Big River tidal estuary, the longest undeveloped estuary in Northern California. Years of conservation efforts have protected this area from highways and buildings. Bring a picnic and a camera to enjoy the marshes, log-strewn beaches, abundant wildlife and ramshackle remnants of century-old train trestles

THE DRIVE
The next stop, Mendocino, is just north of the bridge over the Big River.

06 MENDOCINO

Perched on a gorgeous headland, Mendocino is the North Coast's salt-washed gem, with B&Bs and rose gardens, white picket fences and New England–style redwood water towers.

Bay Area weekenders walk along the headland among berry bramble and wildflowers, where cypress trees stand over dizzying cliffs. A stroll through this dreamy little village is a highlight of a trip through the region. To get a sense for the village's thriving art scene, drop in at the **Mendocino Art Center** (mendocinoartcenter.org), a hub for visual, musical and theatrical arts. The center is also home to the **Mendocino Theatre Company** (mendocinotheatre.org), which

Photo Opportunity
Otters swimming alongside your canoe on the Big River.

stages contemporary plays in the 81-seat Helen Schoeni Theatre. The town itself is loaded with galleries, all of which host openings on the second Saturday evening of the month, when doors are thrown open to strolling connoisseurs of art and wine, and Mendocino buzzes with life.

Of course, the natural setting here is a work of art itself. The spectacular **Mendocino Headlands State Park** (parks.ca.gov) surrounds the village, with trails crisscrossing the bluffs and rocky coves. Ask at the **Ford House Museum & Visitor Center** (mendoparks.org) about guided weekend walks, including spring wildflower walks and whale-watching jaunts.

THE DRIVE
Just south of town, turn inland at Comptche Ukiah Rd. It will make a loop taking you back toward the trip's beginning. All the turns make the next 30 miles eastbound slow going, but the views are impressive.

07 MONTGOMERY WOODS STATE NATURAL RESERVE

Two miles west of Orr, this 2743-acre **park** (parks.ca.gov) protects some of the best old-growth redwood groves within a day's drive from San Francisco. A 2-mile loop trail, starting near the picnic tables and toilets, crosses the creek, winding through the serene forest. It's out of the way, so visitors are likely to have it mostly to themselves. The trees here are impressive – some up to 367ft tall – but remember to admire them from the trail, both to protect the trees' root systems and to protect yourself from poison oak, which is all over the park.

THE DRIVE
Continue 2 miles east on Comptche Ukiah Rd (which may be called Orr Springs Rd on some maps) to reach Orr Hot Springs.

08 ORR HOT SPRINGS

After all the hiking, canoeing and beachcombing, a soak in the thermal waters of **Orr Hot Springs Resort** (orrhotsprings.org) is heavenly, the ultimate zen-out to end the journey.

While it's not for the bashful, this clothing-optional resort is beloved by locals, back-to-the-land hipsters, backpackers and liberal-minded tourists. Still, you don't have to let it all hang out to enjoy Orr Hot Springs.

The place has private tubs, a sauna, a spring-fed rock-bottomed swimming pool, a steam room, massage and lovely, slightly shaggy gardens. Soaking in the rooftop stargazing tubs on a clear night is magical. Reservations are almost always necessary, even for day visits.

11

Lost Coast & Southern Redwoods

DURATION	DISTANCE	GREAT FOR
3-4 days	105 miles / 170km	Families, Nature

BEST TIME TO GO	May to September, when the weather is most manageable.

With its secluded trails and pristine beaches, the gorgeous 'Lost Coast' is one of the state's most untouched coastal areas and most exciting hiking adventures. The region became 'lost' when the state highway system bypassed it in the 20th century and it has since developed an outsider culture of political radicals, marijuana farmers and nature lovers. Inland, take a magical drive through the big trees of California's largest redwood park.

Link Your Trip

12 Northern Redwood Coast

Link this trip with a jaunt to the forests of the Redwood National Park by continuing north past Ferndale on Hwy 101.

03 Pacific Coast Highways

Keep riding along the Pacific edge of California, either north toward Redwood National Park or south to San Diego.

01 GARBERVILLE

The introductory stop on a Lost Coast romp is scrappy little Garberville, the first town beyond the so-called 'Redwood Curtain' of Humboldt County. It has an alluring laissez-faire attitude, but is not everyone's cup of tea. There's an uneasy relationship here between the old-guard loggers and the hippies, many of whom came in the 1970s to grow marijuana after the feds chased them out of Santa Cruz. The three-block downtown works best as a pit stop to grab lunch and stock up on supplies before you zip over to the coast.

BEST FOR COASTAL HIKES

Hike out to Needle Rock to see an unspoilt Californian shore.

Hiking, Lost Coast

🚗 THE DRIVE
Take it easy and in a low gear on the steep, twisting drive down Briceland Rd (which becomes Shelter Cove Rd eventually) – managing the 21 miles from Redway to Shelter Cove can be a challenge. Best to heed the 'No Trespassing' signs on this part of the drive, as the local marijuana farmers don't take kindly to strangers.

02 SHELTER COVE
At the end of the road – and what seems like the end of the earth – is the isolated community of Shelter Cove, gateway to the **Lost Coast**. The tiny encampment of restaurants and shops sometimes seems equally populated by humans and Roosevelt elk. Although primarily used as a launching point for the nearby wilds, it makes a relaxing destination in its own right. From town, scan the water for migrating gray whales (look for mothers and their calves in early spring) and explore tide pools teeming with crabs, snails, sea stars and sponges; locals even spot an octopus on occasion

🚗 THE DRIVE
There are trailheads for exploring the Lost Coast Trail both north and south of town. That's where the drive pauses; the trail has to be done on foot.

03 LOST COAST
The North Coast's superlative backpacking destination is a rugged, mystifying stretch of coast with trails crossing seafront peaks and volcanic black-sand beaches. The **King Range** boldly rises 4000ft within 3 miles of the coast, which became 'lost' when the state's highway system deemed the region impassable in the mid-20th century.

Made up of **Sinkyone Wilderness State Park** and the **King Range National Conservation Area**, the region is best explored on a multiday hike. Leaving from Shelter Cove, a three-day trek north on the Lost

BEST ROAD TRIPS: CALIFORNIA

Coast Trail ends at the mouth of the Mattole River. Equally challenging and rewarding, it passes the abandoned Punta Gorda Lighthouse near the end. You can arrange shuttle service back to your car through **Lost Coast Adventure Tours** (lostcoastadventures.com). From Shelter Cove, you can take a day hike to Black Sand Beach, or overnight at **Needle Rock Campground** (parks.ca.gov), about 9 miles south of the Hidden Valley Trailhead. The **visitor center** (parks.ca.gov) there affords gorgeous coastal views.

THE DRIVE
Retrace the twisting drive back to Garberville, then continue north on Hwy 101. Exit Hwy 101 when you see the 'Avenue of the Giants' sign, 6 miles north of Garberville, near Phillipsville, and be sure to pick up one of the free driving guides at the roadside stand by the exit. This is the heart of the big-tree country.

04 AVENUE OF THE GIANTS & HUMBOLDT REDWOODS STATE PARK

The incredible, 32-mile, two-lane stretch of highway known as the **Avenue of the Giants** is one of the most justifiably celebrated drives in California, and a place where travelers stand with jaws agape and necks craned upward at the canopy. The route connects a number of small towns with mid-20th-century motels, diners serving 'lumberjack' meals and pull-offs parked with Harleys. Visitors would be remiss to drive right past these majestic groves along the avenue without stopping at the **California Federation of Women's Clubs Grove**, home to an interesting four-sided hearth designed by renowned architect Julia Morgan, and the **Founders Grove**, where the 370ft Dyerville Giant was knocked down in 1991 by another falling tree.

Much of the Avenue of the Giants snakes in and out of **Humboldt Redwoods State Park** (parks.ca.gov). At 53,000 acres – 17,000 of which are old-growth – it boasts three-quarters of the world's tallest 100 trees. These groves rival those in Redwood National Park further north.

The 100-plus miles of trails can be taken on foot, horse or bike and range in difficulty from the kid-friendly **Drury-Chaney Loop Trail** to the rugged **Grasshopper Peak Trail**, which climbs to a fire lookout (3379ft). The primeval **Rockefeller Forest**, 4.5 miles west of the avenue via the incredibly picturesque Mattole Rd, appears as it did a century ago. It's the world's largest contiguous old-growth redwood forest, and contains about 20% of all such remaining trees.

TOP TIP:
Accessing the Lost Coast

Backpackers who wish to hike the entirety of the Lost Coast often go from north to south in order to avoid northerly winds. Many hikers start at the Mattole Campground, just south of Petrolia, which is on the northern border of the King Range.

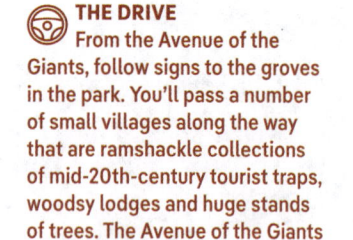

THE DRIVE
From the Avenue of the Giants, follow signs to the groves in the park. You'll pass a number of small villages along the way that are ramshackle collections of mid-20th-century tourist traps, woodsy lodges and huge stands of trees. The Avenue of the Giants ends at Hwy 101 near Pepperwood, from where it's a 5-mile drive north to Scotia.

05 SCOTIA

For years, Scotia was California's last 'company town,' entirely owned and operated by the Pacific Lumber Company, which built cookie-cut houses and had an open contempt for long-haired outsiders who liked to get between their saws and the big trees. The company went belly-up in 2008, sold the mill to another redwood company and, though the town still has a creepy *Truman Show* vibe, you no longer have to operate by the company's posted 'Code of Conduct.'

There are dingy diners and a couple of bars in Rio Dell, across the river from Scotia. Back in the day, this is where the debauchery went down: because it wasn't a company town, **Rio Dell** had saloons and prostitutes. In 1969 the freeway bypassed the town and it withered.

THE DRIVE
Follow Hwy 101 for almost 8 miles north to exit 687 for Kenmar Rd. At the south end of the town in Fortuna, turn right onto Alamar Way.

06 FORTUNA

The penultimate stop is at **Eel River Brewing Company** (eelriverbrewing.com) in Fortuna for a cold, refreshing pint of beer. This place is completely in step with its amazing natural surrounds – it was the USA's first certified organic brewery and uses 100% renewable energy (there's a bit of irony in the fact that most of their beer is brewed in an old redwood mill that formerly belonged to the Pacific Lumber Company). The breezy beer garden and excellent burgers make it an ideal pit stop.

THE DRIVE
Back on Hwy 101, go just over 2 miles north and take exit 691 for Fernbridge/Ferndale. Follow Hwy 211 for 5 miles southwest past rolling dairy farms to Ferndale.

07 FERNDALE
The trip ends at one of the region's most charming towns, stuffed with impeccable Victorians – known locally as 'butterfat palaces' because of the dairy wealth that built them. The entire town is a **State Historical Landmark** with several nationally registered historic sites. A stroll down Main St offers a taste of super wholesome, small-town America, from galleries to old-world emporiums and soda fountains. Half a mile from downtown via Bluff St, enjoy short tramps through fields of wildflowers, beside ponds and past a mature Sitka spruce forest at 110-acre **Russ Park**. The cemetery, also on Bluff St, has graves dating to the 1800s and expansive views to the ocean.

To end the trip with whimsy, show up over Memorial Day weekend in late May to see the fanciful, astounding, human-powered contraptions of the annual **Kinetic Grand Championship** (kineticgrandchampionship.com) race from Arcata to Ferndale. Shaped like giant fish and UFOs, these colorful piles of junk propel racers over roads, water and marsh in a three-day event.

Photo Opportunity
Queen Charlotte Sound snapped from the Snout Track.

Ferndale

12

Northern Redwood Coast

DURATION	DISTANCE	GREAT FOR
3–4 days	110 miles / 175km	Nature

BEST TIME TO GO	April to October for usually clear skies and the region's warmest weather.

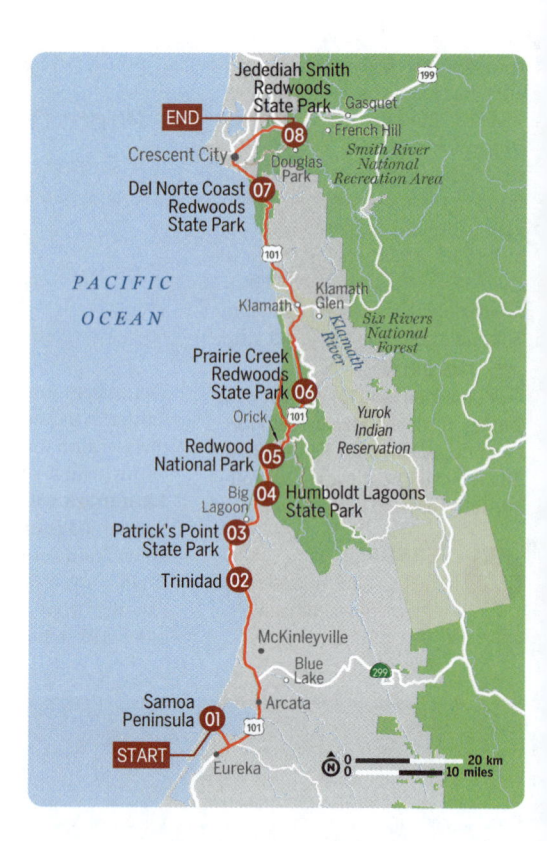

This trip may have been charted in the glory days of the mid-20th-century American road trip – roadside attractions include a giant Paul Bunyan statue, drive-through trees and greasy burger stands – but that might as well be yesterday in this land of towering, mystical, ancient redwood forests. Curving roads and misty trails bring visitors to lush, spectacular natural wonders that are unlike any other place on earth. Prepare to be impressed.

Link Your Trip

11 Lost Coast & Southern Redwoods

Head south on Hwy 101 from Eureka for more redwood wonders and the untouched Lost Coast for the North Coast's best hiking adventures.

13 Trinity Scenic Byway

Cut inland on Hwy 299 from Arcata and get lost in the wild country of California's northern mountains.

01 SAMOA PENINSULA

Even though this trip is about misty primeval forest, the beginning is a study of opposites: the grassy dunes and windswept beaches of the 10-mile long Samoa Peninsula. At the peninsula's south end is **Samoa Dunes Recreation Area** (blm. gov), part of a 34-mile-long dune system. It's great for picnicking or fishing, and the wildlife viewing is excellent. Or, leave the landlubbers behind and take a **Harbor Cruise** (humboldtbaymaritimemuseum. com) aboard the 1910 *Madaket*, America's oldest continuously operating passenger vessel.

BEST SCENIC DRIVE

Howland Hill Rd through old-growth redwood forests.

Patrick's Point State Park

Leaving from the foot of C St in the nearby city of Eureka, it ferried mill workers before the Samoa Bridge was built in 1971. The $15 sunset cocktail cruise serves drinks from the smallest licensed bar in the state.

THE DRIVE
Head north on Hwy 101 from Eureka, passing myriad views of Humboldt Bay. Fifteen miles north of Arcata, take the first Trinidad exit. Note that the corridor between Eureka and Arcata is a closely watched safety corridor (aka speed trap).

02 TRINIDAD
Perched on an ocean bluff, cheery Trinidad somehow manages an off-the-beaten-path feel despite a constant flow of visitors. A free town map available at the tiny **Trinidad Museum** (trinidad museum.org) will help you navigate the town's cute little shops and several fantastic hiking trails, most notably the Trinidad Head Trail with superb coastal views and excellent **whale-watching** (December to April).

If the weather is nice, stroll the exceptionally beautiful cove at **Trinidad State Beach**.

THE DRIVE
Head back north of town on Patrick's Point Dr to hug the shore for just over 5 miles.

03 PATRICK'S POINT STATE PARK
Coastal bluffs jut out to sea at 640-acre **Patrick's Point State Park** (parks.ca.gov) where sandy beaches abut rocky headlands. Easy access to dramatic coastal bluffs makes this the best bet for families, but any age will find a feast for the senses as they climb rock formations, search for breaching whales, carefully navigate tide pools and listen to barking sea lions and singing birds.

The park also features **Sumêg**, an authentic reproduction of an indigenous Yurok village, with hand-hewn redwood buildings. The 2-mile **Rim Trail**, a former Yurok trail around the bluffs, circles the point with access to huge rocky outcrops. Don't miss Wedding Rock, one of the park's most romantic points, or Agate Beach, where lucky visitors spot bits of jade and sea-polished agate.

THE DRIVE
Make your way back out to Hwy 101 through thick stands of redwoods. Another 5 minurtes north will bring you to the sudden clearing of Big Lagoon, part of Humboldt Lagoons State Park. Continue 6 more miles north to the visitor center, which is closed, but has toilets and an information board.

04 HUMBOLDT LAGOONS STATE PARK
Stretching out for miles along the coast, Humboldt Lagoons State Park has long, sandy beaches and a string of coastal lagoons. **Big Lagoon** and prettier **Stone Lagoon** are both excellent for kayaking and bird-watching. Sunsets are spectacular, with no structures in sight. At the **Stone Lagoon Visitor Center**, on Hwy 101, there are restrooms plus a bulletin board displaying information. Just south of Stone Lagoon, tiny **Dry Lagoon** (a freshwater marsh) has a fantastic day hike. Park at Dry Lagoon's picnic area and hike north on the unmarked trail to Stone Lagoon; the trail skirts the southwestern shore and ends up at the ocean, passing through woods and marshland rich with wildlife. Mostly flat, it's about 2.5 miles one way.

Photo Opportunity
Misty redwoods clinging to rocky cliffs at Del Norte Coast Redwoods State Park.

THE DRIVE
Keep driving north on Hwy 101. Now, at last, you'll start to lose all perspective among the world's tallest trees. This is likely the most scenic part of the entire trip; you'll emerge from mist-shrouded shores dotted with rocky islets into curvy two-lane roads through awe inspiring redwood groves.

05 REDWOOD NATIONAL PARK
Heading north, **Redwood National Park** (nps.gov/redw) is the first park in the patchwork of state and federally administered lands under the umbrella of Redwood National & State Parks. After picking up a map at the **Thomas H Kuchel Visitor Center** (nps.gov/redw), you'll have a suite of choices for hiking. A few miles further north along Hwy 101, a trip inland on Bald Hills Rd will take you to **Lady Bird Johnson Grove**, with its 1.5-mile kid-friendly loop

Redwood National Park

trail, or get you lost in the secluded serenity of **Tall Trees Grove**.

To protect the latter grove, a limited number of cars per day are allowed access; get free permits at the visitor center. This can be a half-day trip itself, but you're well rewarded after the challenging approach (a 6-mile rumble on an old logging road behind a locked gate, then a moderately strenuous 4.5-mile round-trip hike).

THE DRIVE
Back on Hwy 101, less than 2 miles north of Bald Hills Rd, turn left onto Davison Rd, which trundles for 7 miles (mostly unpaved) out to Gold Bluffs Beach.

06 PRAIRIE CREEK REDWOODS STATE PARK

The short stroll to Gold Bluffs Beach will lead you to the best spot for a picnic. Past the campground, you can take a longer hike beyond the end of the road into **Fern Canyon**; its 60ft-high fern-covered sheer rock walls appear in *The Lost World: Jurassic Park*. This is one of the most photographed spots on the North Coast – damp and lush, all emerald green – and totally worth getting your toes wet to see.

Back on Hwy 101, head 2 miles further north and exit onto the 8-mile Newton B Drury Scenic Pkwy, which runs parallel to the highway through magnificent untouched ancient redwood forests. Family-friendly nature trails branch off from roadside pullouts, including the wheelchair-accessible Big Tree Wayside, and also start outside the **Prairie Creek Redwoods State Park Visitor Center** (parks.ca.gov), including the Revelation Trail for visually impaired visitors.

DRIVE-THRU TREES & GONDOLA RIDES
With lots of kitschy mid-20th-century appeal, the following destinations are a throwback to those bygone days of the great American road trip.

Trees of Mystery (treesofmystery.net) In Klamath, it's hard to miss the giant statues of Paul Bunyan and Babe the Blue Ox towering over the parking lot at this shameless, if lovable, tourist trap. It has a gondola running through the redwood canopy.

Chandelier Drive-Thru Tree Park (drivethrutree.com) Fold in your mirrors and inch forward, then cool off in the uber-kitschy gift shop, in Leggett.

Shrine Drive Thru Tree Look up to the sky as you roll through, on the Avenue of the Giants in Myers Flat. It's the oldest but least impressive of the three drive-thru trees.

THE DRIVE:
Follow the winding Newton B Drury Scenic Pkwy through beautiful inland forests with views of the east and its layers of ridges and valleys. On returning to Hwy 101, head north to Klamath, with its bear bridge. Del Norte Coast Redwoods State Park is just a few minutes further north.

07 DEL NORTE COAST REDWOODS STATE PARK

Marked by steep canyons and dense woods, this **park** (nps.gov/redw) contains 15 miles of hiking trails and several old logging roads that are a mountain biker's dream. Tall trees cling precipitously to canyon walls that drop to the rocky, timber-strewn coastline. t's almost impossible to get to the water, except via gorgeous but steep **Damnation Creek Trail** or Footsteps Rock Trail. The former may be only 4 miles round trip, but the 1100ft elevation change and cliffside redwoods make it the park's best hike.

THE DRIVE
Leaving Del Norte Coast Redwoods State Park and continuing on Hwy 101, you'll enter dreary little Crescent City, a fine enough place to gas up or grab a bite, but not worth stopping at for long. About 4 miles northeast of town, Hwy 199 splits off from Hwy 101; follow it east for 6 miles to Hiouchi, entry point for Jedediah Smith Redwoods State Park.

08 JEDEDIAH SMITH REDWOODS STATE PARK

The final stop on the trip is loaded with worthy superlatives – the northernmost park has the densest population of redwoods and the largest natural undammed free-flowing river in California, the sparkling Smith. **Jedediah Smith Redwoods State Park** (nps.gov/redw) is a treat for the senses. The redwood stands here are so dense that few hiking trails penetrate the park, so you can drive the outstanding 10-mile Howland Hill Rd, which cuts through otherwise inaccessible areas, heading back toward Crescent City. It's a rough, unpaved road, and it can close if there are fallen trees or washouts, but you'll feel as if you're visiting from Lilliput as you cruise under the gargantuan trunks. To spend the night, reserve at the park's superb riverbank campground.

BEST ROAD TRIPS: CALIFORNIA

13

Trinity Scenic Byway

BEST FOR FAMILIES

Lake Shasta Caverns tour includes a boat ride and wildlife-watching.

DURATION	DISTANCE	GREAT FOR
3 days	245 miles / 395km	Literary landscapes

BEST TIME TO GO | June through October, when the lakes and rivers are full and the air crisp.

Mt Shasta

The back-to-landers, outdoorsy types and new-age escapists in this remote corner of Northern California proudly count the number of stoplights and fast-food joints in their counties on one hand. An epic cruise along the Trinity Scenic Byway takes visitors from one of California's most distinctive mountains to the Pacific shore, passing ample natural wonders and sophisticated small towns along the way.

Link Your Trip

12 Northern Redwood Coast
Head north on Hwy 101 from Arcata to link this epic mountain journey with a visit to the proud redwood stands of the far North Coast.

14 Volcanic Legacy Byway
Take a trip around California's untouched northern volcanic wilds by going east of Redding on Hwy 44.

01 MT SHASTA

'When I first caught sight of it I was 50 miles away and afoot, alone and weary. Yet all my blood turned to wine, and I have not been weary since,' wrote naturalist John Muir in 1874 of Mt Shasta. Though not California's highest (at 14,179ft it ranks fifth), the sight of this solitary peak is truly intoxicating. Start this trip near the top: you can drive almost all the way up via the Everitt Memorial Hwy (Hwy A10) to enjoy exquisite views any time of year. By the time you reach Bunny Flat (6860ft), you'll be gasping at the sights (and the thin air), but if the

82 BEST ROAD TRIPS: CALIFORNIA

NORTHERN CALIFORNIA 13 TRINITY SCENIC BYWAY

road is clear of snow continue the ascent for more amazing views. You'll see Lassen Peak to the south. Look west for a bird's-eye preview of the rest of this trip, toward the Marble Mountains and the green hills along the Trinity Scenic Byway. For information about hikes, contact the in-town **Mt Shasta Ranger Station** (fs. usda.gov/stnf), which issues permits and good advice.

THE DRIVE
Follow Everitt Memorial Hwy back down the mountain. It'll take about 30 minutes to get down to Mt Shasta City, a new-agey town that's easy to love. Go south on I-5 for more than 40 miles to Shasta Lake.

DETOUR
Dunsmuir
Start: 01 Mt Shasta

Built by Central Pacific Railroad, Dunsmuir (population 1570) was originally named Pusher, for the auxiliary 'pusher' engines that muscled the heavy steam engines up the steep mountain grade. The town's reputation is still inseparable from the trains, making the stop essential for rail buffs. You can also stop here to quench your thirst; it could easily be – as locals claim – 'the best water on earth.' Maybe that water is what makes the beer at **Dunsmuir Brewery Works** (dunsmuirbreweryworks.com) so damn good. The crisp ales and malty porter are perfectly balanced. Go south from Mt Shasta on I-5 for almost 8 miles and take exit 730 for central Dunsmuir.

02 SHASTA LAKES

The largest reservoir in California, Shasta Lake has the state's biggest population of bald eagles, an endless network of hiking trails, and great fishing. On the north side, stop to tour the crystalline caves of the **Lake Shasta Caverns** (lakeshastacaverns.com). Tours include a boat ride that's great for families (bring a sweater – it's chilly!). The **Shasta Dam visitors center** (usbr.gov/mp/ncao/shasta-dam.html) to the south has maps of hiking trails and a view of Shasta Dam. The colossal, 15-million-ton dam is second only in size to Hoover Dam in Nevada; its 487ft spillway is nearly three times as

BEST ROAD TRIPS: CALIFORNIA   83

high as Niagara Falls. At the visitor center, join a fascinating free guided tour of the structure's rumbling interior.

🚗 **THE DRIVE**
Retrace your path back to I-5 and head south about 9 miles to Redding.

03 REDDING
Redding's sprawl – malls, big-box stores and large housing developments – might be discordant with the north's natural wonders, but it's the launching point for the Trinity Scenic Byway, which starts west of town. It's worth stopping for the **Turtle Bay Exploration Park** (turtlebay.org). Situated on 300 acres, the complex has an art and natural-science museum with interactive exhibits for kids, extensive gardens, a butterfly conservatory and a 22,000-gallon, walk-through river aquarium with regional aquatic life. The futuristic **Sundial Bridge** connects the park to the north bank of the Sacramento River and was designed by renowned Spanish architect Santiago Calatrava.

🚗 **THE DRIVE**
The banner stretch of the trip starts here: the Trinity Scenic Byway (Hwy 299) begins west of Redding and traces a winding path through the mountains to the Pacific Coast. Forests, mountain lakes, crumbling cabins and rushing rivers accompany the drive.

04 WHISKEYTOWN NATIONAL RECREATION AREA
An old mining town lent the rich name to **Whiskeytown Lake** (nps.gov/whis), this lovely, multi-use reservoir. Much of the lake's serene 36 miles of forested

📷 **Photo Opportunity**
Santiago Calatrava's futuristic Sundial Bridge.

shoreline was devastated in the 2018 Carr fire but it's slowly opening up as an excellent place to camp, swim, sail, mountain bike and pan for gold. The **visitor center**, on the northeast point, provides information and free maps. From here, the hike to roaring **Whiskeytown Falls** (3.4 miles round-trip) follows a former logging road. On the western side, the **Tower House Historic District** contains the El Dorado Mine ruins and the pioneer Camden House, open for summer tours. In winter, it's an atmospheric place to explore.

🚗 **THE DRIVE**
Leaving Whiskeytown Lake, Hwy 299 enters more-remote country – cellphone service gets iffy. About 10 miles west of the lake the road becomes steep with white-knuckled turns and excellent lake vistas. Cut north on Trinity Dam Blvd for Lewiston.

05 LEWISTON
Blink and you might miss Lewiston, a collection of buildings beside a rushing stretch of the Trinity River known for fishing. Stop at the **Country Peddler**, a drafty old barn filled with antiques. The owners, avid outdoor enthusiasts, know the area like the backs of their hands.

Lewiston Lake is about 1.5 miles north of town and is a serene alternative to the other area lakes. Early in the evening you may see ospreys and **bald eagles** diving for fish. Still, the best natural sights are deeper afield – particularly the **Trinity Alps Wilderness**, west of Hwy 3. Look no further for rugged adventure: it hosts excellent hiking and backcountry camping, with over 600 miles of trails that cross granite peaks and skirt deep alpine lakes.

🚗 **THE DRIVE**
Take Lewiston Lake Rd back south to Hwy 299, then head west about 12 miles to Weaverville, the next village on this trip.

06 WEAVERVILLE
The walls of the **Weaverville Joss House State Historic Park** (parks.ca.gov) actually talk – they're papered inside with 150-year-old donation ledgers from the once-thriving Chinese community, a testament to the rich culture of immigrants who built Northern California's infrastructure. The rich blue-and-gold Taoist shrine contains an ornate 3000-year-old altar, which was brought here from China. Sadly, state budget issues have made the future of this park uncertain, but it still makes a surprising gem within this far-flung mountain community.

🚗 **THE DRIVE**
Gas up and get ready for awe-inspiring views of granite mountains, the nationally designated Wild and Scenic Trinity River and sun-dappled forest in every direction. There are no turnoffs; simply continue west on Hwy 299.

07 WILLOW CREEK
Stay sharp as you navigate the road to Willow Creek – this remote community

Whiskeytown Lake, Whiskeytown National Recreation Area

was the site of some of the most convincing homemade footage ever captured of a Sasquatch. This makes an obligatory stop of the **Willow Creek–China Flat Museum** (bigfootcountry.net) for the fun Big Foot Exhibit that includes casts of very large footprints and some provocative (if blurry) photos.

The 25ft-tall redwood sculpture of the hairy beast in the parking lot is hard to miss. Willow Creek is also the beginning of the Bigfoot Scenic Byway (Hwy 96) – a route that winds north through breathtaking mountain and river country, with the most Bigfoot sightings in the country.

THE DRIVE
About 10 miles west of Willow Creek, you'll pass the Berry Summit Vista Point (Mile 28.4) and then start to drop toward the Pacific. Continue just over 25 twisting miles on Hwy 299 to Hwy 101, turning south to Arcata.

08 ARCATA
Congratulations, you've finally arrived in Arcata, an idiosyncratic college town on the sparkling shores of the Pacific and in the middle of California's majestic redwood country.

Park at **Arcata Plaza** (north coastgrowersassociation.org) and stroll around the historic downtown to find a bite to eat (the restaurants are top-notch) or explore the campus of **Humboldt State University** (ccat.humboldt.edu), home to a world-class sustainability program.

14

Volcanic Legacy Byway

BEST FOR ADVENTURES

Rent a boat and make the trip to Ahjumawi Lava Springs.

DURATION	DISTANCE	GREAT FOR
3 days	225 miles / 360km	Families, Nature

BEST TIME TO GO	July and August when the snow finally clears from the highest passes.

Lassen Volcanic National Park

Looping the big, green patches of the map is perfect for hiking, fishing, camping or getting lost. This is a place where few people venture, but those who do come back with stories. Settlements in this neck of the woods are mostly just places to gas up and buy some jerky, but adventurers are drawn here for just that reason. This is the deeply satisfying final frontier of California's wilderness.

Link Your Trip

25 Feather River Scenic Byway
Join this epic mountain journey 40 miles southeast of Lassen National Park in Chester for an inland trip along Hwy 70 and the river.

13 Trinity Scenic Byway
From Mt Shasta, go via the rugged Trinity Alps to the sparkling sea, following Hwy 299 past pristine wilderness.

01 LASSEN VOLCANIC NATIONAL PARK

As you drive through the surrounding fields studded with volcanic boulders, **Lassen Volcanic National Park** (nps.gov/lavo) glowers in the distance. Lassen Peak rises 2000 dramatic feet over the surrounding landscape to 10,457ft above sea level. Lassen's dome has a volume of half a cubic mile, making it one of the world's largest plug-dome volcanoes – its most recent eruption took place in 1915, when it blew a giant billow of smoke, steam and ash many miles high into the atmosphere.

Approaching the park, the road begins to climb, entering corridors of dense forest and emerging at the

best way to visit is to silently glide across these waters in a canoe or kayak. These can often be rented in nearby towns such as **Fall River Mills**. After you paddle out, the hikes are glorious: there are basalt outcroppings, lava tubes, cold springs bubbling and all kinds of volcanic features. For more information about boat rentals and primitive camping, contact McArthur-Burney Falls Memorial State Park.

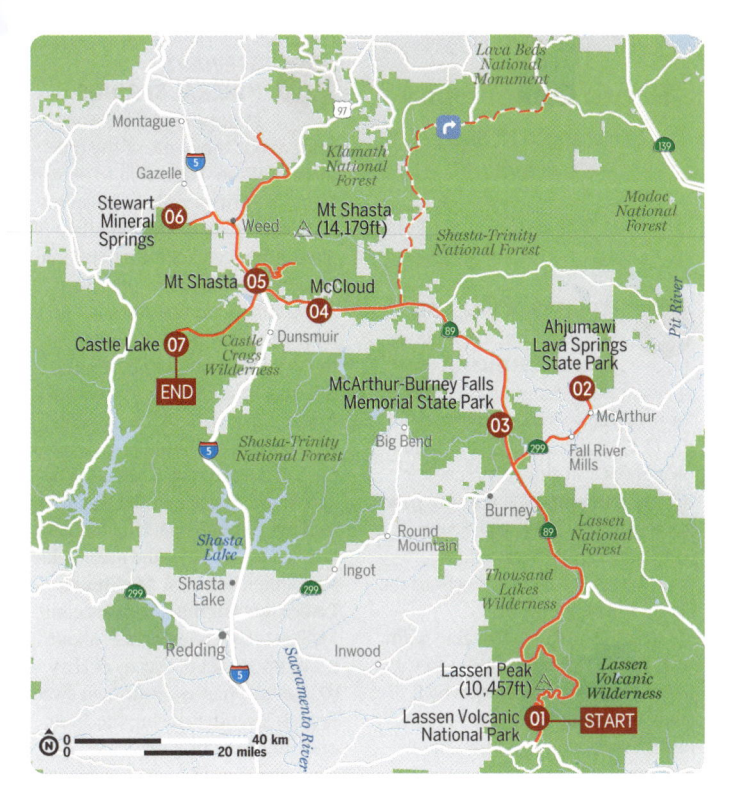

THE DRIVE
Backtrack more than 20 miles west of McArthur on Hwy 299, then turn right on Hwy 89 and take it 6 miles north to McArthur-Burney Falls Memorial State Park.

03 MCARTHUR-BURNEY FALLS MEMORIAL STATE PARK

After all the volcanic rock and sulfur fields, there's a soothing stop up the road in **McArthur-Burney Falls Memorial State Park** (parks.ca.gov). Fed by a spring, the splashing 129ft-tall waterfalls flow at the same temperature, 42°F (5.5°C), year-round. Rangers are quick to point out that it might not be California's highest waterfall, but it may be the most beautiful. Clear, lava-filtered water surges over the top and also from springs in the waterfall's face. Hiking trails include a portion of the Pacific Crest Trail, which continues north to Castle Crags State Park. The 1.3-mile **Burney Falls Trail** is the one you shouldn't miss. Upgraded with guardrails, it's an easy loop for families and allows close-up views of water rushing right out of the rock.

THE DRIVE
Continue northwest on Hwy 89 for about 40 miles to McCloud.

LEED platinum-certified **Kohm Yah-mah-nee Visitor Facility**. Stop in to pick up maps and the handy park newspaper, which outlines campsites and over 150 miles of hiking trails. Heading north, you can roam the tawny stone slopes of burbling Sulfur Works – you'll know it by the ripe scent in the air and the gaseous bursts hissing over the roadway. The moderate 1.5-mile hike to **Bumpass Hell** traverses an active geothermal area festooned with otherworldly colored pools and billowing clouds of steam.

THE DRIVE
Follow Hwy 89 for 29 miles through the park, looping east of Lassen Peak. Go right on Hwy 299 for Fall River Mills, where you may be able to rent a kayak or canoe. Entering McArthur, turn left onto Main St by the Inter-Mountain fairgrounds, cross a canal and continue on a dirt road to the Rat Farm boat launch.

02 AHJUMAWI LAVA SPRINGS STATE PARK

Of all the stops along this trip, none is more remote and more rewarding than the **Ahjumawi Lava Springs State Park** (parks.ca.gov). A visit here comes with serious bragging rights as the abundant springs, aquamarine bays and islets, and jagged flows of black basalt lava are truly off the beaten path, and can be reached only by boat. The

04 MCCLOUD

An old logging town, McCloud sits serenely on the southern slopes of Mt Shasta, with the peak looming in the distance. It is a mellow, comfortable place from which to explore the pristine wilderness that surrounds it. Bump along the tiny, partially paved **McCloud River Loop**, which begins off Hwy 89 about 11 miles east of McCloud, to find the lovely **McCloud River Trail**, which passes three waterfalls on the lower reaches of Mt Shasta. The easy 1.8-mile trail passes gorgeous, secluded falls, and you'll discover a lovely habitat for bird-watching in Bigelow Meadow. Other good hiking trails include the **Squaw Valley Creek Trail** (not to be confused with the ski area near Lake Tahoe), an easy 5-mile loop trail south of town, with options for swimming, fishing and picnicking.

THE DRIVE
Hwy 89 climbs steeply to reach the city of Mt Shasta. Along the way you'll pass Mt Shasta Ski Park, which has ski and snowboard trails that are converted into mountain-biking runs..

DETOUR
Lava Beds National Monument
Start: 04 McCloud
Lava Beds National Monument (nps.gov/labe), perched on a shield volcano, is a truly remarkable 72-sq-mile landscape – lava flows, craters, cinder cones and amazing lava tubes. Nearly 750 caves have been found in the monument and they average a comfortable 55°F (13°C) no matter what the outside temperature. Spy Native American petroglyphs throughout the park. From McCloud, go southeast several miles on Hwy 89, then take Harris Spring Rd northeast; the one-way drive takes about 2¼ hours.

Photo Opportunity
Snowcapped Mt Shasta at sunset.

05 MT SHASTA VILLAGE

Still classified as an active volcano, **Mt Shasta** (fs.usda.gov/stnf) remains a magnet for mystics. Seekers are attracted to the 14,179ft peak's reported cosmic properties, but this reverence for the great mountain is nothing new: for centuries Native Americans have honored it as sacred, considering it to be no less than the Great Spirit's wigwam.

Reach its highest drivable point by heading through Mt Shasta City to Everitt Memorial Hwy, which leads to **Bunny Flat**, one of the lower access points on the mountain for excellent hikes. An amble around the town at the base of the mountain will provide you with an opportunity to duck into book shops and excellent eateries.

Visitors can also fill their water bottles at the **Sacramento River Headwaters** off Mt Shasta Blvd, about a mile north of downtown. Pure water gurgles up from the ground in a large, cool spring amid a city park with walking trails, picnic spots and a children's playground.

THE DRIVE
From the north side of Mt Shasta City go 10 miles north on I-5, past Weed to the Edgewood exit, then turn left at Stewart Springs Rd and follow the signs.

06 STEWART MINERAL SPRINGS

Make all the jokes you want about the name of the little town of Weed, but a visit to Stewart Mineral Springs will only inspire a satisfied sigh. At this popular alternative (read clothing optional) hangout on the banks of a clear mountain stream guests soak in a private claw-foot tub or cook in the dry-wood sauna. There's also massage, body wraps, a Native American–style sweat lodge and a riverside sunbathing deck.

You'll want to call ahead to be sure there is space in the steam and soaking rooms, especially on busy weekends. While in the area, tickle your other senses at **Mt Shasta Lavender Farms** (facebook.com/MtShastaLavenderFarms), about 19 miles northeast of Weed off Hwy 97. You can harvest your own sweet French lavender during the June and July blooming season.

THE DRIVE
Castle Lake can be reached by driving south on I-5 and taking exit 736. Go under the highway and the service road to the north on the west side of the highway to connect with Castle Lake Rd. The lake is approximately 7 miles beyond Lake Siskiyou. En route you'll pass Ney Springs and the short hike to Faery Falls.

07 CASTLE LAKE

Castle Lake is an easily accessible yet pristine mountain pool surrounded by granite formations and pine forest. In the distance you'll see two of Northern California's most recognizable rocks: Castle Crags and Mt Shasta. Swimming, fishing, picnicking and camping are popular in summer.

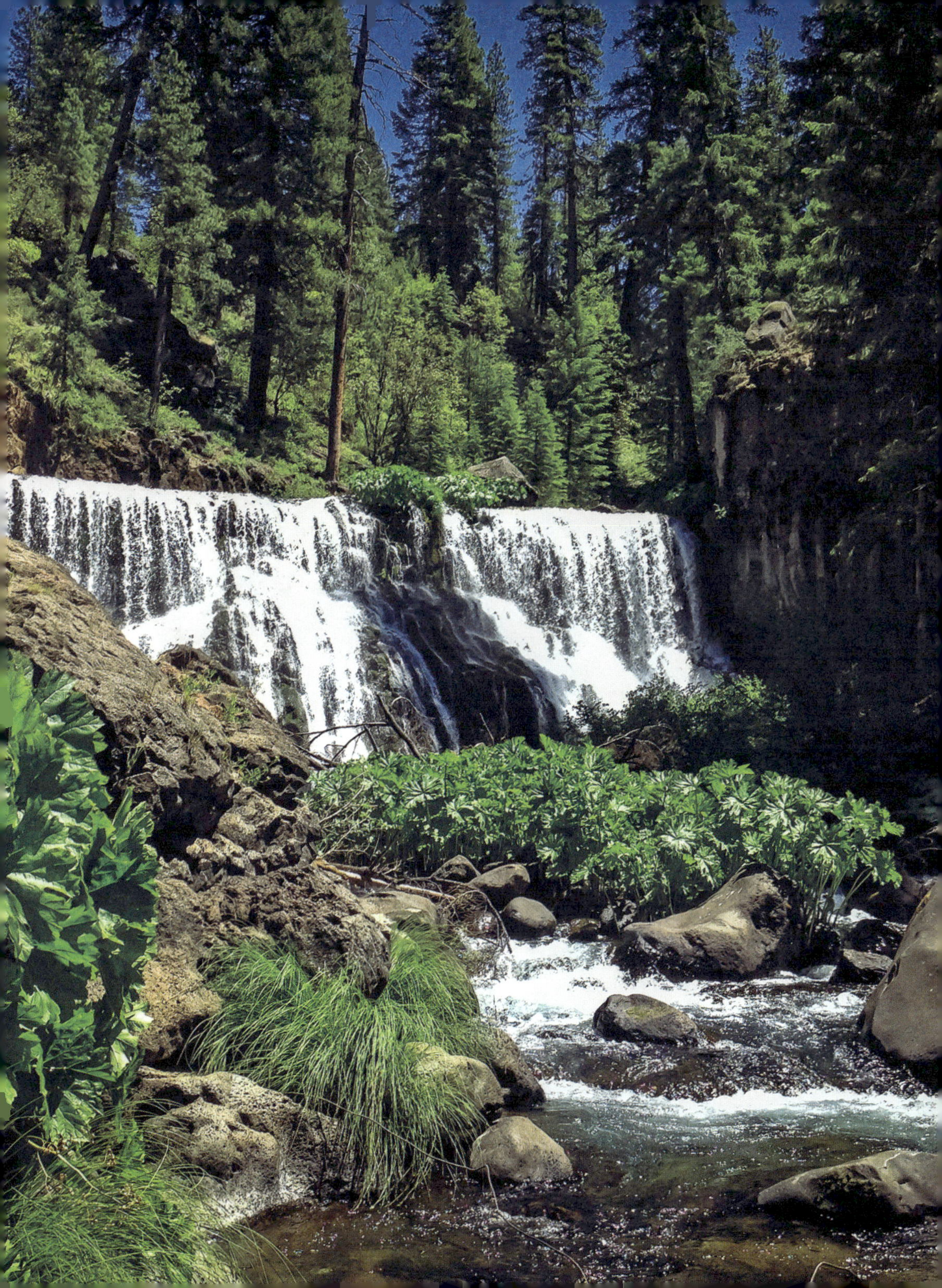

Shasta-Trinity National Forest
Red Bluff
Lassen National Forest
Honey Lake
Pyramid Lake
Carson Sink
25
Quincy
Paradise
Chico
Mendocino National Forest
Downieville
Oroville
Reno
Fallon
Nevada City
Truckee
Grass Valley
20
Lake Tahoe
Carson City
NEVADA
Yuba City
Clearlake
Auburn
South Lake Tahoe
Placerville
Walker Lake
Woodland
Markleeville
Davis
Sacramento
Santa Rosa
Vacaville
24
Sutter Creek
Inyo National Forest
Fairfield
26
23
22
Bodie
Port Costa
Murphys
Stockton
Yosemite National Park
Sausalito
Berkeley
Sonora
Lee Vining
San Francisco
Oakland
Manteca
White Mountain (14,246ft)
Yosemite Village
Pacifica
Modesto
Mammoth Lakes
Turlock
Wawona
San Jose
Merced
Bishop
16
Los Banos
21
Death Valley National Park
Gilroy
Santa Cruz
Watsonville
Madera
Kings Canyon National Park
Cedar Grove
Monterey
Salinas
Fresno
Mt Whitney (14,505ft)
Lone Pine
Kings River
Reedley
17
Visalia
Sequoia National Park
King City
15
Coalinga
Sequoia National Forest
Porterville
Big Sur
Gorda
Ragged Point
Paso Robles
18
Point Piedras Blancas
Lake Isabella
Morro Bay
San Luis Obispo
Kern River
Bakersfield
PACIFIC OCEAN
Pismo Beach
Taft
Mojave
Santa Maria
Guadalupe
Ventucopa
Los Alamos
Los Olivos
Lompoc
19
Palmdale
Point Conception
Santa Barbara
0 100 km
0 50 miles
5
80
99
101
1
395
198
58
166
33
14

Willow Creek Bridge (p94)

Central California

15 Big Sur
Get lost on this classic American road trip, at wild beaches and camps along coastal Hwy 1. **p94**

16 Along Highway 1 to Santa Cruz
Take serpentine Highway 1 through the scenic charms of the Big Sur coastline. **p98**

17 Around Monterey & Carmel
Putter around the idyllic peninsula, then immerse yourself in wildlife-rich Monterey Bay. **p102**

18 Around San Luis Obispo
The laid-back college town of San Luis Obispo is a gateway to coastal adventures in beach towns and fishing villages. **p106**

19 Santa Barbara Wine Country
Spend a weekend in Sideways country, from pretty Santa Barbara to Los Olivos and the Santa Rita Hills. **p110**

20 Lake Tahoe Loop
Encircled by mountains, adventures abound in this year-round natural summer and winter sports location. **p114**

21 Yosemite, Sequoia & Kings Canyon National Parks
Be awed by Sierra Nevada peaks, giant trees and waterfalls. **p118**

22 Eastern Sierra Scenic Byway
Ramble rugged Hwy 395, gateway to hot springs, hikes, ghost towns and soaring Mt Whitney. **p124**

23 Highway 49 Through Gold Country
Explore crumbling falsefront saloons and rusting mining parks on one of California's most enchanting scenic byways. **p130**

24 Ebbetts Pass Scenic Byway
For outdoor fanatics, this gold-rush-era mining route is a trip through paradise. **p136**

25 Feather River Scenic Byway
Rushing streams, daunting mountains and forest lakes are the backdrop to this scenic roadtrip. **p140**

26 Sacramento Delta & Lodi
Discover a maze of orchards, vineyards and waterways on this river delta drive. **p144**

Explore

Central California

The fabled, fairy-tale stretch of coast between San Francisco and LA is a road tripper's dream. Packed with beautiful beaches, historic lighthouses and tall redwood forests that hide magical waterfalls and hot springs, especially in bohemian Big Sur, it inspires both adventure and contemplation.

In central California's agricultural heartland, you can taste the goodness of the land, from juicy strawberries to prickly artichokes to wine, including around Santa Barbara and Santa Cruz. Further east rises the Sierra Nevada, uplifted along fault lines and weathered by wind and rain. Soothe your soul with natural wonders, from Yosemite Valley to Lake Tahoe.

Hub Towns

While you could start or end your Central California trip in the Bay Area or Los Angeles, consider easing your travel by flying directly into one of the regional towns. Airports here are smaller and eliminate tangling with big-city traffic, and in town you'll find all the supplies and restaurants you'll need.

Monterey

Jumping-off spot for Big Sur and points south, Monterey's biggest draw is its world-class aquarium overlooking Monterey Bay, where dense kelp forests house a sublime variety of marine life, including seals and sea lions, dolphins and whales. Nearby, Cannery Row made Monterey the sardine capital of the world in the 1930s; today it's an unabashedly touristic strip lined with souvenir shops and standard eateries in faux-retro buildings. For more authenticity, stroll past downtown's cluster of restored buildings from the Spanish and Mexican periods.

Sacramento

California's state capital, Sacramento is a city of contrasts. It's a former cow town where today's legislators' SUVs go bumper-to-bumper with farmers' muddy, half-ton pickups at rush hour. It has sprawling suburbs, but also new lofts and upscale boutiques squeezed between aging mid-century storefronts. For road-trippers it's a good place to stop between the Bay Area and greater Lake Tahoe.

WHEN TO GO

Along the Central Coast, expect mild winters and warm to hot summers, with the most rain between December and April (average 8in/20cm). In the Lake Tahoe region, winters are cold and snowy while summer days average up to about 80°F (27°C), with cool nights. Check snow conditions before crossing mountain passes in winter; chains may be required.

Lake Tahoe

Driving around the spellbinding 72-mile scenic shoreline of Lake Tahoe (the USA's second-deepest lake and, at 6245ft high, also one of the nation's highest-elevation lakes) will give you quite a workout behind the wheel. Generally, the north shore is quiet and upscale; the west shore, rugged and old-timey; the east shore, undeveloped; the south shore, busy and tacky, with aging motels and flashy casinos – that scene continues in nearby Reno, Nevada.

Santa Barbara

At the southern end of the Central Coast, low-slung between lofty mountains and the shimmering Pacific, chic Santa Barbara's red-tiled roofs, white stucco buildings and Mediterranean vibe give credence to its claim of being the 'American Riviera.' Loll on the beach, eat and drink extraordinarily well, shop a bit and push your cares off to another day. While in town, you can go car-free with the city's electric shuttle buses, urban bike trails and earth-friendly wine tours. And if you get out into nature, it will return the love with hiking, biking, surfing, kayaking, scuba-diving and camping opportunities galore.

TRANSPORT

Central California sits between the state's main international gateways, Los Angeles and San Francisco International Airports (LAX, SFO). Airports in Sacramento (SMF) and Reno-Tahoe (RNO) offer a handful of international flights.

By rail, Amtrak California's Pacific Surfliner connects San Diego and LA through Santa Barbara to San Luis Obispo (LA to Santa Barbara/SLO: from $30/44). Capitol Corridor trains connect Emeryville (Bay Area) to Sacramento (from $29).

WHERE TO STAY

Post Ranch Inn in Big Sur is the last word in luxurious coastal getaways, an adults-only retreat with ocean views, infinity pools, private hot tubs and the option to stay in a 'tree house.'

HI Pigeon Point Lighthouse Hostel, in Pescadero, goes far beyond your average hostel for its absolutely stunning location; contemplate roaring waves while the lighthouse beacon races through a starburst sky. And in Yosemite, the **Ahwahnee** is the *crème de la crème* of national park lodgings; classic rooms have views of Glacier Point, Half Dome and Yosemite Falls.

WHAT'S ON

Santa Barbara International Film Festival
Offers more than 200 films and talks in February.

Elevation Gay Ski Week
In Mammoth in March.

Paso Wine Fest
Over 150 wineries from Paso Robles pour each May..

Monterey Jazz Festival
Gigs with big global jazz headliners; in September.

Aftershock & Golden Sky
Rock and country-music festivals in Sacramento; on consecutive weekends in October.

Resources

National Park Service
(nps.gov) Yosemite, Sequoia and Kings Canyon..

Visit Santa Barbara
(santabarbaraca.com) Downtown Santa Barbara to Wine Country.

Visit Half Moon Bay
(visithalfmoonbay.org) Lodgings to trail guides.

Lake Tahoe Visitors Authority
(visitlaketahoe.com) Official site.

15
Big Sur

BEST FOR FAMILIES

Pfeiffer Big Sur State Park for camping, cabins and easy hikes.

DURATION	DISTANCE	GREAT FOR
2-3 days	60 miles / 95km	Nature, Families

BEST TIME TO GO	April to May for waterfalls and wildflowers; September to October for sunny, cloudless days.

Point Sur State Historic Park

Much ink has been spilled extolling the raw beauty of this craggy land shoehorned between the Santa Lucia Mountains and the Pacific. Yet nothing quite prepares you for that first glimpse through the windshield of Big Sur's wild, unspoiled coastline. There are no traffic lights, banks or strip malls, and when the sun goes down, the moon and the stars are the only streetlights – if coastal fog hasn't extinguished them.

Link Your Trip

03 Pacific Coast Highways

Big Sur is just one famous stretch of Hwy 1 along the California coast, which you can drive along from Mexico to Oregon.

17 Around Monterey & Carmel

From Bixby Bridge, drive almost 20 miles north on Hwy 1 to Monterey for maritime-history lessons and one of the world's best aquariums.

01 BIXBY BRIDGE

Big Sur is more a state of mind than a place you can pinpoint on a map, but the photogenic Bixby Bridge lets you know you've finally arrived. Arching above **Rainbow Canyon**, this landmark is one of the world's highest single-span bridges, completed in 1932 by prisoners eager to lop time off their sentences. Off-road parking is limited and can create a traffic hazard, so consider stopping at other safer pull-offs taking in equally stellar coastal scenery further south.

BEST ROAD TRIPS: CALIFORNIA

a trail-laced collage of grassy meadows, ocean bluffs and sandy beaches, all offering excellent wildlife-watching. Hike for about a mile to where the Big Sur River meets the driftwood-strewn beach, whipped by surf and strong winds. At the parking lot, walk south to the **Big Sur Discovery Center** (ventanaws.org/discovery_center) to learn all about endangered California condors.

THE DRIVE
Speeds rarely top 35mph along Hwy 1, which narrows and becomes curvier further south. A few miles beyond the state park, watch for pedestrians in 'the village,' Big Sur's hub for shops, services, motels and cafes. About 5 miles south of Andrew Molera State Park, the entrance to Pfeiffer Big Sur State Park is on the inland side of the highway.

04 PFEIFFER BIG SUR STATE PARK
Big Sur's biggest draw is **Pfeiffer Big Sur State Park** (parks.ca.gov). Named after Big Sur's first European settlers, who arrived in 1869, it's the largest state park along this coast. Hiking trails loop through redwood groves and run uphill to 60ft-high Pfeiffer Falls, a delicate forested cascade that usually flows between December and May. Near the park entrance, inside a rustic lodge built in the 1930s by the Civilian Conservation Corps (CCC), is a general store selling drinks, snacks, camping supplies and road-trip souvenirs.

THE DRIVE
Just 2 miles south of Pfeiffer Big Sur State Park, about half a mile past ranger-staffed Big Sur Station, make a sharp right turn off Hwy 1

THE DRIVE
From Bixby Bridge, it's about 6 miles south along Hwy 1, rolling beside pastureland, to Point Sur State Historic Park. Watch out for cyclists and use signposted roadside pull-offs to let fast-moving traffic pass by.

02 POINT SUR STATE HISTORIC PARK
Rising out of the sea, **Point Sur State Historic Park** (pointsur.org) looks like an island, but it's connected to the mainland by a sandbar. On the volcanic rock sits California's only turn-of-the-20th-century light station that's still open to the public. Ocean views combine with engrossing tales of the facility's importance in tracking Soviet submarines during the Cold War. Call ahead to confirm schedules; arrive early, because space is limited (no reservations).

THE DRIVE
Lighthouse tours meet at the locked farm gate a quarter-mile north of Point Sur Naval Facility. Afterwards, drive south on Hwy 1 another 2 miles along the coast to Andrew Molera State Park.

03 ANDREW MOLERA STATE PARK
Named after the farmer who first planted artichokes in California, **Andrew Molera State Park** (parks.ca.gov) is

BEST ROAD TRIPS: CALIFORNIA   95

onto Sycamore Canyon Rd, marked only by a small yellow sign saying 'Narrow Road.' Partly unpaved, this road (RVs and trailers prohibited) corkscrews down for over 2 miles to Pfeiffer Beach.

05 PFEIFFER BEACH
Pfeiffer Beach (campone.com) is definitely worth the trouble it takes to reach it. This crescent-shaped strand is known for its huge double rock formation, through which waves crash powerfully. It's often windy, and the surf is too dangerous for swimming. Dig into the wet sand to find sand that's purple because manganese garnet washes down from hillsides above.

THE DRIVE
Backtrack up Sycamore Canyon Rd for more than 2 miles, then turn right onto Hwy 1 southbound. After two more twisting, slow-moving miles, look for Nepenthe restaurant on your right. The Henry Miller Memorial Library is another 0.4 miles south, at a hairpin turn on your left.

06 HENRY MILLER MEMORIAL LIBRARY
'It was here at Big Sur that I first learned to say Amen!' wrote Henry Miller in *Big Sur and the Oranges of Hieronymus Bosch*. A surrealist novelist, Miller was a local from 1944 to 1962. A beatnik memorial, alt-cultural venue and bookstore, the **Henry Miller Memorial Library** (henrymiller.org) was never actually the writer's home. The house belonged to a friend of his, painter Emil White. Inside are copies of all of Miller's published books, many of his paintings and a collection of Big Sur and Beat Generation material. Stop by to browse and hang out on the front deck with coffee, or join the bohemian carnival of live music, open-mic nights and independent film screenings.

THE DRIVE
You'll leave most of the traffic behind as Hwy 1 continues southbound, curving slowly along the vertiginous cliffs, occasionally opening up for ocean panoramas. It's fewer than 8 miles to Julia Pfeiffer Burns State Park; the entrance is on the inland side of Hwy 1.

07 JULIA PFEIFFER BURNS STATE PARK
If you've got an appetite for chasing waterfalls, swing into **Julia Pfeiffer Burns State Park** (parks.ca.gov). From the parking lot, the short Overlook Trail rushes downhill towards the sea, passing through a tunnel underneath Hwy 1. Everyone is in a hurry to see **McWay Falls**, which tumbles year-round over granite cliffs and free falls into the ocean or onto the beach, depending on the tide. This is the classic Big Sur postcard shot, with tree-topped rocks jutting above a golden beach next to swirling blue pools and crashing white surf. During winter, watch for migrating whales offshore.

Photo Opportunity
McWay Falls dropping into the Pacific.

THE DRIVE
The tortuously winding stretch of Hwy 1 southbound is sparsely populated, rugged and remote, running through national forest. Make sure you've got enough fuel in the tank to at least reach the expensive gas station at Gorda, over 20 miles south of Julia Pfeiffer Burns State Park.

DETOUR
Esalen Hot Springs
Start: 07 Julia Pfeiffer Burns State Park
Ocean beaches and waterfalls aren't the only places to get wet in Big Sur. At the private Esalen Institute, clothing-optional baths (esalen.org; y) fed by a natural hot spring sit on a ledge high above the ocean. Dollars to donuts you'll never take another dip that compares scenery-wise, especially on stormy winter nights. Only two small outdoor pools perch directly over the waves, so once you've stripped and taken a quick shower, head outside immediately. Advance reservations are required. The signposted entrance is on Hwy 1, about 3 miles south of Julia Pfeiffer Burns State Park.

08 LOS PADRES NATIONAL FOREST
If you have any slivers of sunlight left, keep trucking down Hwy 1 approximately 8 miles past Gorda to Ragged Point and the **Salmon Creek Falls**, which usually runs from December through May.

Take a short hike to splash around in the pools at the base of this double-drop waterfall, tucked uphill in a forested canyon. In a hairpin turn of Hwy 1, the roadside turnoff is marked only by a small brown trailhead sign.

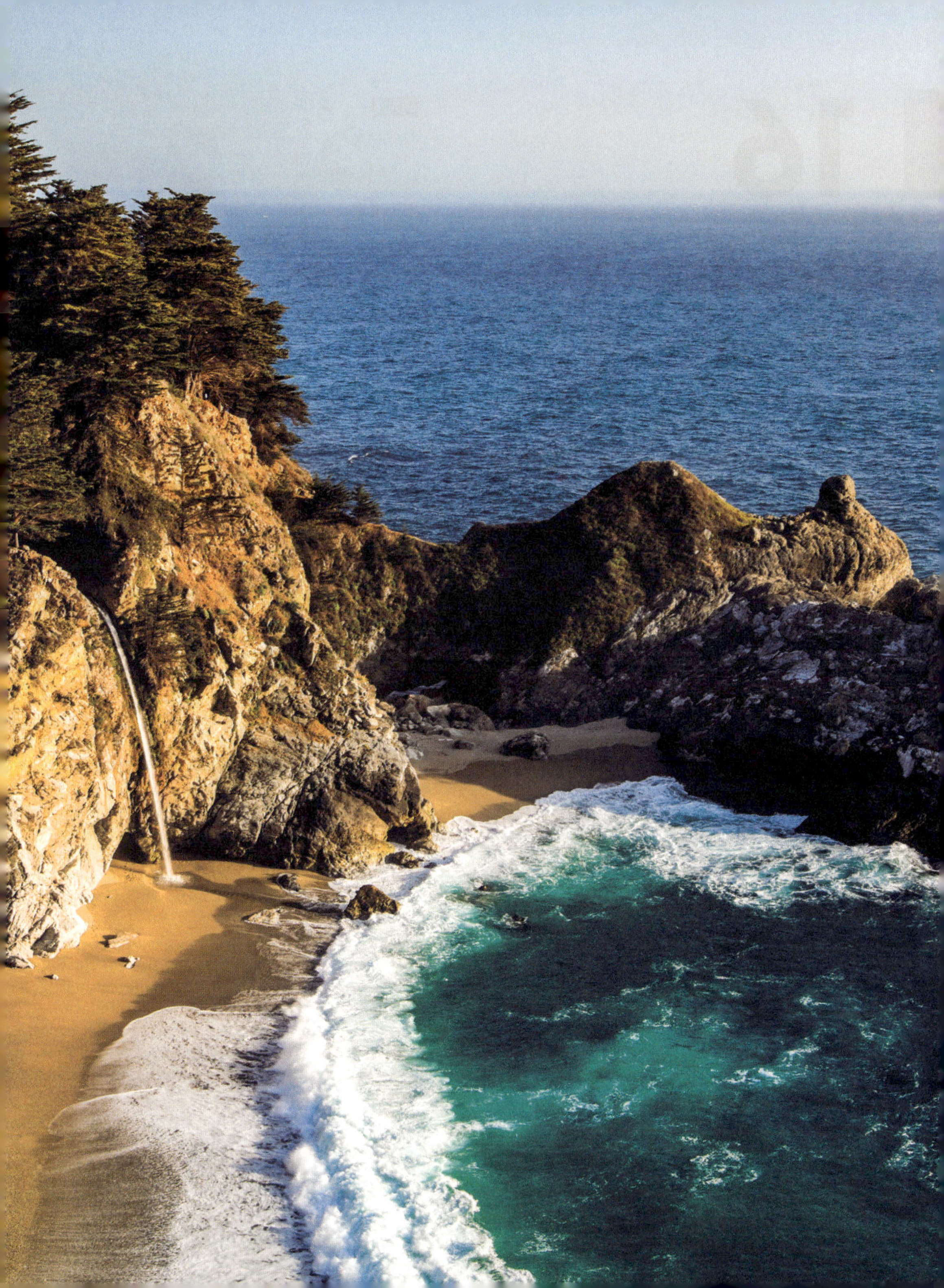

16

Along Highway 1 to Santa Cruz

DURATION	DISTANCE	GREAT FOR
2–3 days	75 miles / 120km	Vineyards, Nature
BEST TIME TO GO	July to October gives you the best chance of sunshine.	

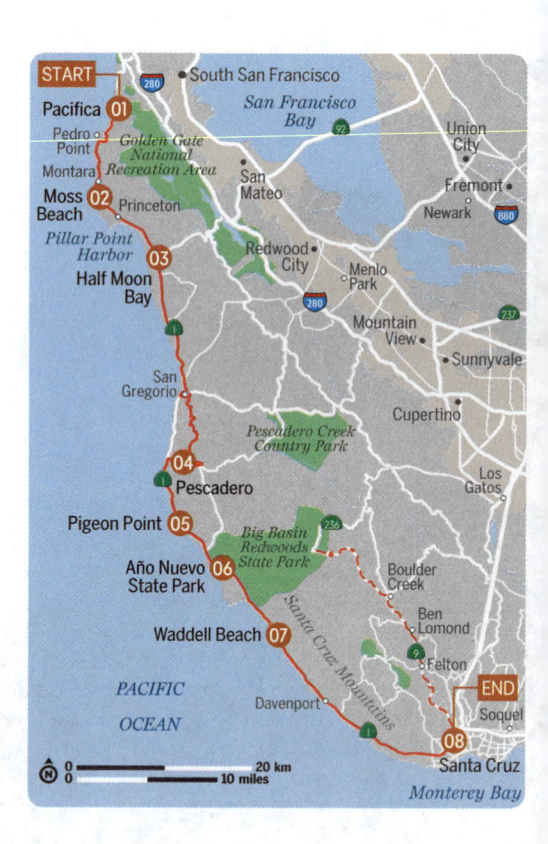

A lazily flowing river of tourism, serpentine Hwy 1 is most celebrated for its scenic charms along the Big Sur coast. But some locals say that the most enchanting stretch of this iconic road starts just south of San Francisco, winding its way slowly down to Santa Cruz. Most beaches are buffeted by wild and unpredictable surf, making them better for tide-pooling than swimming or sunbathing. But, oh, the views!

Link Your Trip

04 Marin County
Starting in San Francisco, follow Hwy 1 in the other direction by crossing north over the Golden Gate Bridge to find redwood groves, beaches and lighthouses.

17 Around Monterey & Carmel
From Santa Cruz, Hwy 1 winds 40 miles south to Monterey, passing more beaches, fishing ports and farms.

01 PACIFICA

In often fog-bound Pacifica, the divided four-lane highway from San Francisco peters out at an intersection overlooking pounding waves, a portent of things to come. Narrowing to two lanes, **Highway 1** jogs inland through thick eucalyptus groves before turning back to the coast. Downhill at **Pacifica State Beach**, stretch your legs or surf, and breath the sea-salted air. Then swerve up through the new tunnels to **Devil's Slide**, where a stretch of the old highway has been converted into a popular hiking and cycling path.

BEST FOR FOODIES

Pescadero's bakery, goat dairy and roadside farms.

Half Moon Bay

THE DRIVE
As Hwy 1 keeps heading south, you'll be enjoying the sea views. Over the next 6 miles, you'll pass Gray Whale Cove and Montara State Beaches. In Moss Beach, turn right onto Vermont Ave, then follow Lake St to its end.

02 MOSS BEACH
South of Point Montara Lighthouse, **Fitzgerald Marine Reserve** (fitzgeraldreserve.org) is a thriving habitat for harbor seals and natural tide pools. Walk out among the pools at low tide to observe (but never pick up) myriad crabs, sea stars, mollusks and rainbow-colored sea anemones. It's illegal to remove creatures, shells or even rocks. Back on Hwy 1 southbound, take the next right onto Cypress Ave, turning left onto Beach Way to find **Moss Beach Distillery** (mossbeachdistillery.com). Overlooking the cove where bootleggers used to unload Prohibition-era liquor, the heated ocean-view deck is perfectly positioned for sunset cocktails.

THE DRIVE
Continue south on Hwy 1 past the airport. Pillar Point Harbor is on the right after 2 miles. For downtown Half Moon Bay, go 4 miles south on Hwy 1, turn left onto Hwy 92, then right onto Main St.

03 HALF MOON BAY
Offshore from the western end of Pillar Point Harbor lies Mavericks, a serious surf break that attracts big-wave riders to battle steep wintertime swells more than 50ft high. Not feeling brave? Paddle in calmer waters with **Half Moon Bay Kayak** (hmbkayak.com), which rents kayaks and guides tours. Further south down Hwy 1, detour inland to amble down this Victorian-era seaside resort's quaint Main St, its tree-lined blocks overstuffed with bookstores, antiques shops and cafes.

THE DRIVE

For the next 11 miles heading south, Hwy 1 gently follows the contours of the coast. Vistas of pounding surf, unspoiled shores and dramatic rock outcrops seem boundless. Turn inland onto Hwy 84 at San Gregorio, then right after less than a mile onto Stage Rd, which narrowly winds through the hills for 7 miles south to Pescadero.

04 PESCADERO

With its long coastline and mild weather, Pescadero has always been prime real estate. Spanish for 'fishmonger,' Pescadero was formally established in 1856, when it was mostly a farming and dairy settlement with a key location along the stagecoach route. Munch on a fresh-baked, pull-apart loaf of Italian garlic-and-herb bread stuffed with juicy artichokes from **Arcangeli Grocery Co** (norms market.com) before traipsing around downtown's art galleries and antiques shops. At the north end of the main drag, turn right onto North St and drive a mile to steal-your-heart **Harley Farms Goat Dairy** (harleyfarms.com). The farm shop sells artisanal goat cheeses festooned with fruit, nuts and edible flowers. Call ahead for a weekend farm tour or show up anytime to chill with goats.

Photo Opportunity

Elephant seal antics at Año Nuevo's beaches.

THE DRIVE

Continue driving past the goat farm on North St to Pescadero Rd. Turn right and head west 2 miles to Pescadero State Beach, passing marshlands where bird-watchers spot waterfowl. Turn left back onto Hwy 1, driving south beside pocket beaches and coves for almost 6 miles to the Pigeon Point turnoff.

05 PIGEON POINT

One of the West Coast's tallest lighthouses stands in **Pigeon Point Light Station State Historic Park** (parks.ca.gov). The 1872 landmark had to close access to its Fresnel lens when chunks of its cornice began to rain from the sky, but the beam still flashes brightly and the bluff is a prime though blustery spot to scan for breaching gray whales.

Año Nuevo State Park

THE DRIVE

Back at Hwy 1, turn right and cruise south along the coast, curving inland as the wind howls all around you, for about 5 miles to Año Nuevo State Park's main entrance.

06 AÑO NUEVO STATE PARK

During winter and early spring, thousands of enormous northern elephant seals noisily mate, give birth, learn to swim, battle for dominance or just laze around on the sands at **Año Nuevo State Park** (parks.ca.gov/anonuevo).

Join park rangers for a guided hike (reservations required) through the sand dunes for up-close views of the huge pinnipeds – a mature male weighs twice as much as your car!

THE DRIVE

Over the next 6 miles, Hwy 1 southbound traces the coast. As you descend a long hill bordered by a sheer cliff face that recalls Devil's Slide, look for Waddell Beach on your right.

07 WADDELL BEACH

These thrilling breaks are usually alive with windsurfers, kitesurfers and other daredevils. Wander the chilly sands and get blasted by the winds and you'll quickly understand that without a wetsuit, you won't be hankering to swim here.

Across Hwy 1 is the end of the popular Skyline-to-the-Sea Trail that descends from Big Basin State Park's redwoods. Just inland, **Rancho del Oso Nature and History Center** (rancho deloso.org) has two kid-friendly nature trails through the marshlands behind the beach.

THE DRIVE

Hwy 1 begins slowly moving away from the rocky shoreline as the coast's limestone and sandstone cliffs regularly shed chunks into the white-capped waters below. Motor past roadside farmstands and barns and more pocket beaches before rolling into Santa Cruz after 15 miles.

08 SANTA CRUZ

SoCal beach culture meets NorCal counterculture in Santa Cruz. Witness the old-school radical and freak-show weirdness along Pacific Ave, downtown's main drag.

Tumble downhill to the West Coast's oldest oceanfront amusement park, **Santa Cruz Beach Boardwalk** (beachboardwalk.com), where the smell of cotton candy mixes with the salt air. Continue up W Cliff Dr, which winds for a mile to Lighthouse Point. Join the gawkers on the cliffs peering down at the floating kelp beds, hulking sea lions, playful sea otters and black wet suit-clad surfers riding Steamer Lane surf break.

Inside the 1960s-era lighthouse is the memorabilia-packed **Santa Cruz Surfing Museum**. Almost 2 miles further west, W Cliff Dr dead-ends at **Natural Bridges State Beach** (parks.ca.gov), named for its sea arches. Starfish, anemones, crabs and more inhabit myriad tide pools carved into the limestone rocks. Find out about sea creatures both great (look at that blue-whale skeleton!) and small at the nearby **Seymour Marine Discovery Center** (seymourcenter.ucsc.edu).

DETOUR
Santa Cruz Mountains
Start: 06 Santa Cruz

Hwy 9 is a sun-dappled backwoods byway into the Santa Cruz Mountains, passing towering redwood forests and a few fog-blessed vineyards (estate-bottled pinot noir is a specialty). Seven miles north of Santa Cruz, **Henry Cowell Redwoods State Park** (parks.ca.gov) has hiking trails through old-growth redwood trees.

Nearby in Felton, **Roaring Camp Railroads** (roaringcamp.com) operates narrow-gauge steam trains up into the redwoods. It's another 7 miles up to Boulder Creek, a tiny mountain town with simple cafes and a grocery store for picnic supplies.

Take Hwy 236 northwest for 10 more twisty miles to **Big Basin Redwoods State Park** (parks.ca.gov), where misty nature trails loop past skyscraping redwoods.

17

Around Monterey & Carmel

BEST FOR FAMILIES

Spend the day at the Monterey Bay Aquarium.

DURATION	DISTANCE	GREAT FOR
2–3 days	70 miles / 115km	Nature, Families

BEST TIME TO GO	August to October for sunniest skies; December to April for whale-watching.

Monterey Bay Aquarium, Monterey

Tourist-choked Cannery Row isn't actually the star attraction on the Monterey Peninsula. Much more memorable are ocean panoramas caught from roadside pull-offs on the edge of the bay, from the hiking trails of Point Lobos or from the open-air decks of a winter whale-watching boat. Historical roots show all along this drive, from well-preserved Spanish Colonial adobe buildings in downtown Monterey to Carmel's jewel-box Catholic mission.

Link Your Trip

15 Big Sur

Big Sur's vertiginous coastal cliffs, hippie-beatnik retreats and redwood forests alongside Hwy 1 start 15 miles south of Carmel-by-the-Sea.

16 Along Highway 1 to Santa Cruz

Santa Cruz's 'Surf City' beaches are about 25 miles north of Moss Landing via Hwy 1, which curves around Monterey Bay.

01 MONTEREY

Working-class Monterey is all about the sea. Start exploring by walking around **Old Monterey**, downtown's historic quarter, which preserves California's Mexican and Spanish colonial roots. It's just inland from the salt-sprayed Municipal Wharf II, overlooking **Monterey Bay National Marine Sanctuary**, which protects kelp forests, seals, sea lions, dolphins and whales. Less than 2 miles northwest of downtown via Lighthouse Ave, **Cannery Row** was the hectic, smelly epicenter of the sardine-canning industry, Monterey's lifeblood till the 1950s, as immortalized by novelist John Steinbeck. Today the eco-conscious

Monterey Bay Aquarium (montereybayaquarium.org) puts aquatic creatures on educational display. Walking south along Cannery Row, peek into the one-room shacks of former cannery workers. Further south along Cannery Row, stop at **Steinbeck Plaza** (Cannery Row) to soak up bay views.

🚗 THE DRIVE
From Cannery Row, Ocean View Blvd slowly traces the bayfront coastline for 2.5 miles west to Point Pinos, curving left onto Sunset Dr. Watch out for cyclists along this route.

02 PACIFIC GROVE
Pacific Grove was where John Steinbeck's family once had a summer cottage. Ocean View Blvd runs from Lovers Point west to Point Pinos, where it becomes Sunset Dr heading south to **Asilomar State Beach**. Tempting turnoffs showcase pounding surf, rocky outcrops and teeming tide pools. **Point Pinos Lighthouse** (point pinoslighthouse.org) has been warning ships of this peninsula's hazards since 1855.

Nearby, golfers crowd the windy **Pacific Grove Golf Links** (playpacificgrove.com), a penny-pincher's version of Pebble Beach. Follow Lighthouse Ave east, turning right onto Ridge Rd after half a mile. Park to stroll around the **Monarch Grove Butterfly Sanctuary** (cityof pacificgrove.org/visiting) between October and February or March, when thousands of migratory monarch butterflies cluster in tall eucalyptus trees.

🚗 THE DRIVE
Drive back north on Ridge Rd to Lighthouse Ave, which heads east toward leafy downtown Pacific Grove, with its shops, cafes and a natural-history museum for kids. To bypass downtown PG, take the next right after Ridge Rd onto 17-Mile Dr. Drive another mile southwest, crossing Sunset Dr/Hwy 68, to the Pacific Grove toll gate.

03 17-MILE DRIVE
Once promoted as 'Mother Nature's Drive-Thru,' **17-Mile Drive** (pebblebeach.com) is a spectacularly scenic private toll road (motorcyclists prohibited) that loops around the Monterey Peninsula, connecting Pacific Grove with Pebble Beach and Carmel-by-the-Sea. Using the self-guided tour map handed out at the toll gates, motor past postcard vistas of the ocean and Monterey cypress trees, world-famous golf courses, a luxury lodge and the bay where Spanish explorer Gaspar de Portolá dropped anchor in 1769.

🚗 THE DRIVE
17-Mile Dr is actually only 9 miles long between the Pacific Grove and Carmel toll gates. After exiting the toll road, continue south to Ocean Ave, then turn left for downtown Carmel-by-the-Sea. Enjoy the 'kiwi crossing' road signs!

04 CARMEL-BY-THE-SEA
Once an artists' colony, this quaint village now has the manicured feel of a country club. On the west side of town, **Carmel Beach City Park** (off Scenic Rd) is a gorgeous

white-sand strand where pampered pups run off-leash. Just inland, 20th-century poet Robinson Jeffers' **Tor House** (torhouse.org) offers insights into bohemian Old Carmel.

Further east, off Rio Rd, the arched basilica and flowering garden courtyard of **Carmel Mission Basilica** (carmelmission.org) will make you feel as if you've landed in old Spain. Established in 1772, this is the second-oldest California mission. Padre Junípero Serra is buried at Carmel-by-the-Sea.

🚗 THE DRIVE
From the mission, continue southeast down Rio Rd to the intersection with Hwy 1. Turn right and drive about 2 miles south to the turnoff for Point Lobos State Natural Reserve on your right.

05 POINT LOBOS STATE NATURAL RESERVE
Sea lions are the stars here at **Punta de los Lobos Marinos** (Point of the Sea Wolves), where a rocky coastline offers excellent tide-pooling. Short walks around **Point Lobos State Natural Reserve** (pointlobos.org) take in wild scenery and wildlife-watching, including Bird Island, shady cypress groves, the historic Whaler's Cabin and the Devil's Cauldron, a whirlpool that gets splashy at high tide.

🚗 THE DRIVE
Back at the park entrance, turn left onto Hwy 1 northbound. Wind 2.5 miles uphill away from the coast to the stoplight intersection with Carmel Valley Rd. Turn right and drive east through farmlands and vineyards toward Carmel Valley village, about 11.5 miles away.

📷 Photo Opportunity
Pebble Beach's trademarked lone cypress tree.

06 CARMEL VALLEY
Carmel Valley is a peaceful and bucolic side trip. At organic **Earthbound Farm** (ebfarm.com), sample fresh-fruit smoothies and homemade soups. Wineries further east offer tastings. The pinot noir bottled by **Boekenoogen Wines** (boekenoogenwines.com) is excellent, and both **I Brand & Family** (ibrandwinery.com) and **Joyce Wine Company** (joycewineco.com) feature stylish tasting rooms. Carmel Valley village is also chock-a-block with excellent cafes. Try **Corkscrew Cafe** (corkscrewcafe.com) for Mediterranean flavors and wood-fired pizza.

🚗 THE DRIVE
Backtrack 2 miles west of the village along Carmel Valley Rd, then turn right onto Laureles Grade. After 6 miles, turn left on Hwy 68, driving west to join Hwy 1 northbound. After passing sand dunes, suburbs and strawberry fields, Hwy 1 swings back toward the coast. Turn left onto Moss Landing Rd.

🧭 DETOUR
Salinas
Start: 06 Carmel Valley

From Salinas farmhands to Monterey cannery workers, the sun-baked Central Valley hills to the fishing coastline, Nobel Prize–winning author John Steinbeck drew a perfect picture of the landscapes and communities he knew. His hometown, Salinas, is a 25-minute drive east of Monterey via Hwy 68.

Downtown, the National Steinbeck Center (steinbeck.org) brings the novels to life with interactive exhibits and short movie clips. Look for Rocinante, the camper Steinbeck drove across America while writing Travels with Charley. Take a moment and listen to Steinbeck's Nobel acceptance speech – it's grace and power combined.

A few blocks west, **Steinbeck House** (steinbeckhouse.com/about-us) is the author's childhood home. A classic Queen Anne Victorian with dainty bird-patterned lace curtains, it's both a mini museum and a high-tea restaurant.

Two miles southeast of downtown, Steinbeck pilgrims can pay their respects at **Garden of Memories Memorial Park** (Memory Dr). An iron sign points the way to the Hamilton family plot, where a simple grave marker identifies where some of Steinbeck's ashes were buried. Around 20 miles southeast of Salinas is the **River Road Wine Trail** (riverroadwinetrail.com).

07 MOSS LANDING
Time to meet the local wildlife. Rent a kayak from outfitters on Hwy 1 and paddle past harbor seals into **Elkhorn Slough National Estuarine Research Reserve** (elkhornslough.org), or take a guided weekend hike and go bird-watching.

From the fishing harbor on Moss Landing Rd, **Sanctuary Cruises** (sanctuarycruises.com) operates year-round whale-watching and dolphin-spotting cruises aboard biodiesel-fueled boats (make advance reservations).

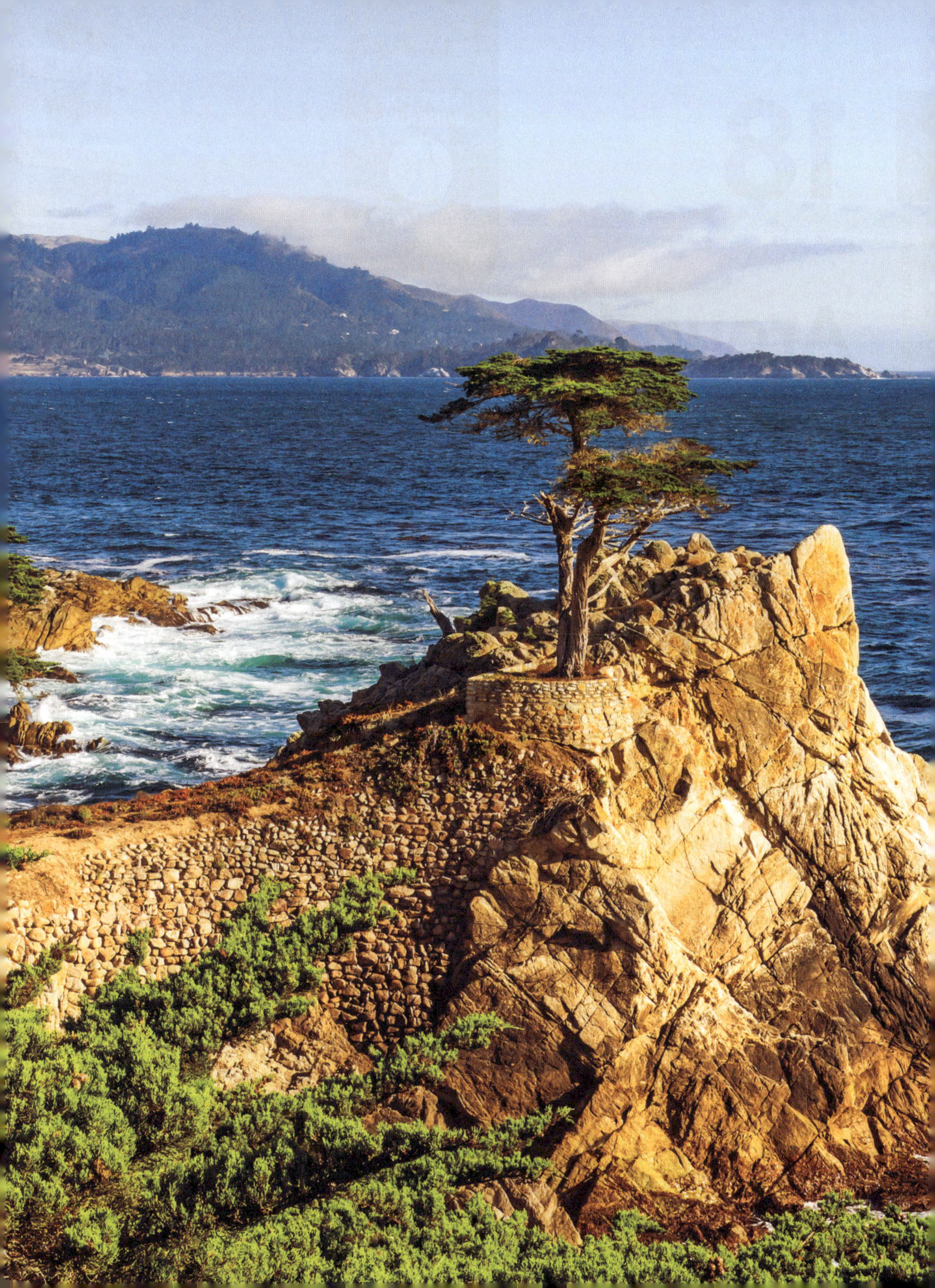

18

Around San Luis Obispo

BEST FOR WINERIES

Explore Hwy 46 east and west of Paso Robles.

DURATION	DISTANCE	GREAT FOR
2–3 days	115 miles / 185km	Nature, Families

BEST TIME TO GO	July through October brings sunniest skies.

Edna Valley wine trail

Halfway between San Francisco and LA, the laid-back college town of San Luis Obispo (aka 'SLO') is a gateway to coastal adventures. Beach towns and fishing villages offer a bucketful of outdoor pursuits, both on land and at sea – and wherever there's natural beauty, it's never too far from Hwy 1. Farm-to-table locavorian restaurants and vineyards abound, especially in Paso Robles' wine country, ideal for lazy weekend or weekday drives.

Link Your Trip

19 Santa Barbara Wine Country
Want more good grapes? Follow Hwy 101 south of Pismo Beach for 45 miles to the Santa Ynez Valley.

15 Big Sur
From Cayucos, cruise Hwy 1 north for 45 miles to the southern Big Sur coast, passing Hearst Castle halfway along.

01 SAN LUIS OBISPO

Oprah Winfrey called it 'the happiest city in America,' and once you spend a few hours downtown, you might agree. CalPoly university students inject a healthy dose of hubbub into the streets, shops, pubs and cafes, especially during the weekly **farmers market** (downtownslo.com), which turns downtown's Higuera St into a street festival with live music and sidewalk food stalls. Like many other California towns, SLO grew up around a Spanish Catholic mission, **Mission San Luis Obispo de Tolosa** (missionsanluisobispo.org), founded in

1772 by missionary Junípero Serra. The creek that once used to irrigate mission orchards still flows through downtown, beside tranquil, shaded walking paths.

THE DRIVE
From downtown SLO, follow Broad St/Hwy 227 for 2.5 miles southeast, turning left before the airport onto Tank Farm Rd. After a mile, curve right and continue onto Orcutt Rd, which rolls up and down past vineyards into Edna Valley.)

02 EDNA VALLEY
Cradled by the rich volcanic soil of the Santa Lucia foothills, thriving **Edna Valley wineries** (slocoastwine.com) are known for their crisp, often unoaked chardonnay and subtle syrah and pinot noir. Pick up a free map from any tasting room. All are signposted along Orcutt Rd and Edna Rd/Hwy 227. These roads run parallel through the peaceful valley, which is cooled by drifting coastal fog in the morning before being brightened by afternoon sunshine.

Niven Family Wine Estates pours inside a 20th-century wooden schoolhouse, while **Edna Valley Vineyard** (ednavalleyvineyard.com) has panoramic windows that overlook vineyards. Further southeast, **Talley Vineyards** (talleyvineyards.com) offers winery tours, but only by appointment.

THE DRIVE
From Talley Vineyards, Lopez Rd winds west toward Arroyo Grande, just over 6 miles away. Turn left onto Branch St, then merge onto Hwy 101 north to Pismo Beach. Exit at Price St, which enters downtown Pismo Beach. Turn left onto Pomeroy Ave and roll downhill to the ocean.

03 PISMO BEACH
By a wooden pier that stretches toward the setting sun, James Dean once trysted with Pier Angeli. Today this classic California beach town feels like somewhere straight out of a 1950s hot-rod dream. Pismo likes to call itself the 'Clam Capital of the World.' Across recent years, clams have been rare on the wide, sandy beach, but the tasty mollusk is now making a slow comeback.

To ride the waves, rent a wetsuit and board from any surf shop, or negotiate the hilltop walking trails of the **Pismo Preserve** (lcslo.org) for excellent coastal views.

After dark, go bar hopping or knock down pins at the retro bowling alley. The next day, drive a mile south of downtown to the **Monarch Butterfly Grove** (monarchbutterfly.org), where migratory monarchs roost in eucalyptus trees, usually from November through February. Join a free docent tour at 11am and 2pm.

THE DRIVE
Follow Hwy 1 north through downtown Pismo Beach, then follow the signs to rejoin Hwy 101 northbound for almost 4 miles to exit 195 for Avila Beach Dr. Keep left at the fork, then wind slowly west downhill to Avila Beach, about 3 miles away.

BEST ROAD TRIPS: CALIFORNIA   107

04 AVILA BEACH

For a perfectly lazy summer day at the beach, rent beach chairs and umbrellas underneath Avila Pier, off downtown's sparkling new waterfront promenade. Two miles further west, the coastal road dead-ends at **Port San Luis.** The barking of sea lions echoes as you stroll past seafood shacks and restaurants to the end of creaky, weather-worn Harford Pier, where you can while away time gazing out over the choppy waters. If you'd like to visit 1890 **Point San Luis Lighthouse** (pointsanluislighthouse.org), guided-tour reservations are required.

Back uphill near Hwy 101, you can pick your own fruit and feed the goats at **Avila Valley Barn** (avilavalleybarn.com) farm stand, or do some stargazing from a private redwood hot tub at **Sycamore Mineral Springs** (sycamoresprings.com).

THE DRIVE
Take Hwy 101 back northbound toward San Luis Obispo. Exit after 4.5 miles at Los Osos Valley Rd, which leaves behind stop-and-go strip-mall traffic to slowly roll past farmland for about 11 miles. After passing through downtown Los Osos, curve left onto Pecho Valley Rd, which enters Montaña de Oro State Park a few miles later.

05 MONTAÑA DE ORO STATE PARK

In spring, the hillsides of **Montaña de Oro State Park** (parks.ca.gov) are blanketed by bright California native poppies, wild mustard and other wildflowers, giving this park its Spanish name, which means 'mountain of gold.' Along the winding access road, sand dunes and the wind-tossed bluffs of the Pacific appear. Pull over at **Spooner's Cove**, a postcard-perfect sandy beach once used by smugglers. Here the grinding of the Pacific and North American plates has uplifted and tilted sedimentary layers of submarine rock, visible from shore.

Hike along the beach and the park's grassy ocean bluffs, or drive uphill past the visitor center to tackle the 4-mile round-trip trail up rocky **Valencia Peak** – the summit views are exhilarating.

THE DRIVE
Backtrack on Pecho Rd out of the park, curving right onto Los Osos Valley Rd. East of Los Osos, turn left onto Bay Blvd, winding north alongside Morro Bay's estuary. Before reaching Hwy 101, turn left onto Morro Bay State Park Rd, continuing on Main St into downtown Morro Bay. Turn left on Marina St and drive downhill to the Embarcadero.

06 MORRO BAY

This fishing village is home to **Morro Rock**, a volcanic peak jutting up from the ocean floor. (Too bad about those power-plant smokestacks obscuring the views, though.) You're likely to spot harbor seals and sea otters as you paddle around the bay in a kayak rented from the waterfront Embarcadero, crowded with seafood shacks. Or drive a mile north of the marina to walk partway around the base of the landmark rock. West of downtown in **Morro Bay State Park** (parks.ca.gov) is the **Museum of Natural History**, where kids can touch interactive models of the bay's ecosystem and stuffed wildlife mounts.

Photo Opportunity
Morro Rock silhouetted at sunset.

Montaña de Oro State Park

Morro Bay

🚗 THE DRIVE
Follow Main St north to Hwy 1. For 4 miles, Hwy 1 northbound rides above ocean beaches. In Cayucos, turn right onto Old Creek Rd, a winding, narrow back road, passing citrus farms and cattle ranches. Turn right after 9 miles onto Hwy 46, which heads east through wine country for 11 miles to meet Hwy 101 in Paso Robles.

07 PASO ROBLES WINE COUNTRY
Franciscan missionaries brought the first grapes to this region in the late 18th century, but it wasn't until the 1920s that the now-famous zinfandel vines took root in Paso Robles. Coasting through golden-brown hills and grassy pastureland, Hwy 46 passes family-owned vineyards, olive orchards and rustic farm stands.

Pick up a free **winery tour map** (pasowine.com) from any tasting room and sniff out boutique winemakers such as **Chronic Cellars** (chroniccellars.com) as well as big-name producers like **Eberle Winery** (eberlewinery.com). For many more wine-tasting rooms and bars, restaurants and urbane boutiques, explore around downtown Paso's leafy central park square.

📍 DETOUR
James Dean Memorial
Start: 7 Paso Robles Wine Country

On Hwy 46 about 25 miles east of Paso Robles, there's a monument near the spot where *Rebel Without a Cause* star James Dean fatally crashed his Porsche on September 30, 1955, at the age of 24.

Ironically, the actor had recently filmed a public-safety-campaign TV spot against drag racing and speeding on US highways. Look for the shiny brushed-steel memorial wrapped around an oak tree outside the Jack Ranch Cafe truck stop, which has a few old photographs and some dusty movie-star memorabilia inside.

19
Santa Barbara Wine Country

BEST FOR WALKING

Los Olivos' wine-tasting rooms and boutique shops.

DURATION	DISTANCE	GREAT FOR
2–3 days	145 miles / 235km	Food & Drink, Outdoors

BEST TIME TO GO	April to October for optimal sunshine.

Lake Piru, Los Padres National Forest

The 2004 Oscar-winning film *Sideways*, an ode to wine-country living as seen through the misadventures of middle-aged buddies Miles and Jack, may have brought the spotlight to Santa Barbara's wine country. But passionate winegrowers and vintners direct the ongoing viticultural play in this gorgeous, climatically blessed setting. More than 100 wineries spread across the landscape, with five small towns all clustered within a 10-mile drive of one another.

Link Your Trip

18 Around San Luis Obispo
Want more wine, but beaches too? Drive Hwy 101 north of the Santa Ynez Valley for 45 miles to Pismo Beach.

03 Mission Trail
Trace the path of Spanish-colonial history at La Purísima Mission, 18 miles northwest of Solvang via Hwy 246.

01 SANTA BARBARA

Start pretending to live the luxe life in Santa Barbara, a coastal Shangri-la where the air is redolent with citrus, and flowery bougainvillea drapes whitewashed buildings with Spanish Colonial–style red-tiled roofs, all fringed with beaches and oceanside bluffs. Before heading out of town into the wine country for the day or weekend, make time to visit landmark **Mission Santa Barbara** (santa barbaramission.org), California's 'Queen of the Missions.' Then walk around downtown's courthouse, historical buildings and museums, all on or just off

State St, which leads downhill to the ocean and splintered wooden **Stearns Wharf** (stearnswharf.org), the West Coast's oldest continuously operating pier. A few blocks inland from the beach, follow Santa Barbara's **Urban Wine Trail** (urbanwinetrailsb.com), where boutique wine-tasting rooms are typically open from noon to 6pm daily.

🚗 **THE DRIVE**
In the morning, take a short drive north on Hwy 101, then follow winding, narrow Hwy 154 up into the Santa Ynez Mountains and over San Marcos Pass. About 9 miles from Hwy 101, turn left onto Stagecoach Rd, passing the 1860s Cold Springs Tavern. After 2 miles, turn right onto Paradise Rd.

02 LOS PADRES NATIONAL FOREST
Off Paradise Rd, the oak-covered hills of **Los Padres National Forest** (fs.usda.gov/lpnf) contain several good hiking trails for all ages, all easily accessed off Hwy 154.

Starting beyond the family campgrounds and river crossing on Paradise Rd, the creekside **Red Rock Trail** leads for a mile to rocky pools and waterfalls where you can sunbathe or swim.

🚗 **THE DRIVE**
Backtrack along Paradise Rd, then turn right and follow Hwy 154 northbound past Lake Cachuma and the rolling hillsides for over 13 miles. Turn left onto Hwy 246 and keep motoring five more flat miles through the Santa Ynez Valley west to Solvang.

03 SOLVANG
Loosely translated as 'sunny fields,' this touristy Danish village was founded in 1911 on what was once a Mexican *rancho* (land grant). Filled with knickknack stores and storybook motels, the town is almost as sticky-sweet as the Scandinavian pastries gobbled by day-trippers. Wine-tasting rooms and windmills decorate the village's pedestrian-friendly streets. For a break from the grapes, seek out tiny speakeasy the **Backroom** (valleybrewers.com/the-backroom), where locals cozy up with

pints from a rotating selection of intriguing local and international beers. Of cultural interest is the petite **Wildling Museum** (wildlingmuseum.org), exhibiting nature-themed California and American Western art. On a residential side street, the tiny **Elverhøj Museum of History & Art** (elverhoj.org) uncovers the real roots of Danish life in Solvang. Tranquil today, **Old Mission Santa Inés** (missionsantaines.org) witnessed an 1824 Chumash revolt against Spanish colonial cruelty.

THE DRIVE
Continue west on Hwy 246 past equestrian ranches and the famous ostrich farm (as seen during Jack's predawn run in Sideways) for just a few miles to Buellton. Continue across Hwy 101 and drive west toward Lompoc.

Photo Opportunity
The graceful and spectacular arch of Cathedral Cove.

04 SANTA RITA HILLS
When it comes to rolling scenery, eco-conscious farming practices and top-notch pinot noir and chardonnay grapes kissed by coastal fog, the **Santa Rita Hills** (staritahills.com) undoubtedly hold their own. Almost a dozen tasting rooms open their doors daily along this 36-mile scenic loop west of Hwy 101. Be prepared to share these slow-moving roads with sweaty cyclists, Harley-Davidson bikers and an occasional John Deere tractor. Head west of Buellton on Hwy 246 into the countryside to small-lot estate winery **Melville Winery** (melvillewinery.com), which talks about pounds per plant, not tons per acre. Turn left onto Hwy 1 south, then left again on Santa Rosa Rd, where **Sanford Winery** (sanfordwinery.com) was the first to plant pinot noir in the Santa Rita Hills; stop to taste the wine and the vineyard scenery. Just west of Hwy 101 by a hillside olive orchard, **Mosby Winery** pours unusual Cal-Italian varietals inside a red carriage house.

THE DRIVE
At the eastern end of Santa Rosa Rd, merge onto fast-tracked Hwy 101 northbound. After 6 miles, take the Hwy 154 exit for Los Olivos, driving 3 miles further east past more rolling vineyards.

05 LOS OLIVOS
The local saddlery occupies the same block as one of the best restaurants in the ranching town of Los Olivos. Its four-block-long downtown is bursting with wine-tasting rooms, little eateries, art galleries and fashionable shops seemingly airlifted straight out of Napa Valley. You can easily walk between downtown's inviting tasting rooms and brewery on a long, lazy afternoon. Taste estate small-lot artistry at **Blair Fox** (blairfoxcellars.com) and compare nuances of terroir at **Liquid Farm** (liquidfarm.com), among the numerous diverse tasting rooms in town.

THE DRIVE
From Los Olivos, drive west on Hwy 154 for 3 miles. Before reaching Hwy 101, turn right onto Zaca Station Rd, then follow it for three winding miles northwest onto Foxen Canyon Rd.

LOCAL TIPS: WINE TASTING
To make the most of your wine tour, travel the wine country in small groups and with an itinerary focused on just a handful of wineries. Keep an open mind: don't tell the staff you never drink chardonnay or merlot – who knows, the wine you try that day may change your mind. Picnicking is usually cool, if you complement your lunch with a bottle of wine purchased on the premises. Not so cool? Heavy perfume and smoking. Otherwise, enjoy yourself and don't be afraid to ask questions – most tasting rooms welcome novices. And be sure to tip your knowledgeable server.

Foxen Canyon

06 FOXEN CANYON

On the celebrated wine trail through **Foxen Canyon** (foxencanyonwinetrail.net), tidy rows of grapevines border some of Santa Barbara County's prettiest wineries. This country lane meanders north all the way to the Santa Maria Valley before finally reaching the 1875 **San Ramon Chapel**, a good turnaround point after about 15 miles.

Furthest south, tour buses crowd **Firestone Vineyards** (firestonewine.com), Santa Barbara's oldest estate winery (it's where Miles, Jack and their dates sneak into the barrel room in *Sideways*). You'll have to make an appointment to visit the hidden beauty of **Demetria Estate** (demetriaestate.com), where Rhône varietals and pinot grapes are farmed biodynamically. On a former cattle ranch, sustainable **Foxen** (foxenvineyard.com) pours chardonnay and full-fruited pinot noir in a solar-powered tasting room; up the road, Foxen's old 'shack' – with a corrugated-metal roof and funky decor – pours award-winning Bordeaux-style and Italian varietals.

THE DRIVE
Backtrack just over 17 miles along Foxen Canyon Rd, keeping left at the intersection with Zaca Station Rd to return to Los Olivos. Turn left onto Hwy 154 southbound for 2 miles, then turn right onto Roblar Ave for Ontiveros Rd.

07 SANTA YNEZ VALLEY

Further inland in the warm Santa Ynez Valley, Rhône-style grapes do best, including syrah and viognier. Some of the most popular tasting rooms cluster between Los Olivos, Solvang and Santa Ynez, but noisy tour groups, harried staff and stingy pours too often disappoint.

Thankfully, that's not the case at **Beckmen Vineyards** (beckmenvineyards.com), where biodynamically farmed, estate-grown varietals flourish on the unique terroir of Purisima Mountain. For more natural beauty, backtrack east on Roblar Ave to family-owned **Clairmont Farms** (clairmontfarms.com), where purple lavender fields bloom like a Monet masterpiece in early summer. Turn right onto Refugio Rd, which flows south past more vineyards, fruit orchards and farms and straight across Hwy 154 to **Kalyra Winery** (kalyrawinery.com), where an Australian traveled halfway around the world to combine two loves: surfing and winemaking. Try his shiraz made with imported Australian grapes or locally grown varietals, all in bottles with Australian indigenous art–inspired labels.

20
Lake Tahoe Loop

BEST FOR ROAD VIEWS

Stunning vistas from South Lake Tahoe to Tahoe City.

DURATION	DISTANCE	GREAT FOR
2–3 days	105 miles / 170km	Families, nature

BEST TIME TO GO	
	May to September for sunshine; January to March for snow.

Emerald Bay, Lake Tahoe

Encircled by mountains, cis open for adventure year-round. During summer, hit the sapphire waters fringed by sandy beaches or trek and mountain-bike forest trails. In winter, powder-hungry skiers and boarders bombard scores of slopes. The north shore is quiet and upscale; the west shore, rugged and old-timey; the east shore, blissfully undeveloped; and the south shore, always busy. The lake straddles the California–Nevada state line.

Link Your Trip

22 Eastern Sierra Scenic Byway
Downtown Reno's casinos are just over 30 miles northeast of Truckee via I-80.

24 Ebbetts Pass Scenic Byway
From South Lake Tahoe, it's 20 miles south along Hwy 89 to Hope Valley, although Ebbetts Pass is closed during winter and spring.

01 SOUTH LAKE TAHOE

South Lake Tahoe is a chockablock commercial strip bordering the lake, which is framed by postcard-pretty mountains. In winter, go swooshing down the double-black diamond runs and monster vertical drops of **Heavenly** (skiheavenly.com), a behemoth ski resort. From the top, you're on the spine of the Sierra Nevada between mountains and desert flatlands. For killer lake views in summer, ascend the **gondola** from Heavenly Village, or board the paddle wheelers of **Lake Tahoe Cruises** (zephyrcove.com) that ply the 'Big Blue.' Survey the azure expanse of the lake at eye level from in-town beaches or aboard a kayak launched from **Zephyr Cove**, which also has sandy swimming beaches. It's about 3 miles north of Stateline, NV, where you can bet a stack of chips at the hulking casinos, all buzzing with bars, nightclubs and 24-hour restaurants.

🚗 THE DRIVE
Unless the road has been closed by heavy snowfall, set a course heading northwest from South Lake Tahoe's 'The Y' intersection onto scenic lakeside Hwy 89. You'll pass USFS Tallac Historic Site and Taylor Creek Visitor Center, both of which have nature trails and educational exhibits, before reaching Inspiration Point and, further along, the parking lot of Vikingsholm Castle ($10 per vehicle).

02 EMERALD BAY & DL BLISS STATE PARKS

Sheer granite cliffs and a jagged shoreline mark glacier-carved **Emerald Bay** (parks.ca.gov), a teardrop cove that will have you digging for your camera. Panoramic pullouts all along Hwy 89 peer over the uninhabited granite speck of Fannette Island, which harbors the vandalized remains of a 1920s teahouse once belonging to heir Lora Knight. She also built **Vikingsholm Castle** (vikingsholm.com), a Scandinavian-style mansion on the bay that's reached via a steep 2-mile round-trip hiking trail. Heading north, the 4.5-mile Rubicon Trail ribbons along the lakeshore past hidden coves to **DL Bliss State Park** (parks.ca.gov), with its old lighthouse and sandy beaches.

🚗 THE DRIVE
Head north on Hwy 89 past the sandy beach at Meeks Bay, forested Ed Z'berg Sugar Pine Point State Park and the lakeshore hamlets of Tahoma and Homewood. At the intersection with N Lake Blvd/Hwy 28, Tahoe City's commercial strip, turn left to stay on Hwy 89 for another 5 miles northwest to Squaw Valley Rd.

03 SQUAW VALLEY

After stopping in Tahoe City for supplies and to refuel your stomach and the car, it's a short drive up to **Squaw Valley Alpine Meadows** (squawalpine.com), a mega-size ski resort that hosted the 1960 Winter Olympics. You could spend a whole winter weekend here and not ski the same run twice. Hold on tight as the aerial tram rises over the granite ledges of the **Tram Face** to **High Camp** at a lofty 8200ft, where you can sip a cocktail while being mesmerized by vistas of the lake so very far below. In summer, families crowd the outdoor swimming pool, disc-golf course, ziplines and the hiking and mountain-biking trails radiating from High Camp. The thrilling **Tahoe Via Ferrata** (tahoevia.com) takes climbers, who are clipped to cables, along a network of steel anchors ascending the Tram Face, which looms over the ski village. Hold on tight – there's more than 1000ft of elevation gain.

THE DRIVE
LBacktrack out of Squaw Valley, turning left onto Hwy 89 and driving north for about 8 miles. Before reaching I-80, turn right onto W River St for another mile to downtown Truckee.

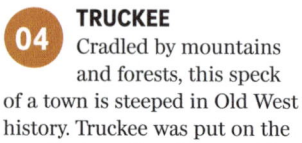

04 TRUCKEE

Cradled by mountains and forests, this speck of a town is steeped in Old West history. Truckee was put on the map by the railroad, grew rich on logging and ice harvesting, and found Hollywood fame with the 1924 filming of Charlie Chaplin's *The Gold Rush*.

The aura of the Old West still lingers over Truckee's teensy one-horse downtown, where railroad workers and lumberjacks once milled about in raucous saloons, bawdy brothels and shady gambling halls. But an influx of entrepreneurs and youthful newcomers from the San Francisco Bay Area and beyond has infused the town with a fun energy. Most of the late 19th-century buildings now contain festive restaurants and bars, and upscale boutiques.

Truckee is close to a dozen downhill and cross-country ski resorts, most famously **Northstar California** (northstarcalifornia.com), where ski lifts also transport summer hikers and mountain bikers into the highlands.

THE DRIVE
In downtown Truckee, cross over the railroad tracks and the river, following Brockway Rd southeast for 1.5 miles. Turn right onto Hwy 267 back toward Lake Tahoe, passing Northstar ski resort before cruising downhill to the lakeshore town of Kings Beach, 10 miles away.

Photo Opportunity
Inspiration Point above Emerald Bay.

DETOUR
Donner Lake
Start: 04 Truckee

Donner Summit is where the infamous Donner Party became trapped during the fierce winter of 1846–47. Their grisly tale of survival – and cannibalism – is chronicled inside the visitor center at **Donner Memorial State Park** (parks.ca.gov), where tree-lined Donner Lake (donnerlakemarina.com) offers sandy beaches. Further west, popular municipal **West End Beach** (tdrpd.com) has a roped-off swimming area for kids, and kayak, paddleboat and stand-up paddleboarding (SUP) rentals. Pull over for delicious homemade ice cream at **Little Truckee Ice Creamery** (truckeeicecream.com), a nice pit stop on the way back to Truckee from West End Beach. The state park and lakeshore are just a few miles east of Truckee via Donner Pass Rd.

05 KINGS BEACH & TAHOE VISTA

On summer weekends, sun-seekers converge on picturesque **Kings Beach State Recreation Area** (parks.ca.gov), especially the picnic tables, barbecue grills and boat rentals. **Adrift Tahoe** (standuppaddletahoe.com) handles kayak, outrigger canoe and SUP rentals, paddling lessons and tours. Just inland, the 1920s **Old Brockway Golf Course** (oldbrockwaygolf.com) runs along pine-bordered fairways where Hollywood celebs once hobnobbed. Spread southeast along Hwy 28, Tahoe Vista has more public beaches than any other lakeshore town. Lose the crowds on the hiking and mountain-biking trails or disc-golf course at **North Tahoe Regional Park** (northtahoeparks.com), which also has a snow-sledding hill and cross-country ski and snowshoe trails in winter. In summer, local hikers, picnickers and disc-golf fans keep the park just as busy.

THE DRIVE
East of Kings Beach, Hwy 28 barrels uphill across the California–Nevada border past the small-potatoes casinos of Crystal Bay before reaching Incline Village just a few miles later.

06 CRYSTAL BAY & INCLINE VILLAGE

Crossing into Nevada, the neon starts to flash and old-school gambling palaces appear. Try your luck at the gambling tables or catch a live-music show at the **Crystal Bay Casino** (crystalbaycasino.com). Straddling the state border, the currently closed **Cal-Neva Resort & Casino** evokes a colorful history of ghosts, mobsters and ex-owner Frank Sinatra. Oracle co-founder and billionaire Larry Ellison purchased the property in 2018, and slow-moving plans are afoot to develop a new resort here. Ask about the secret tunnels if it ever reopens.

One of Lake Tahoe's ritziest communities, Incline Village is a gateway to winter ski resorts.

Truckee

During summer, you can tour the eccentric **Thunderbird Lodge** (thunderbirdtahoe.org), a historical mansion only accessible by bus, boat or kayak. Or drive northeast up Hwy 431 into the **Mt Rose Wilderness**, a gateway to miles of unspoiled terrain, including easy wildflower walks at Tahoe Meadows. The new **East Shore Trail** (tahoefund.org) is a paved 3-mile path linking Incline Village with Sand Harbor State Park. Open to walkers and cyclists, the trail overlooks the lake and is lined with viewpoints and interpretive markers.

THE DRIVE
Beyond the stop-and-go traffic of Incline Village, Hwy 28 winds south, staying high above Lake Tahoe's east shore, offering peekaboo lake views and roadside pull-offs, from where locals scramble down the cliffs to hidden beaches. It's a slow-moving 13 miles south to Spooner Lake.

07 LAKE TAHOE-NEVADA STATE PARK

With pristine beaches and miles of wilderness trails for hikers, mountain bikers, skiers and snowshoers, the **Lake Tahoe-Nevada State Park** (parks.nv.gov) is the east shore's big draw. Summer crowds splash in the warm, turquoise waters and sun themselves on the white, boulder-strewn beaches of **Sand Harbor**, a few miles south of Incline Village.

The 15-mile **Flume Trail**, a mountain biker's holy grail, starts further south at Spooner Lake, where anglers fish along the shore (no swimming – too many leeches). It's just north of the Hwy 50 junction.

21

Yosemite, Sequoia & Kings Canyon

BEST SCENIC DRIVE

Don't miss Kings Canyon Scenic Byway to Cedar Grove.

DURATION	DISTANCE	GREAT FOR
5-7 days	450 miles / 725km	Nature, Families

BEST TIME TO GO	April and May for waterfalls; June to September for full access.

Cathedral Peak, Yosemite National Park

Glacier-carved valleys resting below dramatic peaks make Yosemite an all-ages playground. Here you can witness earth-shaking waterfalls, clamber up granite domes and camp out by high-country meadows where wildflowers bloom in summer. Home to the USA's deepest canyon and the biggest tree on the planet, Sequoia and Kings Canyon National Parks justify detouring further south into the Sierra Nevada, which conservationist John Muir called 'The Range of Light.'

Link Your Trip

22 Eastern Sierra Scenic Byway

From Yosemite's Tuolumne Meadows, roll over high-elevation Tioga Pass and downhill toward Mono Lake, a 20-mile trip.

23 Highway 49 Through Gold Country

En route between Yosemite Valley and Tuolumne Meadows, turn west onto Hwy 120, then follow Hwy 49 north to Sonora, a 70-mile drive away.

01 TUOLUMNE MEADOWS

Tuolumne Meadows makes for an impressive introduction to the Yosemite area. These are the Sierra Nevada's largest subalpine meadows, with fields of wildflowers, bubbling streams, ragged granite peaks and cooler temperatures at an elevation of 8600ft. Hikers can find a paradise of trails to tackle, or unpack a picnic basket by the stream-fed meadows.

Note that the route crossing the Sierra and passing by the meadows, Tioga Rd (a 19th-century wagon road and Native American trading route), is

and blown aloft by the wind. Spread below you are the pine forests and meadows of the valley floor, with the sheer face of El Capitan rising on the left and, in the distance straight ahead, iconic granite Half Dome.

THE DRIVE
Merge carefully back onto eastbound Wawona Rd, which continues downhill into Yosemite Valley, full of confusingly intersecting one-way roads. Drive east along the Merced River on Southside Dr past the Bridalveil Fall turnoff. Almost 6 miles from Tunnel View, turn left and drive across Sentinel Bridge to Yosemite Village's day-use parking lots. Ride free shuttle buses that circle the valley.

03 YOSEMITE VALLEY
From the bottom looking up, this dramatic valley cut by the meandering Merced River is song-inspiring, and not just for birds: rippling meadow grasses; tall pines; cool, impassive pools reflecting granite monoliths; and cascading, glacier-cold white-water ribbons.

At busy Yosemite Village, start inside the **Yosemite Valley Visitor Center** (nps.gov/yose), with its thought-provoking history and nature displays and free *Spirit of Yosemite* film screenings. At the nearby **Yosemite Museum** (nps.gov/yose), Western landscape paintings are hung beside Native American baskets and beaded clothing.

The valley's famous waterfalls are thunderous cataracts in May but mere trickles by late July. Triple-tiered **Yosemite Falls** is North America's tallest, while Bridalveil Fall is hardly less impressive. A strenuous, often slippery staircase beside **Vernal**

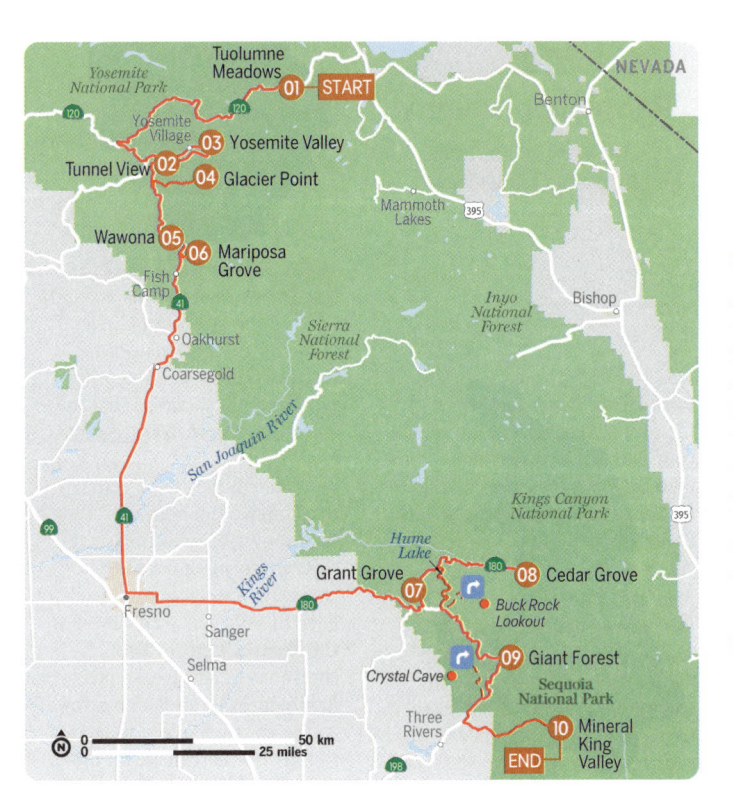

completely closed by snow in winter. It usually reopens in May or June and remains passable until October or November.

Nine miles west of the meadows, a sandy half-moon beach wraps around **Tenaya Lake**, tempting you to brave some of the park's coldest swimming. Sunbathers lie upon rocks that rim the lake's northern shore. A few minutes further west, stop at **Olmsted Point**. Overlooking a lunar-type landscape of glaciated granite, you can gaze deeply down Tenaya Canyon to Half Dome's backside.

THE DRIVE
From Tuolumne Meadows it's 50 miles to Yosemite Valley, following Tioga Rd (Hwy 120), turning south onto Big Oak Flat Rd, then east onto El Portal Rd. There's one must-do stop before entering the valley proper, Tunnel View, so follow Wawona Rd west for a few miles where it forks with Southside Dr. You'll know you've arrived when you see all the other parked cars.

02 TUNNEL VIEW
For your first, spectacular look into Yosemite Valley, pull over at Tunnel View, a vista that has inspired painters, poets, naturalists and adventurers for centuries. On the right, **Bridalveil Fall** swells with snowmelt in late spring, but by late summer it's a mere whisper, often lifted

Fall leads you, gasping, right to the top edge of the waterfall, where rainbows pop in clouds of mist. Keep hiking up the same Mist Trail to the top of **Nevada Fall** for a heady 5.5-mile round-trip trek.

In midsummer you can rent a raft at Curry Village and float down the Merced River. The serene stretch between Stoneman Bridge and Sentinel Beach is gentle enough for kids. Or take the whole family to see the stuffed wildlife mounts at the hands-on Nature Center at **Happy Isles**, east of Curry Village.

THE DRIVE
Use Northside Dr to loop round and join Wawona Rd again. Follow Wawona Rd/Hwy 41 up out of the valley. After 9 miles, turn left onto Glacier Point Rd at the Chinquapin intersection, driving 15 more miles to Glacier Point.

04 GLACIER POINT
In just over an hour you can zip from Yosemite Valley up to head-spinning **Glacier Point**. Note that the final 10 miles of Glacier Point Rd are closed by snow in winter, usually from November through April or May. During winter the road remains open as far as the Badger Pass Ski Area, but snow tires and tire chains may be required.

Rising over 3000ft above the valley floor, dramatic Glacier Point (7214ft) practically puts you at eye level with Half Dome. Glimpse what John Muir and US president Teddy Roosevelt saw when they camped here in 1903: the waterfall-strewn Yosemite Valley below and the distant peaks ringing Tuolumne Meadows.

To get away from the crowds, hike a little way down the

Photo Opportunity
Yosemite Valley from panoramic Tunnel View.

Panorama Trail, just south of the crowded main viewpoint. On your way back from Glacier Point, take time out for a 2-mile hike up Sentinel Dome or out to Taft Point for incredible 360-degree valley views.

THE DRIVE
Drive back downhill past Badger Pass Ski Area, turning left at the Chinquapin intersection and winding south through thick forest on Wawona Rd/Hwy 41. After almost 13 curvy miles you'll reach Wawona, with its lodge, visitor center, general store and gas station, all on your left.

05 WAWONA
At Wawona, a 45-minute drive south of the valley, drop by the **Pioneer Yosemite History Center**, with its covered bridge, pioneer-era buildings and historic Wells Fargo office.

In summer you can take a short, bumpy stagecoach ride and really feel like you're living in the past. Peek inside the **Wawona Visitor Center** at the recreated studio of 19th-century artist Thomas Hill, hung with romantic Sierra Nevada landscape paintings. On summer evenings, imbibe a civilized cocktail in the lobby lounge of the **Wawona Hotel**.

THE DRIVE
By car, follow Wawona Rd/Hwy 41 south for 4.5 miles to the park's south entrance, where you must leave your car at the new parking lot. A free shuttle will take you to Mariposa Grove.

06 MARIPOSA GROVE
Wander giddily around the Mariposa Grove, home of the 1800-year-old **Grizzly Giant** and 500 other monumental sequoias that tower above your head. Nature trails wind through this popular grove, but you can only hear yourself think above the noise of vacationing crowds during the early morning or evening. Notwithstanding a cruel hack job back in 1895, the walk-through **California Tunnel Tree** continues to survive, so pose your family in front and snap away. If you've got the energy, make a round-trip pilgrimage on foot to the fallen **Wawona Tunnel Tree** in the upper grove.

THE DRIVE
From Yosemite's south entrance station, it's a 115-mile, three-hour trip to Kings Canyon National Park. Follow Hwy 41 south 60 miles to Fresno, then slingshot east on Hwy 180 for another 50 miles, climbing out of the Central Valley back into the mountains. Keep left at the Hwy 198 intersection, staying on Hwy 180 toward Grant Grove.

07 GRANT GROVE
Through **Sequoia** and **Kings Canyon National Parks** (nps.gov/seki), roads seem barely to scratch the surface of the twin parks' beauty. To see real treasures, you'll need to get out and stretch your legs. North of Big Stump entrance station in

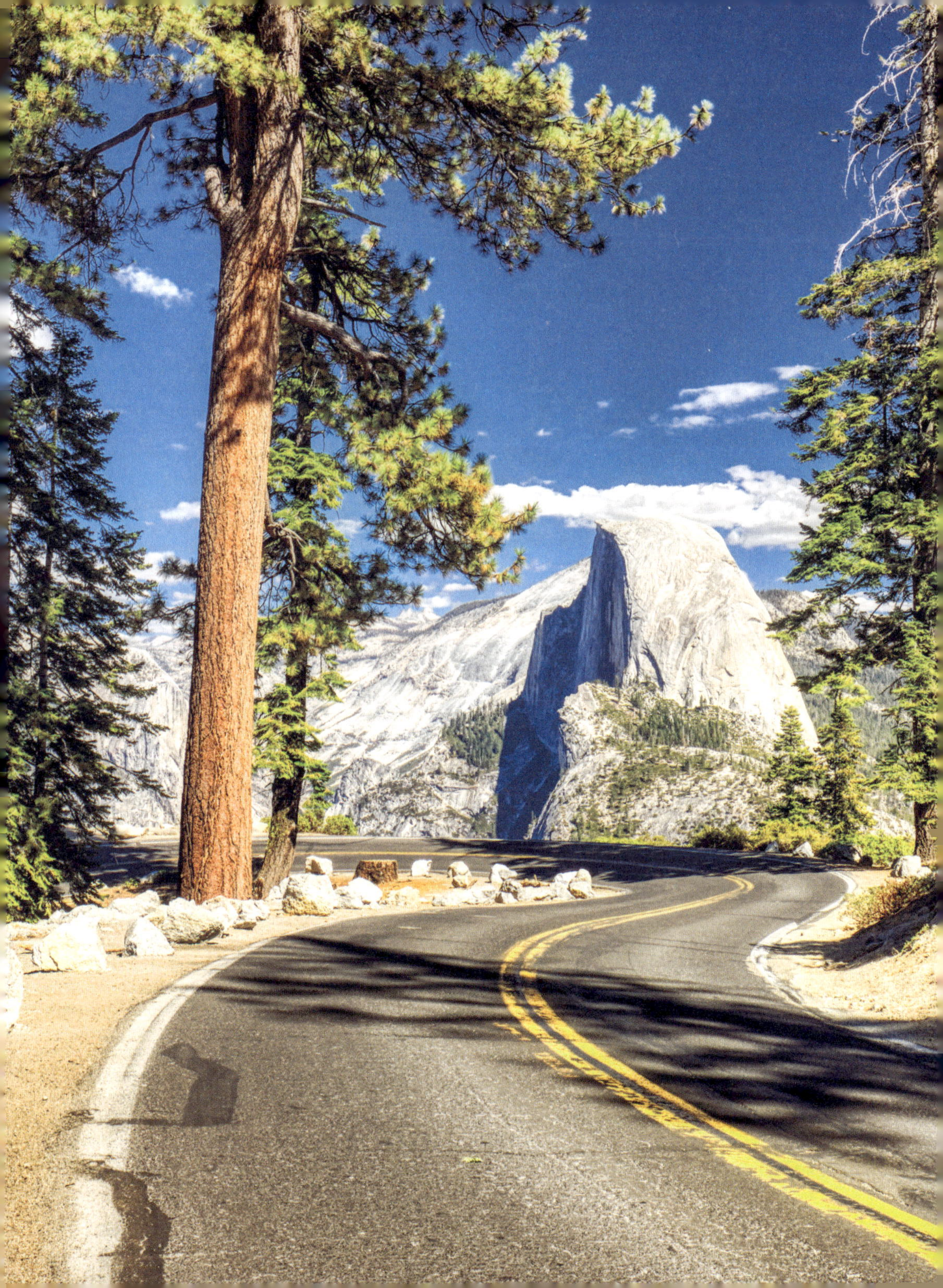

HIKING HALF DOME & AROUND YOSEMITE VALLEY

Over 800 miles of hiking trails in **Yosemite National Park** fit hikers of all abilities. Take an easy half-mile stroll on the valley floor or underneath giant sequoia trees, or venture out all day on a quest for viewpoints, waterfalls and lakes in the mountainous high country.

Some of the park's most popular hikes start right in **Yosemite Valley** (pictured), including to the top of Half Dome (16-mile round trip), the most famous of all. It follows a section of the **John Muir Trail** and is strenuous, difficult and best tackled in two days with an overnight in Little Yosemite Valley.

Reaching the top can only be done in summer after park rangers have installed fixed cables; depending on snow conditions, this may occur as early as late May and the cables usually come down in mid-October. To limit the cables' notorious human logjams, the park now requires permits for day hikers, but the route is still nerve-racking because hikers must share the cables. Advance permits go on sale by preseason lottery in early spring, with a limited number available via another daily lottery two days in advance during the hiking season. Permit regulations and prices keep changing; check the **park website** (nps.gov/yose) for current details.

The less ambitious or physically fit will still have a ball following the **Mist Trail** as far as Vernal Fall (2.5-mile round trip), the top of **Nevada Fall** (5.5-mile round trip) or idyllic **Little Yosemite Valley** (8-mile round trip). The **Four Mile Trail** (9-mile round trip) up to Glacier Point is a strenuous but satisfying climb to a glorious viewpoint. If you've got the kids in tow, nice and easy valley walks include to **Mirror Lake** (2-mile round trip) and viewpoints at the base of thundering **Yosemite Falls** (1-mile round trip) and lacy **Bridalveil Fall** (0.5-mile round trip).

Grant Grove Village, turn left and wind downhill to **General Grant Grove** where you'll see some of the park's landmark giant sequoia trees along a paved path. You can walk right through the **Fallen Monarch**, a massive, fire-hollowed trunk that's done duty as cabin, hotel, saloon and horse stable. For views of Kings Canyon and the peaks of the Great Western Divide, follow a narrow, winding side road (closed during winter; no RVs or trailers) starting behind the John Muir Lodge for over 2 miles up to Panoramic Point (high summer only).

THE DRIVE
The tortuously winding stretch of Hwy 1 southbound is sparsely populated, rugged and remote, running through national forest. Make sure you've got enough fuel in the tank to at least reach the expensive gas station at Gorda, over 20 miles south of Julia Pfeiffer Burns State Park.

08 CEDAR GROVE
Serpentining past chiseled rock walls laced with waterfalls, Hwy 180 plunges down to the **Kings River**, where roaring white water ricochets off the granite cliffs of North America's deepest canyon, technically speaking.

Pull over partway down at **Junction View overlook** for an eyeful, then keep rolling down along the river to Cedar Grove Village. East of the village, **Zumwalt Meadow** is the place for spotting birds, mule deer and black bears.

If the day is hot and your swimming gear is handy, stroll from Road's End to **Muir Rock**, a large flat-top river boulder where John Muir once gave outdoor talks that's now a popular summer swimming hole. Starting from Road's End, a very popular day hike climbs 4 miles each way to Mist Falls, which thunders in late spring.

THE DRIVE
Backtrack from Road's End nearly 30 miles up Hwy 180. Turn left onto Hume Lake Rd. Curve around the lake past swimming beaches and campgrounds, turning right onto 10 Mile Rd. At Hwy 198, turn left and follow the Generals Hwy (often closed from January to March) south for about 23 miles to the Wolverton Rd turnoff on your left.

DETOUR
Buck Rock Lookout
Start: 08 Cedar Grove
To climb one of California's most evocative fire lookouts, drive east of the Generals Hwy on Big Meadows Rd into the Sequoia National Forest between Grant Grove and the Giant Forest. Follow the signs to staffed Buck Rock Fire Lookout (buckrock.org). Constructed in 1923, this active fire lookout allows panoramic views from a dollhouse-sized cab lording it over the horizon from 8500ft atop a granite rise, reached by 172 spindly stairs. It's not for anyone with vertigo. Opening hours may vary seasonally, and the lookout closes during lightning storms and fire emergencies.

09 GIANT FOREST
We dare you to try hugging the trees in Giant Forest, a 3-sq-mile grove protecting the park's most gargantuan specimens. Park off Wolverton Rd and walk downhill to reach the world's biggest living tree, the **General Sherman Tree**, which towers 275ft into the sky. With sore arms and sticky sap fingers, you can lose the crowds on any of many forested trails nearby. The trail network stretches all the way south to Crescent Meadow, a 5-mile one-way ramble.

By car, drive 2.5 miles south along the Generals Hwy to get schooled on sequoia ecology and fire cycles at the **Giant Forest Museum** (nps.gov/seki).

Starting outside the museum, Crescent Meadow Rd makes a 6-mile loop into the Giant Forest, passing right through Tunnel Log. For 360-degree views of the Great Western Divide, climb the steep quarter-mile staircase up **Moro Rock**. Note: Crescent Meadow Rd is closed to traffic by winter snow; during summer, ride the free shuttle buses around the loop road.

WHY I LOVE THIS TRIP
Michael Grosberg, writer

When city life gets claustrophobic, the Sierra Nevada region beckons me. This drive takes you through scenery out of an Albert Bierstadt painting or a CGI version of the American West. Out of the car and into the wilderness, your thoughts become meditative as the rhythm of your walking pace and the challenge of the terrain are the only concerns.

THE DRIVE
Narrowing, the Generals Hwy drops for more than 15 miles into the Sierra Nevada foothills, passing Amphitheater Point and exiting the park beyond Foothills Visitor Center. Before reaching the town of Three Rivers, turn left on Mineral King Rd, a dizzyingly scenic 25-mile road (partly unpaved, no trailers or RVs allowed and closed in winter) that switchbacks up to Mineral King Valley.

10 MINERAL KING VALLEY
Navigating over 700 hairpin turns, it's a winding 1½-hour drive up to the glacially sculpted **Mineral King Valley** (7500ft), a 19th-century silver-mining camp and lumber settlement, and later a mountain retreat. Trails into the high country begin at the end of Mineral King Rd, where historic private cabins dot the valley floor, flanked by massive mountains.

Your final destination is just over a mile past the ranger station, where the valley unfolds all of its hidden beauty, and hikes to granite peaks and alpine lakes.

Note that Mineral King Rd is typically open only from late May through late October. In summer, Mineral King's marmots like to chew on parked cars, so wrap the undercarriage of your vehicle with a tarp and rope (which can be bought, though not cheaply, at the hardware store in Three Rivers).

BEST ROAD TRIPS: CALIFORNIA

22

Eastern Sierra Scenic Byway

DURATION	DISTANCE	GREAT FOR
3–5 days	360 miles / 580km	Families, Nature

BEST TIME TO GO	June to September for warm days and (mostly) snow-free mountain ramblings.

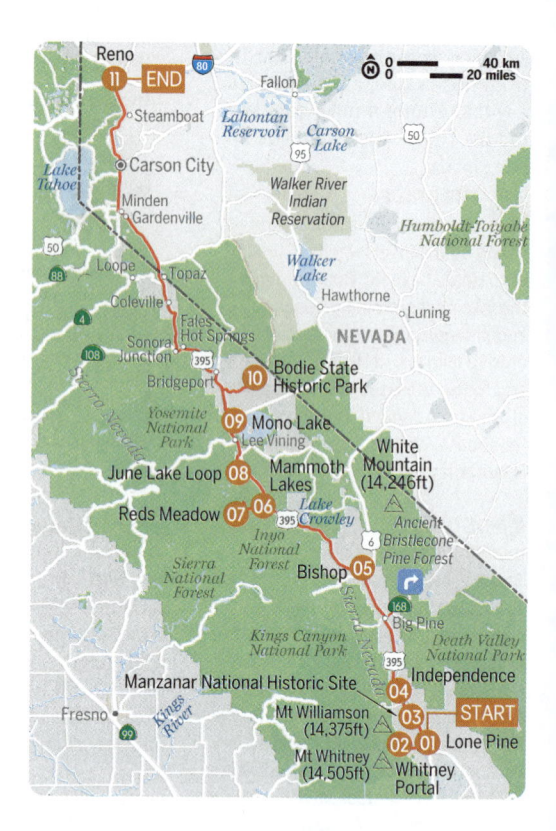

The gateway to California's largest expanse of wilderness, Hwy 395 – also called the Eastern Sierra Scenic Byway – borders towering mountain vistas, glistening blue lakes and the seemingly endless forests of the eastern Sierra Nevada mountains. A lifetime of outdoor activities beckons beyond the asphalt (parts of which get traffic clogged in summer), and desolate Old West ghost towns, unique geological formations and burbling natural hot springs await exploration.

Link Your Trip

21 Yosemite, Sequoia & Kings Canyon

In Lee Vining, go west on Hwy 120 to enter Yosemite National Park via the 9945ft Tioga Pass

31 Life in Death Valley

From Lone Pine, head southeast on Hwys 136 and 190 to reach Panamint Springs, a western access point for Death Valley.

01 LONE PINE

The diminutive town of Lone Pine stands as the southern gateway to the craggy jewels of the Eastern Sierra. At the southern end of town, drop by the **Museum of Western Film History** (museumofwesternfilmhistory.org), which contains exhibits of paraphernalia from the over 450 movies shot in the area. Don't miss the occasional screenings in its theater or the tricked-out Cadillac convertible in its foyer.

Just outside the center of town on Whitney Portal Rd, an otherworldly orange alpenglow makes the **Alabama Hills** a must for watching a slow-motion

BEST FOR OUTDOORS

Hike tranquil mountain trails and camp in Mammoth Lakes.

Museum of Western Film History, Lone Pine

sunset. A frequent backdrop for movie Westerns and the *Lone Ranger* TV series, the rounded earthen-colored mounds stand out against the steely gray foothills and jagged pinnacles of the Sierra range, and a number of graceful rock arches are within easy hiking distance of the roads.

THE DRIVE
From Lone Pine, the jagged incisors of the Sierra surge skyward in all their raw and fierce glory. Continue west past the Alabama Hills and then brace yourself for the dizzying ascent to road's end – a total of 13 miles from Hwy 395. The White Mountains soar to the east, and the dramatic Owens Valley spreads below.

02 WHITNEY PORTAL
At 14,505ft, the celestial granite giant of **Mt Whitney** (fs.usda.gov/inyo) stands as the loftiest peak in the lower 48 and the obsession of thousands of high-country hikers every summer. Desperately coveted permits (assigned by advance lottery) are your only passport to the summit, though drop-in day-trippers can swan up the mountain as far as Lone Pine Lake – about 6 miles round-trip – to kick up some dust on the iconic Whitney Trail.

Ravenous hikers can stop by the **Whitney Portal Store** (facebook.com/WhitneyPortalStore) for enormous burgers and plate-size pancakes.

As you get a fix on this majestic megalith cradled by scores of smaller pinnacles, remember that the country's lowest point is only 80 miles (as the crow flies) east of here: Badwater in Death Valley.

THE DRIVE
Double back to Lone Pine and drive 9 miles north on divided Hwy 395. Scrub brush and tumbleweed desert occupy the valley between the copper-colored foothills of the Sierra Nevada and the White Mountain range. Well-signed Manzanar sits along the west side of the highway.

03 MANZANAR NATIONAL HISTORIC SITE
A monument to one of the darkest chapters in US

history, Manzanar unfolds across a barren and windy sweep of land cradled by snow-dipped peaks. During the height of WWII, the federal government interned more than 10,000 people of Japanese ancestry here following the attack on Pearl Harbor. Though little remains of the infamous war concentration camp, the camp's former high-school auditorium houses a superb **interpretive center** (nps.gov/manz). Watch the 22-minute documentary film, then explore the thought-provoking exhibits chronicling the stories of the families that languished here yet built a vibrant community. Afterwards, take a self-guided 3.2-mile driving tour around the grounds, which include a recreated mess hall and barracks, vestiges of buildings and gardens, as well as the haunting camp cemetery.

Photo Opportunity

Sunrise or sunset in the Alabama Hills, framed by the snowy Sierra Nevada.

Often mistaken for Mt Whitney, 14,375ft Mt Williamson looms above this flat, dusty plain, a lonely expanse that bursts with yellow wildflowers in spring.

THE DRIVE
Continue north 6 miles on Hwy 395 to the small town of Independence. In the center of town, look for the columned Inyo County Courthouse and turn left onto W Center St. Drive six blocks through a residential area to the end of the road.

04 INDEPENDENCE
This sleepy highway town has been a county seat since 1866 and is home to the **Eastern California Museum** (inyocounty.us/ecmsite). An excellent archive of Eastern Sierra history and culture, it contains one of the most complete collections of Paiute and Shoshone baskets in the country, as well as historic photographs of local rock climbers scaling Sierra peaks – including Mt Whitney – with huge packs and no harnesses. Other highlights include artifacts from Manzanar and an exhibit about the fight to keep the region's water supply from being diverted to Los Angeles.

Fans of Mary Austin (1868–1934), renowned author of *The Land of Little Rain* and vocal

Alabama Hills (p124)

foe of the desertification of the Owens Valley, can follow signs leading to her **former house** at 253 Market St.

🚗 THE DRIVE
Depart north along Hwy 395 as civilization again recedes amid a buffer of dreamy granite mountains, midsize foothills and (for most of the year) an expanse of bright blue sky. Tuffs of blackened volcanic rock occasionally appear roadside. Pass through the blink-and-you'll-miss-it town of Big Pine, and enter Bishop.

🧭 DETOUR
Ancient Bristlecone Pine Forest
Start: **04** Independence

For encounters with some of the earth's oldest living things, plan at least a half-day trip to the **Ancient Bristlecone Pine Forest** (fs.usda.gov/inyo). These gnarled, otherworldly-looking trees thrive above 10,000ft on the slopes of the seemingly inhospitable White Mountains, a parched and stark range that once stood even higher than the Sierra. One of the oldest trees – called Methuselah – is estimated to be over 4700 years old, beating even the Great Sphinx of Giza by about two centuries.

To reach the groves, take Hwy 168 east 12 miles from Big Pine to White Mountain Rd, then turn left (north) and climb the curvy road 10 miles to Schulman Grove, named for the scientist who first discovered the trees' biblical age in the 1950s. The entire trip takes about one hour one way from Independence. There's access to self-guided trails near the solar-powered **Schulman Grove Visitor Center** (fs.usda.gov/inyo). White Mountain Rd is usually closed from November to April.

05 BISHOP
The second-largest town in the Eastern Sierra and about a third of the way north from Lone Pine to Reno, Bishop is a major hub for hikers, cyclists, anglers and climbers. To get a taste of what draws them here, head to the Happy and Sad Boulders areas in the strikingly unique rocky Volcanic Tablelands not far north of town.

Where Hwy 395 swings west, continue northeast for 4.5 miles on Hwy 6 to reach the **Laws Railroad Museum & Historic Site** (lawsmuseum.org), a remnant of the narrow-gauge Carson and Colorado rail line that closed in 1960. Train buffs will hyperventilate over the collection of antique railcars, and kids love exploring the 1883 depot and clanging the brass bell. Dozens of historic buildings from the region have been reassembled with period artifacts to create a time-capsule village.

🚗 THE DRIVE
Back on Hwy 395, continue over 40 miles north to Hwy 203, passing Lake Crowley and the southern reaches of the Long Valley Caldera seismic hot spot. On Hwy 203 before the center of town, stop in at the Mammoth Lakes Welcome Center for excellent local and regional information.

06 MAMMOTH LAKES
Splendidly situated at 8000ft, Mammoth Lakes is an active year-round outdoor-recreation town buffered by alpine wilderness and punctuated by its signature 11,053ft peak, **Mammoth Mountain** (mammothmountain.com). This ever-growing resort complex has 3100 vertical feet – enough to whet any snow-sports appetite – and an enviably long season that may last from November to June. When the snow finally melts, the ski and snowboard resort does a quick costume change and becomes the massive **Mammoth Mountain Bike Park** and with a slew of mountain-bikers decked out in body armor, it could be mistaken for the set of an apocalyptic *Mad Max* sequel. With more than 80 miles of well-tended single-track trails and a crazy terrain park, it draws those who know their knobby tires.

Year-round, a vertiginous **gondola** hisks sightseers to the apex for breathless views of snow-speckled mountaintops.

🚗 THE DRIVE
Keep the car parked at Mammoth Mountain and catch the mandatory Reds Meadow shuttle bus from the Gondola Building. However, you may want to drive up 1.5 miles west and back on Hwy 203 as far as Minaret Vista to contemplate eye-popping views of the Ritter Range, the serrated Minarets and the remote reaches of Yosemite National Park.

07 REDS MEADOW
One of the most beautiful and varied landscapes near Mammoth is the Reds Meadow Valley, west of Mammoth Mountain. The most fascinating attraction in Reds Meadow is the surreal 10,000-year-old volcanic formation of **Devils Postpile National Monument** (nps.gov/depo). The 60ft curtains of near-vertical, six-sided basalt columns formed when rivers of molten lava slowed, cooled and cracked with perplexing symmetry. This honeycomb design is best appreciated from atop the columns, reached by a short trail. The columns are an easy half-mile hike from the Devils Postpile Ranger Station.

From the monument, a 2.5-mile hike passing through

fire-scarred forest leads to the spectacular **Rainbow Falls**, where the San Joaquin River gushes over a 101ft basalt cliff. Chances of actually seeing a rainbow forming in the billowing mist are greatest at noon. The falls can also be reached via an easy 1.5-mile walk from the Reds Meadow shuttle stop.

THE DRIVE
Back on Hwy 395, continue north to Hwy 158 and pull out the camera for the alpine lake and peak vistas of the June Lake Loop.

08 JUNE LAKE LOOP
Under the shadow of massive Carson Peak (10,909ft), the stunning 16-mile June Lake Loop (Hwy 158) meanders through a picture-perfect horseshoe canyon, past the relaxed resort town of **June Lake** and four sparkling, fish-rich lakes: Grant, Silver, Gull and June. It's especially scenic in fall when the basin is ablaze with golden aspens. Hardy ice climbers scale its frozen waterfalls in winter. June Lake is backed by the Ansel Adams Wilderness, which runs into Yosemite National Park. From Silver Lake, Gem and Agnew Lakes make spectacular **day hikes**, and boat rentals and horseback rides are available.

THE DRIVE
Rejoin Hwy 395 heading north, where the rounded Mono Craters dot the dry and scrubby eastern landscape and the Mono Lake Basin unfolds into view..

09 MONO LAKE
North America's second-oldest lake is a quiet and mysterious expanse of deep blue water, whose glassy surface reflects jagged Sierra peaks, young volcanic cones and the unearthly tufa (too-fah) towers that make the lake so distinctive. Protruding from the water like drip sand castles, tufas form when calcium bubbles up from subterranean springs and combines with carbonate in the alkaline lake waters.

The salinity and alkaline levels are unfortunately too high for a pleasant swim. Instead, paddle a kayak or canoe around the weathered towers of tufa, drink in wide-open views of the **Mono Craters volcanic field**, and discreetly spy on the water birds that live in this unique habitat.

The **Mono Basin Scenic Area Visitor Center** (fs.usda.gov/inyo), half a mile north of Lee Vining, has interpretive displays, a bookstore and a 20-minute movie about Mono Lake

THE DRIVE
About 10 miles north of Lee Vining, Hwy 395 arrives at its highest point, Conway Summit (8148ft). Pull off at the vista point for awe-inspiring

EASTERN SIERRA HOT SPRINGS

Nestled between the White Mountains and the Sierra Nevada near Mammoth is a tantalizing slew of natural pools with snowcapped panoramic views (pictured). When the high-altitude summer nights turn chilly and the coyotes cry, you'll never want to towel off. About 9 miles southeast of Mammoth Lakes, Benton Crossing Rd juts east off Hwy 395, accessing a delicious bounty of hot springs.

To overnight with your very own private hot-springs tub, head to the Inn at **Benton Hot Springs** (bentonhotsprings.org), a small, historic resort in a 150-year-old former silver-mining town nestled in the White Mountains.

For detailed directions and maps, pick up Matt Bischoff's excellent *Touring Hot Springs California and Nevada: A Guide to the Best Hot Springs in the Far West* or seemammothweb.com/recreation/hottubbing.cfm for directions to a few.

Mono Lake

panoramas of Mono Lake, backed by the Mono Craters and June and Mammoth Mountains. Continue approximately 8 miles north, and go 13 miles east on Hwy 270 (closed in winter); the last 3 miles are unpaved.

10 BODIE STATE HISTORIC PARK

For a time warp back to the gold-rush era, swing by **Bodie** (parks.ca.gov/bodie), one of the West's most authentic and best-preserved ghost towns. Gold was discovered here in 1859, and the place grew from a bare-bones mining camp to a lawless boomtown of 10,000.

Fights and murders occurred almost daily, fueled by liquor from 65 saloons, some of which doubled as brothels, gambling halls or opium dens.

The hills disgorged some $35 million worth of gold and silver in the 1870s and '80s, but when production plummeted, Bodie was abandoned, and about 200 weather-beaten buildings now sit frozen in time in this cold, barren and windswept valley. Peering through dusty windows you'll see stocked stores, furnished homes, a schoolhouse with desks, the jail and more. The former **Miners' Union Hall** now houses a museum and visitor center, and rangers conduct free tours in summer.

THE DRIVE

Retrace your way back to Hwy 395, where you'll soon come to the big-sky settlement of Bridgeport. From here, it's approximately two hours to Reno along a lovely two-lane section of the highway that traces the bank of the snaking Walker River.

11 RENO

Nevada's second-largest city has steadily carved a non-casino niche as an all-season outdoor-recreation spot. The Truckee River bisects the heart of the mountain-ringed city, and in the heat of summer the **Truckee River Whitewater Park** (reno.gov) teems with urban kayakers and swimmers bobbing along on inner tubes. Two kayak courses wrap around Wingfield Park, a small river island that hosts free concerts in summertime. **Sierra Adventures** (wildsierra.com) offers kayak rentals, tours and lessons.

23

Highway 49 Through Gold Country

DURATION	DISTANCE	GREAT FOR
3-4 days	200 miles / 322km	Families, Nature

BEST TIME TO GO	May to October for sunny skies.

When you roll into Gold Country on a sunny afternoon, the adventures along Hwy 49 recall the days when newspaper headlines screamed about gold discoveries and the Golden State was born. Today this rural region offers different riches: exploring crumbling false-front saloons, rusting mining parks, wineries in the Sierra Nevada foothills and a parade of patinaed bronze historical markers along Hwy 49, one of California's most enchantingly scenic byways.

Link Your Trip

24 Ebbetts Pass Scenic Byway
From Columbia, wind 13 miles northwest on Parrots Ferry Rd and Hwy 4 to Murphys, in Calaveras County wine country.

26 Sacramento Delta & Lodi
Sacramento is an hour's drive or less from such Gold Country towns as Placerville via Hwy 50 or Auburn via I-80.

01 SONORA
Settled in 1848 by Mexican miners, Sonora soon became a cosmopolitan center with ornate saloons patronized by gamblers, drunkards and gold diggers. Its downtown district is so well preserved that it's frequently a location for Hollywood films, such as Clint Eastwood's *Unforgiven*. Likewise, **Railtown 1897 State Historic Park** (parks.ca.gov) and the surrounding hills of Jamestown, about 4 miles southwest of Sonora along Hwy 49, have been a backdrop for more than 200 Western movies and TV shows, including *High Noon*.

BEST FOR SWIMMING

Take a dip at South Yuba River State Park.

South Yuba River State Park (p135)

There's a lyrical romance to the historical railway yard, where orange poppies bloom among the rusting shells of steel goliaths. On some weekends and holidays, you can board the narrow-gauge railroad that once transported ore, lumber and miners. Making a 45-minute, 6-mile circuit, it's the best train ride in Gold Country. The park is five blocks east of Jamestown's pint-size Main St.

THE DRIVE
Follow Hwy 49 just over 2 miles north of Sonora, then turn right onto Parrots Ferry Rd at the sign for Columbia. The state historic park is 2 miles further along this two-lane country road.

02 COLUMBIA
Grab suspenders and a floppy hat for **Columbia State Historic Park** (parks.ca.gov), near the so-called 'Gem of the Southern Mines.' It's like a miniature gold-rush Disneyland, but with more authenticity and heart. Four blocks of town have been preserved, around which volunteers perambulate in 19th-century dress and demonstrate gold panning.

The blacksmith's shop, theater, hotels and saloon are all carefully framed windows into California's past. The yesteryear illusion of Main St is shaken only a bit by fudge shops and the occasional banjo picker or play-acting 49er whose cell phone rings. Stop by the **Columbia Museum** (parks.ca.gov) inside Knapp's Store to learn more about historical mining techniques and let your kids dress up in Old West attire.

According to the hotel manager and past guests, there are two ghosts in the atmospheric **Fallon Hotel**. You'll have to spend the night to see if the rumors are true.

THE DRIVE
Backtrack south on Parrots Ferry Rd, veering right and then turning right to stay on Springfield Rd for just over a mile. Rejoin Hwy 49 northbound, which crosses a long bridge over an artificial reservoir. After a dozen miles or so, Hwy 49 becomes Main St through the small town of Angels Camp.

BEST ROAD TRIPS: CALIFORNIA 131

03 ANGELS CAMP

On the southern stretch of Hwy 49, one literary giant looms over all other Western tall-tale tellers: Samuel Clemens, aka Mark Twain, who got his first big break with the short story The Celebrated Jumping Frog of Calaveras County, written in 1865 and set in Angels Camp. With a mix of Victorian and art-deco buildings that shelter antiques shops and cafes, this 19th-century mining town makes the most of its Twain connection.

Visit the engaging **Angels Camp Museum** (angelscamp.gov/museum) for a good overview of Twain and local mining-era history. The annual **Calaveras County Fair & Jumping Frog Jubilee** (frogtown.org) is held at the fairgrounds just south of town on the third weekend in May. You could win $5000 if your frog beats the world-record jump (over 21ft) set by 'Rosie the Ribeter' back in 1986.

THE DRIVE

Hwy 49 heads north of Angels Camp through rolling hillside farms and ranches. Past San Andreas, make a short detour through Mokelumne ('Moke') Hill, another historic mining town. In Jackson, turn right onto Hwy 88 east. After 9 miles, turn left on Pine Grove-Volcano Rd for 3 miles to reach Volcano, passing Indian Grinding Rock State Historic Park en route.

DETOUR
California Cavern
Start: **03** Angel's Camp

A 20-minute drive east of San Andreas via Mountain Ranch Rd, off Hwy 49 about 12 miles north of Angels Camp, **California Cavern State Historic Landmark** (cave touring.com) has the most extensive system of natural underground caverns. John Muir described them as 'graceful flowing folds deeply plicated like stiff silken drapery.' Regular tours take 60 to 80 minutes, or get a group together and reserve ahead for a three- to five-hour 'Middle Earth Expedition', which includes some serious spelunking (over 16 only). There's also a three-hour Mammoth Expedition. The Trail of Lakes walking tour, available only during the wet season in winter and spring, is magical.

Photo Opportunity

Sutter's Mill, California's original gold discovery site.

Sutter Creek

04 VOLCANO

Although the village of Volcano once yielded tons of gold and saw Civil War intrigue, today it slumbers in solitude. Huge sandstone rocks lining Sutter Creek were blasted from the surrounding hills using a hydraulic process before being scraped clean of gold-bearing dirt. Hydraulic mining had dire environmental consequences, but at its peak, miners raked in nearly $100 a day.

Less than a mile southeast of town, **Black Chasm Cavern** (caverntouring.com) has the whiff of a tourist trap, but one look at the helictite crystals – sparkling white formations in rare horizontal clusters – makes the crowds bearable.

For eye-catching rock formations just outside the cavern, head to the on-site **Zen Garden**, where a short trail twists through a cluster of Tolkien-esque marble slabs. Two miles southwest of town at **Indian Grinding Rock State Historic Park** (parks.ca.gov), a limestone outcrop is covered with petroglyphs and more than 1000 chaw'se (mortar holes) used for grinding acorns into meal. Learn more about the Sierra Nevada's indigenous tribes inside the park's museum, shaped like a Native American hun'ge (roundhouse).

THE DRIVE
Backtrack along Pine Grove-Volcano Rd, turning right onto Hwy 88 for about half a mile, then turn right onto Ridge Rd, which winds for around 8 miles back to Hwy 49. Turn right and head north for about a mile towards Sutter Creek.

WHY I LOVE THIS TRIP
Amy C Balfour, writer

Highway 49 rolls through Old West towns and crusty mining sites – all looking much like they did during their gold-rush heyday and offering a fascinating window on the past. The vineyards and wineries scattered near Plymouth, Sutter Creek and Placerville are gorgeous places to savor the history, the old vine grapes and the sweeping views of the Sierra Nevada mountains.

---

05 SUTTER CREEK

Perch on the balcony of one of Main St's gracefully restored buildings and view this gem of a Gold Country town, boasting raised, arcaded sidewalks and high-balconied, false-fronted buildings that exemplify California's 19th-century frontier architecture.

Pick up self-guided walking and driving tour maps at the **visitor center** (suttercreek.org). The nearby **Sutter Creek Theatre** (suttercreektheater.com), an 1860s saloon and billiards hall, now hosts live-music concerts and occasionally plays, films and cultural events.

The rest of the town's four-block-long Main St is crowded with antiques shops, county boutiques, cafes and tasting bars pouring regional wines and craft spirits. Welcoming **Yorba Wines** (yorbawines.com) is a good place to start your tasting. You can learn more about the town's mining past at the **Miner's Bend Park** (suttercreekfoundation.org) at the southern end of downtown. It's loaded with old mining equipment and informative signage.

THE DRIVE
Follow Main St north of Sutter Creek for 3 miles through quaint Amador City. Back at Hwy 49, turn right and continue north toward Plymouth and Shenandoah Valley Rd..

06 AMADOR COUNTY WINE COUNTRY

Amador County is an underdog among California's winemaking regions, but a circuit of welcoming wineries and local characters make for great sipping without any pretension. Planted with California's oldest surviving zinfandel vines, the countryside has a lot in common with its most celebrated grape varietal – bold, richly colored and earthy.

Many wineries are found along Shenandoah Valley Rd and its offshoots. For a true family affair going back 150 years stop by **Deaver Vineyards** (deavervineyards.com), where nearly everyone pouring has their last name on the bottles. Down the road is chic **Iron Hub Winery** (ironhubwines.com). With its hilltop perch and sweeping views of the Sierra Nevada foothills, this is a pretty place to sample wines and socialize.

Continue east on Shenandoah Rd to **Sobon Estate** (sobonwine.com), an environmentally conscious family-run estate with a winemaking history dating to the 1850s. There's a small local history museum on-site. Backtrack to **Jeff Runquist Wines** (jeffrunquistwines.com), which dominates the double-gold winners list at the San Francisco Chronicle Wine Competition every year. Locally sourced favorites here include the zinfandel and barbera.

🚗 THE DRIVE

Turn left back onto Shenandoah Rd for 3 miles, then turn right onto Hwy 49 northbound. Less then 20 miles later, after up-and-down roller-coaster stretches, you'll arrive in downtown Placerville, south of Hwy 50.

07 PLACERVILLE

Things get livelier in 'Old Hangtown,' a nickname Placerville earned for the vigilante-justice hangings that happened here in 1849. Most buildings along Placerville's Main St date from the 1850s. Poke around antiques shops or ho-hum **Placerville Hardware**, the oldest continuously operating hardware store west of the Mississippi River. Downtown dive bars get an annual cleaning at Christmas and are great for knocking elbows with odd birds.

For family-friendly shenanigans, head 1 mile north of town via Bedford Ave to **Hangtown's Gold Bug Park & Mine** (goldbugpark.org), where hard-hatted visitors can descend into a 19th-century mine shaft, or try gem panning (per hour $2).

Around Placerville, El Dorado County's mountainous terrain and volcanic soil combine with intense summertime heat and cooling night breezes off the Sierra Nevada to produce some noteworthy wines. Welcoming wineries on Apple Hill north of Hwy 50 include **Lava Cap Winery** (lavacap.com), which sells stocked picnic baskets, and **Boeger Winery** (boegerwinery.com), whose vineyards were first planted during the gold rush.

🚗 THE DRIVE

Back on Hwy 49 northbound, you'll ride along one of the most scenic stretches of the Gold Country's historic route. Patched with shade from oak and pine trees, Hwy 49 drifts beside Sierra Nevada foothills for the next 9 miles to Coloma.

08 COLOMA

At pastoral, low-key **Marshall Gold Discovery State Historic Park** (parks.ca.gov), a simple dirt path leads to the place along the banks of the American River where James Marshall made his famous discovery of gold flecks below Sutter's Mill on January 24, 1848.

Today, several reconstructed and restored historical buildings are all within a short stroll along grassy trails that pass mining artifacts, a blacksmith's shop, pioneer houses and the **Gold Discovery Museum & Visitor Center** (marshallgold.com).

Panning for gold is always popular at **Bekeart's Gun Shop**. Opposite the pioneer cemetery, you can walk or drive up Hwy 153 – the sign says it's California's shortest state highway (but it's

CHASING THE ELEPHANT

Every gold prospector in the Sierra Nevada foothills (pictured) came to 'see the elephant,' a colloquialism of the '49ers that captured the adventurous rush for gold.

Those on the overland California Trail were 'following the elephant's tracks,' and when they hit it rich, they'd seen the beast from 'trunk to tail.' Like hunting a rare wild animal, rushing Gold Country's hills was a once-in-a-lifetime risk, with potential for a jumbo reward.

Marshall Gold Discovery State Historic Park, Coloma

not really) – to where the James Marshall Monument marks Marshall's final resting place. Ironically, he died bankrupt, penniless and a ward of the state.

THE DRIVE
Rolling northbound, Hwy 49 unfolds more of the region's historical beauty over the next 18 miles. In Auburn, drive across I-80 and stay on Hwy 49 north for another 22 miles, gaining elevation while heading toward Grass Valley. Exit onto Empire St, turning right to follow the signs for Empire Mine State Historic Park's visitor center.

09 AROUND NEVADA CITY

The biggest bonanza of the mother lode is **Empire Mine State Historic Park** (parks.ca.gov), where California's richest hard-rock mine produced 5.8 million ounces of gold between 1850 and 1956. The mine yard is littered with massive mining equipment and buildings constructed from waste rock.

Backtrack west, then follow the Golden Chain Hwy (Hwy 49) about 5 miles further north to Nevada City. On the town's quaint main drag, hilly Broad St, the **National Exchange Hotel** (thenationalexchangehotel.com) was built in 1856. It was scheduled to re-open in 2021, after a renovation. Walk to historic **Firehouse No 1 Museum** (nevadacountyhistory.org), where Native American artifacts join displays about Chinese laborers and creepy Donner Party relics. Last, cool off with a refreshing dip at **South Yuba River State Park** (parks.ca.gov), which has popular swimming holes and forest hiking trails near Bridgeport, the USA's longest covered wooden bridge. It's a 30-minute drive northwest of Nevada City or Grass Valley.

24

Ebbetts Pass Scenic Byway

BEST FOR FAMILIES
Bear Valley's ski resort and summertime trails and lakes.

DURATION	DISTANCE	GREAT FOR
2 days	95 miles / 155kms	Nature, Families

BEST TIME TO GO	June to October, when the pass is open.

Calaveras Big Trees State Park

Stretched along a gold-rush-era mining route, Hwy 4 jogs through a handful of mountain hamlets and forests before crossing Ebbetts Pass, which is only open in summer and fall. For outdoor fanatics, it's practically a road trip through paradise. Go hiking among giant sequoias and on the Sierra Crest, paddle tranquil lakes, climb granite boulders, splash in summer swimming holes, and strap on skis or snowshoes in winter.

Link Your Trip

20 Lake Tahoe Loop
From Hope Valley, it's a 20-mile drive northwest on Hwy 89 past stream-fed meadows to South Lake Tahoe's beaches and ski resorts.

23 Highway 49 Through Gold Country
From Murphys, mosey 13 miles along Hwy 4 and Parrots Ferry Rd to old-time Columbia State Historic Park.

01 MURPHYS

With its white-picket fences, the 19th-century 'Queen of the Sierra' is one of the most picturesque towns along the southern stretch of California's Gold Country. Amble along Main St, which shows off plenty of historical charm alongside its wine-tasting rooms, art galleries, boutiques and cafes.

These rocky, volcanic Sierra Nevada foothills are known for making brambly zinfandel and spicy syrah, which you can sample at a dozen wineries, most crowded together on a four-block stretch downtown. It's best to arrive early if you're visiting

the crowds, drive 8.5 miles along the curving park road to the start of the **South Grove Trail**. This 3.5-mile loop ascends to a peaceful grove that protects 10 times as many giant sequoias; a 1.5-mile round-trip spur trail leads to the Agassiz Tree, the big daddy of them all. Afterward, cool off with a summertime dip in Beaver Creek below the trail's footbridge or in the Stanislaus River along the main park road.

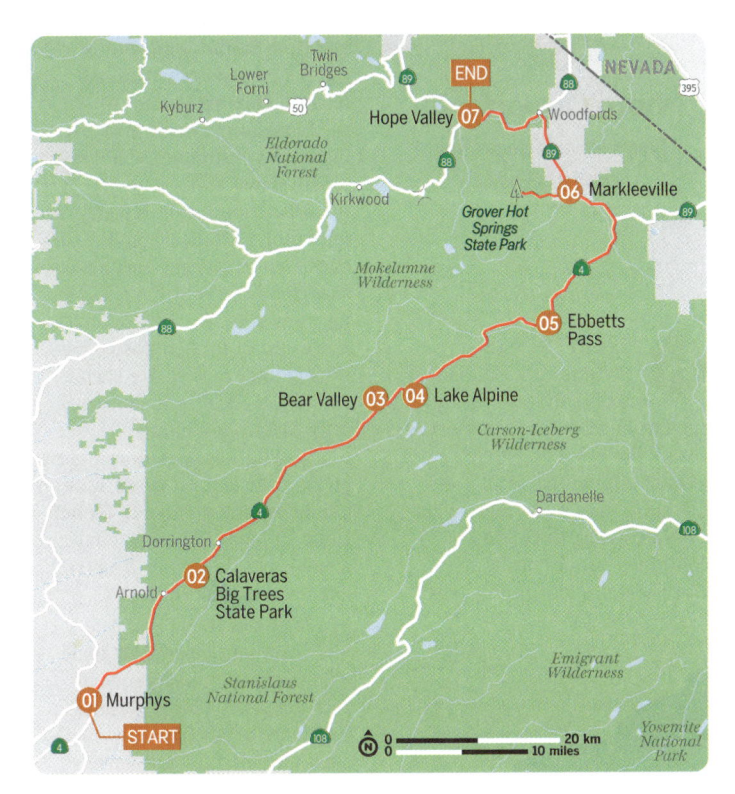

THE DRIVE
Back at Hwy 4, turn right and drive uphill past Dorrington, a 19th-century stagecoach stop and toll-road station, stopping at Hell's Kitchen Vista Point for panoramas of the glaciated volcanic landscape. About 22 miles northeast of the state park lies Bear Valley.

03 BEAR VALLEY
It's all about outdoor family fun here. Sniff out anything from rock climbing to mountain biking and hiking, all within a short distance of Bear Valley Village, which has a gas station, shops and casual restaurants. In winter, **Bear Valley Mountain** (bearvalley.com) ski area will get your brain buzzing with 2000ft of vertical rise and 12 lifts.

The resort's somewhat off-the-beaten-track location gives it a beginner-friendly, locals-only feel. On your left as you pull into Bear Valley Village, **Bear Valley Adventure Company** (bvadventures.com) is a one-stop shop for outdoor gear and supplies – kayak, SUP, mountain-bike and cross-country-ski rentals. Here you'll find insider information on just about everything there is to do in the area. Staff can also arrange mountain-bike

on the weekend. Don't miss the 'Drama Queen' chenin blanc at **Newsome Harlowe** (nhvino.com). If you can, responsibly, hop in the car for the quick drive to **Ironstone Vineyards** (ironstonevineyards.com), with its enormous tasting room, natural-spring waterfall, and landmark amphitheater, which hosts outdoor concerts.

THE DRIVE
Hwy 4 ascends through the workaday small town of Arnold, which has a few cafes and motels strung along the roadside 12 miles east of Murphys. After motoring another 3 miles uphill, turn right into Calaveras Big Trees State Park.

02 CALAVERAS BIG TREES STATE PARK
An on-the-nose name if there ever was one, **Calaveras Big Trees State Park** (parks.ca.gov) is home to giant sequoias. The most massive trees on earth, they grow only in the western Sierra Nevada range. Reaching up to 275ft tall here and with trunk diameters over 35ft, these leftovers from the Mesozoic era are thought to weigh upwards of 2000 tons, or more than 10 blue whales. Close to the park entrance, the **North Grove Big Trees Trail** is a 1.5-mile self-guided loop, where the air is scented with fresh pine, fir and incense cedar. To escape some of

BEST ROAD TRIPS: CALIFORNIA 137

shuttles and will sell you really helpful maps on the area.

🚗 THE DRIVE
From the Bear Valley Village turnoff, it's less than 4 miles up Hwy 4 to Lake Alpine's beaches, campgrounds and day-use parking lots.

04 LAKE ALPINE
Suddenly Hwy 4 reaches the shores of gaspworthy Lake Alpine, a reservoir skirted by slabs of granite and offering several sandy beaches and a handful of rustic US Forest Service (USFS) **campgrounds**. Paddling, swimming and fishing opportunities abound, which means that it's always jammed with people on summer weekends.

No matter how many folks descend upon the lake (and there are far fewer midweek), it's still hard to beat the gorgeous Sierra Nevada setting, 7350ft above sea level. Of several nearby hiking trailheads, the scramble to **Inspiration Point** gets you spectacular views of lakes and the Dardanelles; this 3-mile round-trip hike starts from the lakeshore trail near Pine Marten Campground.

Next to the boat ramp on the lake's northern shore, Lake Alpine Resort's summertime kiosk rents rowboats, paddleboats, kayaks and canoes.

🚗 THE DRIVE
Make sure you've got plenty of gas in the tank before embarking on the 33-mile drive over Ebbetts Pass downhill to Markleeville. There are campgrounds, but no services, gas stations, motels or places to eat along this high-elevation, twisting mountain road, which is only open seasonally during summer and fall.

📷 Photo Opportunity
Sierra Nevada peaks from Ebbetts Pass.

05 EBBETTS PASS
Ebbetts Pass National Scenic Byway officially runs from Arnold to Markleeville, yet it's the dramatic stretch east of Lake Alpine that really gets drivers' hearts pumping.

Narrowing, the highway continues 4 miles past Cape Horn Vista to Mosquito Lakes

✓ TOP TIP:
Crossing Ebbetts Pass

Hwy 4 is usually plowed from the west as far as Lake Alpine year-round, but Ebbetts Pass closes completely after the first major snowfall in November, December or January. The pass typically doesn't open again until April, May or June. Check current road conditions with the California Department of Transportation (dot.ca.gov).

and over Pacific Grade Summit before slaloming through historic **Hermit Valley**, where the Mokelumne River meadow blooms with summer wildflowers. Finally, Hwy 4 winds up and over the actual summit of Ebbetts Pass (elevation 8736ft), where the top-of-the-world scenery encompasses snaggletoothed granite peaks rising above the tree line. About 0.4 miles east of the signposted pass, the highway crosses the Pacific Crest Trail (PCT), which zigzags from Mexico to Canada.

For wildflowers, volcanic cliffs and granite canyon views, take an 8-mile round-trip hike to **Nobel Lake**. Or park the car and have a picnic beside Kinney Reservoir, just over another mile east.

🚗 THE DRIVE
With a maximum 24% grade (no vehicles with trailers or over 25ft long), Hwy 4 loses elevation via dozens of steep hairpin turns, crossing multiple creek and river bridges as forested valley views open up below bald granite peaks. After 13 miles, turn left onto Hwy 89 and drive almost 5 miles northwest to Markleeville.

06 MARKLEEVILLE
Breathlessly coming down from Ebbetts Pass, Hwy 4 winds past remnants of old mining communities long gone bust, including a pioneer cemetery, ghost towns and cattle ranches.

From the junction below Monitor Pass, Hwy 89 runs gently north alongside the Carson River, where anglers fish for trout from pebble-washed beaches that kids love. Crossing Hangman's Bridge, Hwy 89 threads through Markleeville, a historic toll-road outpost that boomed with silver

Cape Horn, Ebbetts Pass

mining in the 1860s. Today it's a quiet spot to refuel and relax. Downtown, turn left onto Hot Springs Rd, then head up School St to **Alpine County Museum** (alpinecountymuseum.org), with its one-room 1882 schoolhouse, log-cabin jail and tiny museum displaying Native American baskets and pioneer-era artifacts. Back on Hot Springs Rd, drive 4 miles west through pine forests to **Grover Hot Springs State Park** (parks.ca.gov), which has a shady picnic area, a campground and a natural-spring-fed swimming pool. Carry tire chains in winter.

THE DRIVE
Drive north out of Markleeville for 6 miles to the unremarkable junction of Hwys 88 and 89 at Woodfords. Turn left and continue lazily west another 6 miles, crossing the bridge over the Carson River to Hope Valley, where Hwys 88 and 89 split at Picketts Junction.

07 HOPE VALLEY
After all the fantastical scenery leading up to and over Ebbetts Pass, what's left? Hope Valley, where wildflowers, grassy meadows and burbling streams are bordered by evergreen pines and aspen trees that turn brilliant yellow in fall.

This panoramic valley is ringed by Sierra Nevada peaks, which remain dusted with snow even in early summer. Incidentally, the historic Pony Express route once ran through this way.

Today, whether you want to dangle a fishing pole or splash around in the chilly mountain waters, or just take a bird-watching stroll or snowshoe trek in winter around the meadows, Hope Valley can feel like the most magical place to be in Alpine County.

Start exploring on the nature trails of **Hope Valley Wildlife Area** (wildlife.ca.gov).

25
Feather River Scenic Byway

BEST SWIM HOLE

Try the riverside Feather River Hot Springs.

DURATION	DISTANCE	GREAT FOR
3-4 days	215 miles / 346km	Nature

BEST TIME TO GO	April to June, September to October.

Lassen Peak

As you cruise the remote two-lane blacktop of the Feather River Scenic Byway you're surrounded by California's northern natural wonders – rushing streams, daunting mountains and forest lakes. Eventually, the route leads to characterful towns, where hikers and mountain bikers shovel down hearty fare and stock up on supplies. The best way to soak up the sights is by camping; a number of cheap (or free) federal campgrounds line the route.

Link Your Trip

23 Highway 49 Through Gold Country

More swimming holes, wild history lessons and winding byways await on the 'Golden Chain.' Link to Hwy 49 in Downieville.

14 Volcanic Legacy Byway

Skirt the volcanic domes of Mt Shasta and Mt Lassen, starting 30 miles northwest of Chester via Hwys 36 and 89.

01 OROVILLE

This journey begins in Oroville, a little town that shares a name with the nearby lake that's filled by the Feather River. There's not much to see in Oroville, save the stunning **Chinese Temple & Museum Complex**, a quiet monument to the 10,000 Chinese people who once lived here. During the 19th century, theater troupes from China toured a circuit of Chinatowns in California, and Oroville was the end of the line, which explains the unrivaled collection of 19th-century Chinese stage finery.

The **Feather River Ranger District** (fs.usda.gov) office is also in town; it issues permits and has

ple of murders, mob rule enforced by horsewhipping and hanging, an attempted suicide and a fatal duel. And she was only here a single month!

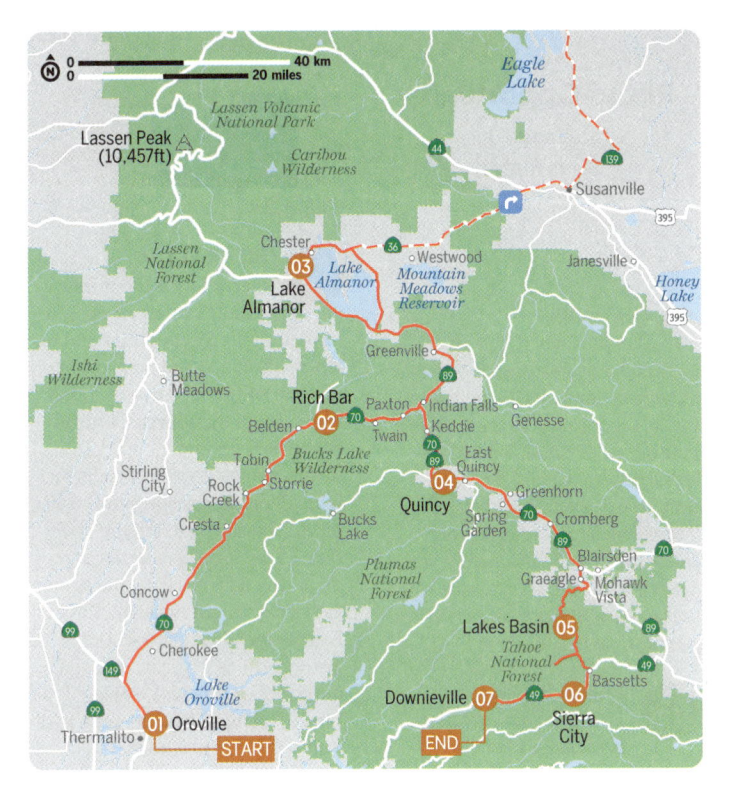

🚗 THE DRIVE
Continue the lovely, sinuous drive on Hwy 70, catching quick views of Lassen and Shasta Peaks in the rearview mirror. Go north on Hwy 89 to reach the south shore of Lake Almanor. Follow the shore around the lake clockwise.

03 LAKE ALMANOR

This artificial lake is a crystalline example of California's beautiful, if sometimes awkward, conservation and land-management policy: the lake was created by the now-defunct Great Western Power Company and is now owned by the Pacific Gas & Electric (PG&E) Company. Lassen Peak's stark silhouette overlooks the lake, which is surrounded by lush meadows and stately pines, mostly in the Lassen National Forest and Caribou Wilderness. Both offer camping with permits from the **Almanor Ranger District** (fs.usda.gov).

The main town near the lake is **Chester**, and though you could whiz right by and dismiss it, don't. This robust little community has a fledgling art scene, decent restaurants and some comfy places to stay. You can rent bicycles for a cruise along the lakeshore at **Bodfish Bicycles & Quiet Mountain Sports** (bodfishbicycles.com).

🚗 THE DRIVE
Continue around the lake and retrace the route south on Hwy 89, which will bring you back to the Feather River Scenic Byway. You'll hit Quincy after hanging left at the T-junction.

---

a handout detailing historic stops along the byway. The nearby **Lake Oroville State Recreation Area** (parks.ca.gov) is an excellent place to hike, camp and hook bass; head north instead of east and you'll find the **North Table Mountain Ecological Reserves**, which offers an off-the-beaten-track hiking experience through volcanic basalt rock formations and wildflower meadows.

🚗 THE DRIVE
Take Hwy 70 into the granite gorge, passing hydroelectric plants, mountain tunnels and historic bridges, including the Pulga Bridge. Four miles past the red bridge to Belden turn off Hwy 70 onto Rich Bar Rd, on your right.

02 RICH BAR

Although the so-called Golden Chain, Hwy 49, is still further up the road, the Feather River area was dotted with its own rough-and-ready encampments of fortune hunters. One of the most successful of these was the aptly named Rich Bar, where little remains today except a crumbling graveyard and a historic marker. This quiet place wasn't so tame in the 1850s, when a resident named Dame Shirley chronicled life at Rich Bar as a part of her fascinating diary of life in California gold towns. Published as *The Shirley Letters*, she paints Rich Bar as a chaotic place of bloody accidents, a cou-

DETOUR
Eagle Lake
Start: 03 **Lake Almanor**

Those who have the time to get all the way out to Eagle Lake, California's second-largest natural lake, are rewarded with one of the most striking sights in the region: a stunningly blue jewel on the high plateau. From late spring until early fall, this lovely lake, over 15 miles northwest of Susanville, attracts a smattering of visitors who come to cool off, swim, fish, boat and camp. On the south shore, you'll find a pristine 5-mile paved recreational trail for cycling and hiking and several busy **federal campgrounds** (recreation.gov) managed by **Eagle Lake Marina** (facebook.com/EagleLakeMarinaNCampgrounds), which offers hot showers, laundry and boat rentals. It also can help you get out onto the lake with a fishing license. To get to Eagle Lake, take Hwy 36 northeast of Lake Almanor toward Susanville, then continue north on Eagle Lake Rd to the south shore.

04 QUINCY
Idyllic Quincy (population 1858) is a mountain community that teeters on the edge of becoming an incorporated town. It's no metropolis, but after the route along the Feather River it may feel like one. Three streets make up Quincy's low-key commercial district, dotted with homey restaurants, bars and bakeries.

Visit the **Plumas County Museum** (plumasmuseum.org) and you'll find that the building houses hundreds of historical photos and relics from the county's pioneer and Maidu days, early mining and timber industries, and construction of the Western Pacific Railroad. The hills surrounding the town also harbor some lovely hiking trails.

Photo Opportunity
The crags of the Sierra Buttes.

THE DRIVE
Continue down Hwy 70/89 passing horse pastures and distant mountain views. At Graeagle take the fork in the road to the right to follow Hwy 89 south, then after less than 3 miles take a right on Gold Lake Hwy and start climbing. If traveling in shoulder season, check road conditions before you make the turnoff; an alternate route follows Hwy 89 until it hits Hwy 49 just north of Sattley.

05 LAKES BASIN
Haven Lake, Gold Lake, Rock Lake, Deer Lake: dotted with crystalline alpine waters, this area is a secluded corner of paradise. Over a dozen of these gems can be reached only on foot, and great trails are virtually endless – you can even connect to the Pacific Crest Trail. The most scenic hike in the area is the **Haskell Peak Trail**, which affords views of both Lassen and Shasta and, on a clear day, Mt Rose in Nevada. To reach the trailhead, turn right from Gold Lake Hwy at Haskell Peak Rd (Forest Rd 9) and follow it for 8.5 miles. The hike is only 4.5 miles round-trip, but it's not for the faint of heart – you'll climb more than 1000ft through dense forest before it opens on an expansive view. From there you can see the rugged **Sierra Buttes**, distinguished from their surrounding mountains by jagged peaks, which look like a miniature version of the Alps.

THE DRIVE
Gold Lake Hwy will now descend and connect to Hwy 49 in Bassetts (a town that consists of little more than a gas station). Go right on Hwy 49 for 5 miles to reach Sierra City...

06 SIERRA CITY
Sierra City is the primary supply station for people headed to the Sierra Buttes and offers more chances at amazing short hikes to summits with panoramic views. From the **Sierra Country Store** (sierracountrystore.com) there's a vast network of trails that is ideal for backpacking and casual hikes. They are listed in the *Lakes Basin, Downieville–Sierra City* map, which is on sale at the store. Sierra City's local museum, the **Kentucky Mine** (sierracountyhistory.org), is a worthy stop that introduces the famed 'Golden Chain Highway.' Its gold mine and stamp mill are just northeast of town.

THE DRIVE
Head west on Hwy 49 along the North Yuba River for a dozen miles to Downieville.

07 DOWNIEVILLE
Even with a population smaller than 300, Downieville is the biggest town in the remote Sierra County, located at the junction of the North Yuba and Downie Rivers. With a reputation that quietly rivals Moab, Utah (before it got big), the town is the premiere place for trail riding in the state, and a staging area for true wilderness adventures. Brave souls bomb down the **Downieville Downhill**, a molar-rattling 4000ft vertical descent, which is rated among the best mountain-bike routes in the USA.

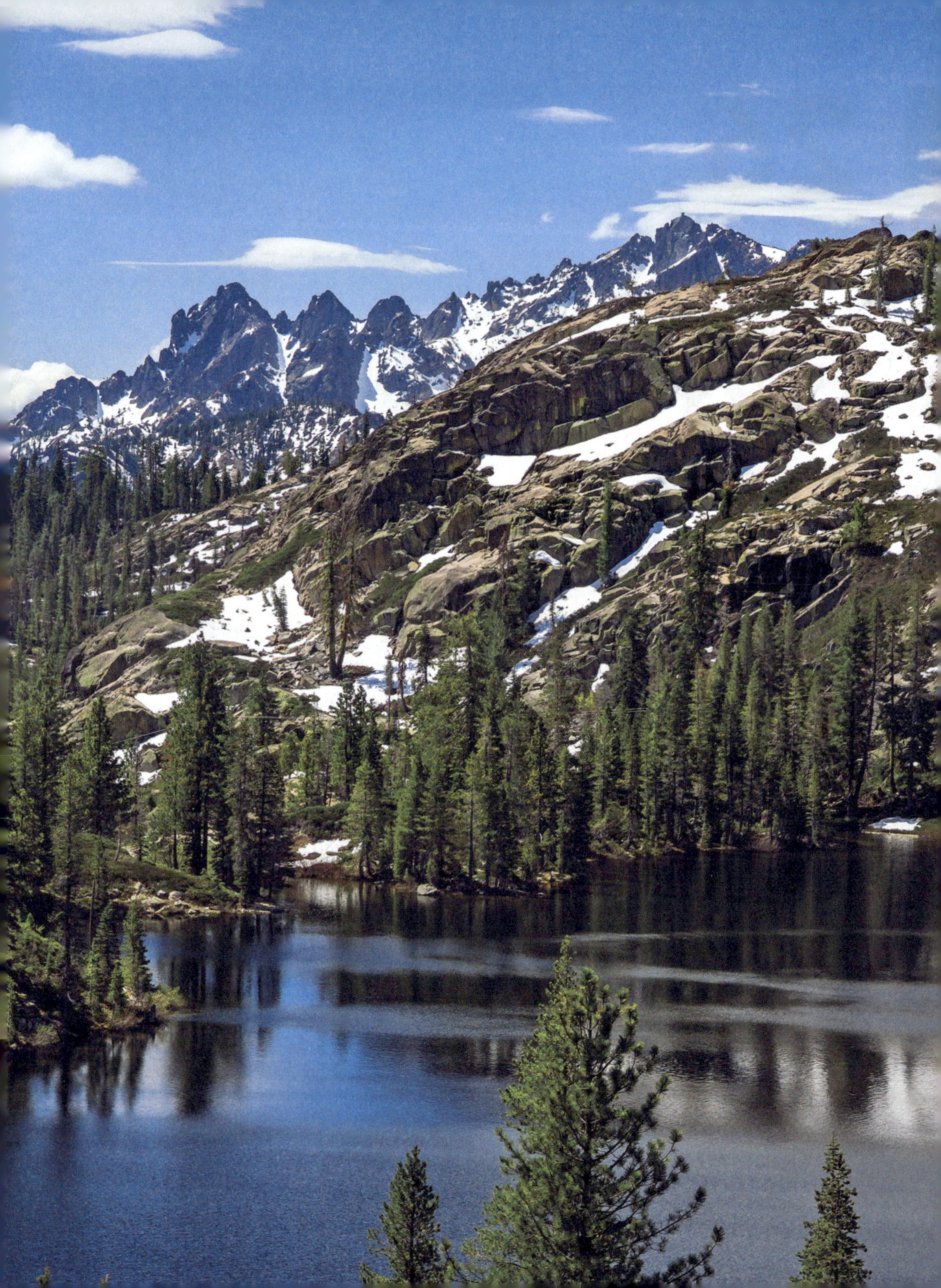

26

Sacramento Delta & Lodi

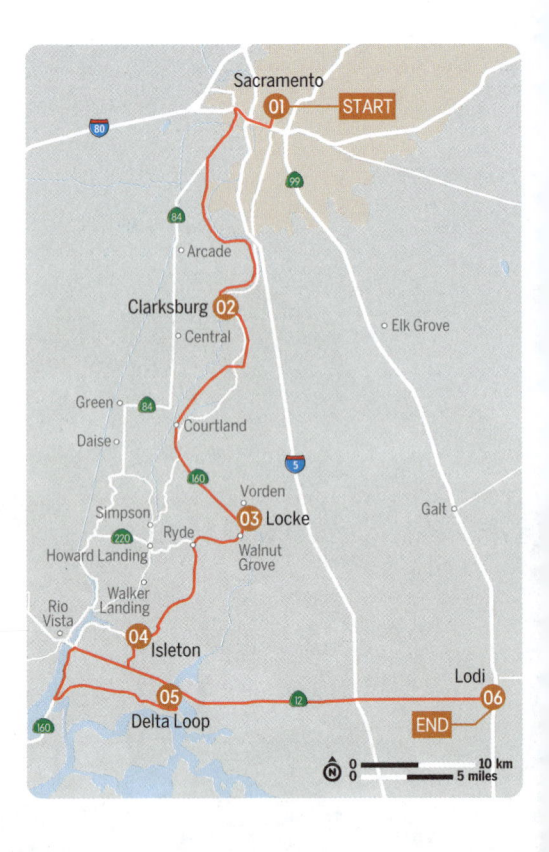

DURATION	DISTANCE	GREAT FOR
2 days	100 miles / 160km	Families, Nature

BEST TIME TO GO	May–October when the 'Delta Breeze' keeps the sweltering heat at bay.

When exploring the network of channels in the 750,000-acre Sacramento–San Joaquin River Delta, you'll take gently sweeping levy roads into a maze of orchards, vineyards and waterways. Although this region of California is squeezed between the crowded urban spaces of the Bay Area and Sacramento, it feels like it's a million miles away. So do the rural wineries of nearby Lodi, one of California's oldest grape-growing regions.

Link Your Trip

24 Ebbetts Pass Scenic Byway
Ready for another off-the-beaten-path excursion? Head east from Lodi via Hwys 12, 49 and 4 for 55 miles to Murphys in Gold Country.

06 Napa Valley
Contrasting with Lodi's humble charms, Northern California's most celebrated wine circuit is off Hwy 12, which runs west from Rio Vista.

01 SACRAMENTO

At the confluence of two of California's most powerful waterways – the American and Sacramento Rivers – lies the tidy grid of streets that make up the state capital. The impressive **California State Capitol** (capitolmuseum.ca.gov) is a mandatory stop, as is **Capitol Park**, the 40-acre garden surrounding the dome.

At the river port neighboring downtown, **Old Sacramento State Waterfront** (oldsacramento.com) remains the city's stalwart tourist draw. The old-fashioned gold-rush atmosphere makes it good

BEST FOR CULTURE

California's last rural Chinese American community.

Old Sacramento State Historic Park

for a stroll, especially on summer evenings. California's largest concentration of buildings on the National Register of Historic Places is found here. At the north end, the **California State Railroad Museum** (csrmf.org) displays a sizable collection of railcars and locomotives, including a fully outfitted Pullman sleeper and vintage dining cars. Foodies and beerheads will be content with a visit to Sac's buzzing **Midtown**, where they will find a large number of breweries and local restaurants sourcing fresh ingredients straight from the Central Valley.

THE DRIVE
Point the car west from over the golden Tower Bridge, a landmark on the Sacramento River that opened in 1935. Across the bridge, turn left by Raley Field onto 5th St, following it south until it connects with S River Rd. It's less than 20 miles to Clarksburg.

02 CLARKSBURG

The fields and arid heat surrounding West Sacramento offer little clue that the 'Thousand Miles of Waterways' is near. But as you follow River Rd into Clarksburg, the breeze begins to blow. Travelers can't miss the **Old Sugar Mill** (oldsugarmill.com), the hub of a thriving community of local winemakers. The wines made in the Clarksburg region of the Sacramento Valley have developed a lot over the last decades, benefiting from the blazing sun and cool breezes. A few miles southwest of town via County Rds 141 and 144, the region's best-known winery, **Bogle** (boglewinery.com), is prettily set among the vineyards of a sixth-generation family farm.

THE DRIVE
Just over a mile south of Bogle, turn east on County Rd 142 to return to S River Rd, which winds beside a wide stretch of the Sacramento River. At the next bridge you come to, cross over to the river's eastern side and continue south another 6 miles. Turn left onto Locke Rd to enter Locke's historic district.

CENTRAL CALIFORNIA 26 SACRAMENTO DELTA & LODI

BEST ROAD TRIPS LOCATION   145

03 LOCKE

Locke was founded by Chinese laborers who built the levies that line nearly every inch of this Delta drive. In its heyday, Locke had a fairly wild reputation; during Prohibition (1920–33) the town's lack of a police force and quiet nearby waterways made it a hotbed of boozing and gambling. As you drop off the main road that parallels the river down into the old town, the view is unlike anywhere else in the country: tightly packed rows of wooden structures with creaking balconies and architecture that blends Western and Chinese details. Locke's wild days are in evidence at **Dai Loy Gambling House Museum** (locke-foundation.org), a former gambling den with exhibits on regional history. Its humble displays are worth a peek, but the best part is the atmospheric building itself.

Nearby, the Chinese cultural shop sells souvenirs, crafts, games, imported teas and books including *Bitter Melon: Inside America's Last Rural Chinese Town*, which contains luminous photographs and oral histories.

> **Photo Opportunity**
>
> One of the many colored metal bridges along S River Rd.

THE DRIVE

Immediately south of Locke in Walnut Grove, cross west over the bridge, then keep motoring south on gently curving Hwy 160, running alongside the Sacramento River. As you approach Isleton, look for the yellow swing bridge, which turns on a pivot so that large ships can pass. Drive east over the bridge, then continue south on Hwy 160 into town.

04 ISLETON

Like Locke and Walnut Grove, Isleton also boasted a thriving Chinese community, which is evident in the historic storefronts that line its main drag. The town is a regular stop for weekend Harley cruisers and Delta boaters, who lend the streets an amiably scruffy atmosphere and ensure the bars are always busy.

Lodi

Isleton also holds the title of 'Crawdad Town USA' and hosts a festival to honor the crustacean every year.

Fishers should drop in to **Bob's Bait Shop** (themaster baiter.tripod.com) for advice from the self-described, 'Master Baiter.' As well as dispensing expert information on fishing in the area, he sells live crayfish that you can cook up yourself for a riverside picnic.

THE DRIVE
Take Jackson Slough Rd south out of town and go left on Hwy 12. Just before the next bridge, go right on Brannan Island Rd and follow it along the Delta Loop for views of bird-filled skies and marshy lowlands. With the air-conditioning off, the rush of heat through the open window smells of tilled earth and river water.

05 DELTA LOOP

The drive along the Delta Loop is best taken at an unhurried pace – proof that sometimes the journey itself is as important as the destination.

This is the heart of the Delta: marinas line the southern stretch where you can charter anything that floats, migratory birds fill the skies and cruisers meander the uncrowded roads. The loop ends at **Brannan Island State Recreation Area** (parks.ca.gov), where sandy picnic areas and grassy barbecue spots draw hard-partying campers.

By day, it's a great place for families: it has lots of space in which to run around and a beach where little ones can wade into the reeds. The park offers excellent bird-watching at **Little Franks Tract**, a protected wetland marsh and riparian habitat, where keen-eyed visitors might also spot mink, beavers or river otters.

CALIFORNIA STATE FAIR

For two weeks every July, the **California State Fair** (pictured; calexpostatefair.com) fills the Cal-Expo fairgrounds, east of I-80 on the north side of the American River, with a small city of cows and carnival rides.

It's likely the only place on earth where you can plant a redwood tree, watch a pig give birth, ride a roller coaster, catch some barrel racing and taste exquisite Napa vintages and California craft beers all in one (exhausting) afternoon. Make time to see some of the auctions ($500 for a dozen eggs!) and the interactive agricultural exhibits run by the University of California, Davis.

THE DRIVE
Take Hwy 160 north to connect with Hwy 12, just across the bridge from Rio Vista, a place to stop and grab a bite. Otherwise, turn right and head east on Hwy 12 for 17 miles toward Lodi, usually a 30-minute drive away. Less than 2 miles.

06 LODI

Lodi used to be the 'Watermelon Capital of the World,' but today wine grapes rule this patch of the valley. Breezes from the delta soothe the area's intensely hot vineyards, where Zinfandel grapes predominate. Some vines have been tended by the same families for more than a century. **Michael David Winery** (michaeldavidwinery.com) sits right off the highway on the way into town. Drive a few miles northeast to the **Lodi Wine & Visitor Center** (lodiwine.com) to snag a free map of Lodi's rural wineries or sample (responsibly) local vintages at the tasting bar.

If you have time, head out to atmospheric wineries like **Jessie's Grove Winery** (jessiesgrovewinery.com) or **Bokisch Vineyards** (bokischvineyards.com); if not, go straight downtown to sip some of the region's boutique wines and more famous labels at several tasting rooms within a few blocks of one another.

Kings Canyon National Park
Death Valley National Park
Rhyolite
Beatty
NEVADA
395
Fresno
Cedar Grove Village
Stovepipe Wells Village
Orange Cove
Lone Pine
Furnace Creek
Three Rivers
Panamint Springs
Sequoia National Park
Harrisburg
Visalia
Badwater
Las Vegas
Shoshone
Porterville
14
31
Tecopa
99
5
15
Kernville
Trona
Prim
Woody
Lake Isabella
Ridgecrest
Kern River
127
Bakersfield
Red Mountain
Baker
Mojave National Preserve
Taft
15
Mojave
58
Barstow
Daggett
166
Ventucopa
Lebec
Ludlow
40
395
15
Palmdale
30
Amboy
Victorville
33
5
Santa Clarita
14
Angeles National Forest
Santa Barbara
Ventura
Joshua Tree
Twentynine Palms
Oxnard
Pasadena
San Bernardino
Joshua Tree National Park
29
Los Angeles
Santa Monica
Channel Islands
Palm Springs
Indio
32
Anaheim
Long Beach
Palomar Mtn (6140ft)
Chiriaco Summit
27
Temecula
Laguna Beach
Capistrano Beach
Borrego Springs
Salton Sea
Santa Catalina Island
Oceanside
33
Ocotillo Wells
San Nicolas Island
Anza-Borrego Desert State Park
28
El Cer
San Clemente Island
La Jolla
8
San Diego
Ocotillo
Mexi
Tijuana
M

Lost Palms Oasis Trail, Joshua Tree National Park (p180)

Southern California

27 Disneyland & Orange County Beaches
Meet Mickey Mouse, then go surfing on the sun-bronzed 'OC' coast. **p152**

28 Fun on the San Diego Coast
The surf's up and the sun almost always shines, from Coronado to Carlsbad. **p156**

29 SoCal Pop Culture
Where film stars, hippies and surf punks collide on the coast with the most. **p162**

30 Route 66
Discover the desert and zoom past retro icons on America's 'Mother Road.' **p166**

31 Life in Death Valley
Old West mining ghost towns, otherworldly geology and soul-touching panoramas. **p172**

32 Palm Springs & Joshua Tree Oases
Desert palm trees shade hot springs and date gardens. Ramble for hours or days in Joshua Tree. **p178**

33 Temecula, Julian & Anza-Borrego
Celebrate the grape harvest in Temecula's vineyards or cool off in its mountain and desert retreats. **p182**

Explore

Southern California

Surf, sand and sex will always sell SoCal, and the reality doesn't disappoint: the swimsuits really are smaller, the water warmer and summers less foggy here than in NorCal. Los Angeles is the place for celebrity spotting. Surf culture rules San Diego and Orange County, where Disneyland proves an irresistible attraction for kids.

Turn up the heat in SoCal's deserts, at the chic resorts of Palm Springs. Then dig deep into the backcountry beauty of Death Valley and Joshua Tree, where dusty 4WD roads lead to remote ghost towns and hidden springs. Finally, leave the crowds behind on SoCal's most iconic road trip: Route 66.

Hub Towns

As the two largest cities in the state, LA and San Diego attract the most visitors, but Orange County and Palm Springs make useful waypoints as well.

Los Angeles

LA is the bajillion megawatt hub of Southern California, America's largest county and home to some 10 million souls. Accordingly, Los Angeles International Airport (LAX) is one of the world's busiest, so it's a good bet you'll arrive here.

But do yourself a favor and get away from the airport. There's a reason LA is such a vacation destination. The beaches of Malibu, the star power of Hollywood, the party scene of West Hollywood and the Sunset Strip, the museums and market districts of Downtown, and hiking in the Santa Monica Mountains are all major draws. And (traffic gods permitting), LA is within an hour or two of other major SoCal destinations, including Disneyland and Santa Barbara.

That said, LA accommodations and restaurants can be pretty pricey compared to elsewhere, so if you're looking to save your pennies you might do well to move on quickly.

San Diego

If you're crossing in from Mexico, your major point of entry will be San Diego. In addition to having America's most perfect weather, it's America's eighth-largest city, although you'd scarcely be able to tell from its easy, breezy atmosphere, lush landscapes and the string of beach cities lining the

WHEN TO GO

There's no off-season in SoCal, but winter tends to be the rainiest. You'll want to pack extra water and crank the AC if traveling in the deserts May to September. If it's been a rainy winter, desert wildflowers bloom brilliantly, typically in late February into April, making a striking contrast to the normal earth tones.

coast like pearls at Tiffany & Co. Have lunch by the ocean in Pacific Beach or mingle with the well-heeled shoppers in La Jolla.

Anaheim

If Orange County had a downtown, it would be fresh-faced Disneyland. Many visitors station themselves nearby for easy access to the parks (lodging pricing varies seasonally), and a crop of surprisingly cool restaurants has sprung up just a few miles away, making Anaheim about more than just the Mouse.

Outside Anaheim awaits a whole other Orange world: surf life in Huntington and Newport Beaches, tidy shops in the retro city of Orange, world-class museums in Santa Ana and the Laguna Beach art scene.

Palm Springs

In the Southern California desert, you'll probably find yourself passing through Palm Springs, anchor of the Coachella Valley. While stocking up on food and supplies, stay for the endless sun, cool architecture and maybe an umbrella-drink cocktail. From here, it's under one hour to Joshua Tree National Park.

TRANSPORT

Car is king in SoCal, although LA's Metro Rail is set to extend to LAX in 2024 and San Diego's MTS rail system serves many local destinations. Amtrak California operates between hubs at the Union Stations in LA and San Diego, with inspiring ocean views through San Diego and southern Orange Counties (LA to San Diego from $36; three hours).

WHAT'S ON

Tournament of Roses
Flower-festooned parade to start the new year right, in Pasadena. January

Coachella Valley Music & Arts Festival
The defining event of US rock culture; in Indio. April

Stagecoach Festival
Country music's annual answer to Coachella. April

Cinco de Mayo
Not Mexican Independence Day but an annual statewide celebration of Mexican culture. May 5

Resources

Visit California
(visitcalifornia.com) State tourism info in a dozen languages.

Discover Los Angeles
(discoverlosangeles.com) One-stop shopping for LA visitors.

San Diego Tourism
(sandiego.org) Explore by land and sea.

LAist
(laist.com) News, podcasts and 'How to LA'.

WHERE TO STAY

Beach, desert, resort or roadside, SoCal has some classic stays. Resort hotels like Disney's **Grand Californian**, **Legoland Hotel**, San Diego's **Hotel del Coronado** and the **Inn at Death Valley** are landmarks in their own right.

Midrange options include the **Ace Hotel & Swim Club** in Palm Springs and some surprising values around West Hollywood, San Diego's Balboa Park and even coastal Santa Monica. Budget travelers will love the **Crystal Cove Beach Cottages** in Orange County (reserve as far ahead as possible) and roadside motels along Route 66, or the myriad campgrounds along the coast

BEST ROAD TRIPS: CALIFORNIA

27

Disneyland & Orange County Beaches

BEST FOR VIEWS
Take a break at Corona del Mar's Lookout Point.

DURATION	DISTANCE	GREAT FOR
3–4 days	65 miles / 105km	Nature, Families

BEST TIME TO GO	June to September for summer beach season.

Huntington Beach Pier

You'll find gorgeous sunsets, prime surf breaks and just-off-the-boat seafood when road-tripping down the OC's sun-kissed coastal Hwy 1. Yet, it's the unexpected, serendipitous discoveries you'll remember long after you've left these blissful 42 miles of surf and sand behind. Start with a couple days at Disneyland's theme parks, and call it a wrap for the perfect SoCal family vacation.

Link Your Trip

03 Pacific Coast Highways
Orange County is California's official section of the Pacific Coast Hwy (PCH), running along Hwy 1 between Seal Beach and Dana Point.

28 Fun on the San Diego Coast
It's just a 30-mile drive from Dana Point along I-5 south to Carlsbad in San Diego's family-friendly North County.

01 DISNEYLAND RESORT

The west coast's most popular attraction, **Disneyland** (disneyland.com) has welcomed untold millions since opening in 1955. From the ghostly skeletons of Pirates of the Caribbean to the screeching monkeys of the Indiana Jones Adventure, the pure adrenaline of Space Mountain to the newest 'land,' Star Wars: Galaxy's Edge, there's magical detail everywhere. After dark, watch fireworks explode over Sleeping Beauty's Castle.

Across the plaza, Disneyland's younger neighbor, **Disney California Adventure** (disneyland.disney.go.com), highlights the best of the Golden State and moviedom in sections like Cars Land, Hollywoodland and Pixar Pier. Catch the World of Color special-effects show at night. The adjacent, pedestrian Downtown Disney District is packed with souvenir shops, family restaurants, after-dark bars and entertainment venues.

THE DRIVE
Follow I-5 south, then take Hwy 22 west through inland Orange County, merging onto I-405 north. After another mile or so, exit onto Seal Beach Blvd, which crawls 3 miles toward the coast. Turn right onto Hwy 1, also known as the Pacific Coast Hwy (PCH) throughout Orange County, then take a left onto Main St in Seal Beach.

02 SEAL BEACH
In the SoCal beauty pageant for pint-sized beach towns, Seal Beach takes the crown, a refreshingly unhurried alternative to the more crowded Orange County coast further south. Its stoplight-free, three-block Main St bustles with mom-and-pop restaurants and indie shops that are low on 'tude and high on nostalgia. Follow barefoot surfers trotting toward the ocean where Main St ends, then walk out onto **Seal Beach Pier**. Down on the beach, you'll find families spread out on blankets, building sandcastles and playing in the water – all of them ignoring that hideous oil derrick offshore. The gentle waves make Seal Beach a great place to learn to surf. **M&M Surfing School** (surfingschool.com) parks its van in the lot just north of the pier, off Ocean Ave at 8th St.

THE DRIVE
Past a short bridge south along Hwy 1, drivers drop onto a mile-long spit of land known as Sunset Beach, with its biker bars and harborside kayak and stand-up paddleboarding (SUP) rental shops. Keep cruising Hwy 1 south another 6 miles past Bolsa Chica State Beach and Ecological Reserve to **Huntington Beach Pier**.

03 HUNTINGTON BEACH
In 'Surf City USA,' SoCal's obsession with wave riding hits its frenzied peak. There's a statue of Hawaiian surfer Duke Kahanamoku at the intersection of Main St and PCH, and if you look down, you'll see names of legendary surfers in the sidewalk **Surfers' Hall of Fame** (hsssurf.com/shof); find out more about them a few blocks east at the **International Surfing Museum** (huntingtonbeachsurfingmuseum.org).

On **Huntington Beach Pier**, you can catch up-close views of daredevils barreling through tubes, though newbie surfers should try elsewhere – locals can be territorial. In summer, the **US Open of Surfing** draws more than 600 world-class surfers and 500,000 spectators with a minivillage of concerts and more. Otherwise, wide, flat **Huntington City Beach** is a perfect place to snooze on the sand on a giant beach towel. Snag a fire pit just south of the pier to build an evening bonfire with friends.

BEST ROAD TRIPS: CALIFORNIA   153

THE DRIVE

From the Huntington Beach Pier at the intersection of Main St, drive south on Hwy 1 alongside the ocean for another 4 miles to Newport Beach. Turn right onto W Balboa Blvd, leading onto the Balboa Peninsula, squeezed between the ocean and Balboa Island, off Newport Harbor.

04 NEWPORT BEACH

As seen on Bravo's *Real Housewives of Orange County* and Fox' *The OC* and *Arrested Development*, in glitzy Newport Beach wealthy socialites, glamorous teens and gorgeous beaches all share the spotlight. Bikini vixens strut down the sandy beach stretching between the peninsula's twin piers, while boogie boarders brave human-eating waves at the Wedge and the ballet of yachts in the harbor makes you dream of being rich and famous. From the harbor, hop aboard a ferry over to old-fashioned **Balboa Island** (balboaisland.com) or climb aboard the Ferris wheel at the pint-sized **Balboa Fun Zone** (balboafunzone.com), near the landmark **1906 Balboa Pavilion** (alboapavilion.com).

THE DRIVE

South of Newport Beach, prime-time ocean views are just a short detour off Hwy 1. First drive south across the bridge over Newport Channel, then after 3 miles turn right onto Marguerite Ave in Corona del Mar. Once you reach the coast, take another right onto Ocean Blvd.

05 CORONA DEL MAR

Savor some of SoCal's most celebrated ocean views from the bluffs of Corona del Mar, a chichi bedroom community south of Newport Channel. Several postcard beaches, rocky coves and child-friendly tide pools beckon

Photo Opportunity

Surfers at Huntington Beach Pier.

Crystal Cove State Park

along this idyllic stretch of coast. One of the best viewpoints is at breezy **Lookout Point** on Ocean Blvd near Heliotrope Ave. Below the rocky cliffs to the east is half-mile-long **Main Beach** (newport beachca.gov), with fire rings and volleyball courts (arrive early on weekends to get a parking spot).

Stairs lead down to Pirates Cove, a great, waveless pocket beach for families – scenes from the classic TV show *Gilligan's Island* were shot here. Head east on Ocean Blvd to **Inspiration Point**, near the corner of Orchid Ave, for more vistas of surf, sand and sea.

THE DRIVE
Follow Orchid Ave back north to Hwy 1, then turn right and drive southbound. Traffic thins out as ocean views become more wild and uncluttered by housing developments that head up into the hills on your left. It's just a couple of miles to the entrance of Crystal Cove State Park.

06 CRYSTAL COVE STATE PARK
With more than 3 miles of open beach and 2400 acres of undeveloped woodland, **Crystal Cove State Park** (parks.ca.gov) lets you almost forget that you're in a crowded metro area. It's also an underwater park where scuba enthusiasts can check out the wreck of a Navy Corsair fighter plane that went down in 1949.

Or just go tide pooling, fishing, kayaking and surfing along Crystal Cove's exhilaratingly wild, windy shoreline. On the inland side of Hwy 1, miles of hiking and mountain-biking trails wait for landlubbers.

THE DRIVE
Drive south on Hwy 1 for another 4 miles or so. As shops, restaurants, art galleries, motels and hotels start to crowd the highway once again, you've arrived in Laguna Beach. Downtown is a maze of one-way streets just east of the Laguna Canyon Rd (Hwy 133) intersection.

07 LAGUNA BEACH
This early 20th-century artist colony's secluded coves, romantic-looking cliffs and arts-and-crafts bungalows come as a relief after miles of suburban beige-box architecture. Laguna celebrates its bohemian roots with summer arts festivals, dozens of galleries and the acclaimed **Laguna Art Museum** (lagunaart museum.org).

In downtown's village, while away an afternoon browsing the chic boutiques. Along the shore, **Main Beac**h is crowded with volleyball players and sunbathers. Just north atop the bluffs, **Heisler Park** winds past public art, palm trees, picnic tables and grand views of rocky shores and tide pools. Drop down to Divers Cove, a deep,

WHY I LOVE THIS TRIP
Andrew Bender, writer

The OC coast is a microcosm of the best of SoCal: 42 miles of gorgeous sunsets, prime surfing, just-off-the-boat seafood, secluded coves and sparkling white sands. Each town offers its own experience – surf lessons in Seal Beach, beach volleyball at Huntington Beach, boating around Newport Harbor, eclectic art in Laguna Beach, whale-spotting off Dana Point – but sometimes the best plan is no plan at all.

protected inlet. Heading south, dozens of public beaches sprawl along just a few miles of coastline. Keep a sharp eye out for 'beach access' signs off Hwy 1, or pull into locals' favorite **Aliso Beach County Park** (ocparks.com).

THE DRIVE
Keep driving south of downtown Laguna Beach on Hwy 1 (PCH) for about 3 miles to Aliso Beach County Park, then another 4 miles into the town of Dana Point. Turn right onto Green Lantern St, then left onto Cove Rd, which winds past the state beach and Ocean Institute onto Dana Point Harbor Dr.

DETOUR
Pacific Marine Mammal Center
Start: 7 Laguna Beach
About 3 miles inland from Laguna Beach is the heart-warming **Pacific Marine Mammal Center** (pacificmmc.org), dedicated to rescuing and rehabilitating injured or ill marine mammals. This nonprofit center has a small staff and many volunteers who help nurse rescued pinnipeds (mostly sea lions and seals) back to health before releasing them into the wild. Stop by and take a self-guided facility tour to learn more about these marine mammals and to visit the 'patients' out back.

08 DANA POINT
Dana Point is all about family fun with whale-watching and sportfishing boats departing from its harbor. Designed for kids, the **Ocean Institute** (ocean-institute.org) has replicas of historic tall ships, maritime-related exhibits and a floating research lab. East of the harbor, **Doheny State Beach** (dohenystatebeach.org) offers picnic tables, volleyball courts, an oceanfront bike path and a sandy beach for swimming, surfing and tide pooling.

28

Fun on the San Diego Coast

DURATION	DISTANCE	GREAT FOR
2-4 days	80 miles / 138km	Families, Nature, Wineries
BEST TIME TO GO	June to September for prime-time beach weather.	

Most Americans work all year for a two-week vacation. San Diegans work all week for a two-day vacation at the beach. Family-fun attractions found just off the county's gorgeous coastal highways include the USS Midway Museum, Balboa Park's zoo and the Legoland theme park, along with dozens of beaches from ritzy to raucous. With SoCal's most idyllic weather, it's time to roll down the windows and chill, dudes.

Link Your Trip

27 Disneyland & Orange County Beaches
Cruise 30 miles north on I-5 to Dana Point for another kid-friendly trip, combining knockout beaches with Disneyland's magic.

33 Temecula, Julian & Anza-Borrego
Escape to wine country, apple farms and desert resorts, starting 35 miles inland from Carlsbad via Hwy 76 east to I-15 north.

01 CORONADO

With the landmark **1888 Hotel del Coronado** (hoteldel.com) and one of the USA's top-rated beaches, the city of Coronado sits across San Diego Bay from Downtown. It's miles from the concrete jungle of the city and the chaos of more crowded beaches further north. After crossing the bay via the curved **Coronado Bay Bridge**, follow the tree-lined, manicured median strip of Orange Ave a mile toward Ocean Blvd, then park your car and walk around. Sprawling in front of the 'Hotel Del' is postcard-perfect **Coronado Municipal**

BEST FOR OUTDOORS

Explore La Jolla's coves, beaches and nature preserves.

Balboa Park

Beach. Around 5 miles further south, **Silver Strand State Beach** (parks.ca.gov) offers calm waters for family-friendly swimming. The strand's long, narrow sand spit connects to the mainland, though people still call this 'Coronado Island.'

THE DRIVE
Follow Hwy 75 south of Silver Strand past San Diego Bay National Wildlife Refuge, curving inland by Imperial Beach. Merge onto I-5 northbound, then exit onto Hwy 163 northbound toward Balboa Park. Take exit 1C and follow the signs for the park and zoo.

02 BALBOA PARK
Spanish Revival–style pavilions from the 1915–16 Panama-California Exposition add a dash of the exotic to a day spent in Balboa Park. This 1200-acre urban retreat is home to gardens, theaters, more than 16 museums and one giant outdoor organ pavilion, all of which you can see on foot. Without a doubt, the highlight is the **San Diego Zoo** (zoo.sandiegozoo.org). If it slithers, crawls, stomps, swims, leaps or flies, chances are you'll find it living inside this world-famous zoo. Conservation signs guide visitors through multilevel walkways, where face-to-snout encounters aren't uncommon.

Arrive early, when the animal denizens are most active – though many perk up again in the afternoon. Nearby at the **Spanish Village Art Center** (spanish villageart.com), where an enclave of small tiled cottages are rented out as artists' studios, you can watch potters, jewelry makers, glassblowers, sculptors and painters at work.

THE DRIVE
Exit Balboa Park to the east via Zoo Pl, turning right onto Florida Dr and right again onto Pershing Dr. Merge onto I-5 north for over a mile, then take exit 17A. Drive almost another mile west on Hawthorn St toward the waterfront, then turn left onto Harbor Dr.

◆ DETOUR
San Diego Zoo Safari Park
Start: 02 Balboa Park

Take a walk on the 'wild' side at **San Diego Zoo Safari Park** (sdzsafaripark.org), where giraffes graze, lions lounge and rhinos romp across 1800 acres of open range. For that instant safari feel, board the Africa Tram, which tours some of the field exhibits in just 25 minutes. Elsewhere, animals are in giant outdoor enclosures so naturalistic it's as if the humans are guests. There's a petting kraal, zookeeper talks and animal encounters too. The park is in Escondido, 30 miles northeast of Balboa Park via Hwy 163 and I-15 northbound; alternatively, it's 25 miles east of coastal Carlsbad via Hwy 78. Parking costs $15.

03 EMBARCADERO

The Coronado ferry and cruise ships moor along downtown San Diego's waterfront Embarcadero. Well-manicured oceanfront promenades stretch along Harbor Dr, where a lineup of historical sailing ships points the way to the **Maritime Museum** (sdmaritime.org). Climb aboard the 1863 *Star of India* and don't miss seeing the B-39 Soviet attack submarine. The even larger **USS Midway Museum** (midway.org) is housed on the Navy's longest-serving aircraft carrier (1945–92); it saw action in WWII, Vietnam and the Gulf War.

📷 Photo Opportunity
The red-turreted Hotel del Coronado.

Top Gun's Goose and Maverick may spring to mind at the sight of this floating city. A self-guided tour is the best way to experience history: crawl into berthing spaces, the galley and sickbay and, of course, peer over the flight deck with its restored aircraft, including an F-14 Tomcat.

🚗 THE DRIVE
Follow Harbor Dr northwest for 3 miles as it curves along the waterfront past the airport. Turn right onto Nimitz Blvd for another mile, then left onto Chatsworth Blvd and right on Narragansett Ave. After a mile, you'll intersect with Sunset Cliffs Blvd in Ocean Beach.

04 OCEAN BEACH

San Diego's most bohemian seaside community, OB is a place of seriously scruffy haircuts and tattooed and pierced

Mission Beach boardwalk

skin. Newport Ave, the main drag, runs perpendicular to the beach through a downtown district of bars, street-food eateries, surf and music shops, and vintage-clothing and antique boutiques.

Half-mile-long **Ocean Beach Pier** has all the architectural allure of a freeway ramp, but at its end you'll get a great perspective on the coast. A bait-and-tackle shop rents fishing poles if you want to try your luck. Further north on **Dog Beach**, pups chase birds around the marshy area where the river meets the sea, or walk a few blocks south of the pier to **Sunset Cliffs Park** for surfing and, yes, brilliant sunsets.

THE DRIVE
Follow stop-and-go Sunset Cliffs Blvd north. Merge onto W Mission Bay Dr, which crosses the water twice and curves past SeaWorld. Less than 4 miles from Ocean Beach, you'll intersect with Mission Blvd; turn left to reach the main beach and Belmont Park.

05 MISSION BEACH & PACIFIC BEACH

This is the SoCal of the movies: buffed surfers and bronzed sun worshippers pack the 3-mile-long stretch of beach from South Mission Jetty north to Pacific Beach Point. San Diego's best people-watching is along Ocean Front Walk, the boardwalk that connects the two beaches. For old-fashioned carnival fun in Mission Beach, Belmont Park (belmontpark.com) has been giving kids a thrill with its Giant Dipper wooden roller coaster since 1925. There are bumper cars, a tilt-a-whirl, a carousel, other classic rides and an escape room. At the ocean end of Garnet Ave in Pacific Beach, **Crystal Pier** is a mellow place to gaze out to

BORDERLANDS: TIJUANA, MEXICO

Just beyond the busiest land border in the western hemisphere is Tijuana, Mexico (population around 2 million). It was for decades a cheap, convivial escape for hard-partying San Diegans, Angelenos, sailors and college kids. Around two decades ago, a double-whammy of drug-related violence and global recession turned once-bustling tourist areas into ghost towns. While there are pockets of hope around the city, there is also a very worrying local methamphetamine market. At the time of research, Tijuana had the highest murder rate in the world. The difference from squeaky-clean San Diego is palpable from the moment you cross the border. However, while travelers should maintain a decent level of caution, many visits are trouble-free and there are numerous reasons to visit.

The main tourist drag is **Avenida Revolución** ('La Revo'; pictured), though its charm is marred by cheap clothing and souvenir stores, strip joints, pharmacies selling bargain-priced medications to Americans, and touts best rebuffed with a firm 'no.' It's a lot more appealing just beyond La Revo, toward and around **Avenida Constitución**, where sightseeing highlights include **Catedral de Nuestra Señora de Guadalupe**, the city's oldest church; **Mercado El Popo**, an atmospheric market hall selling everything from tamarind pods to religious iconography; and **Pasaje Rodríguez**, an arcade filled with youthful art galleries, bars and trendsetters. A short taxi ride away, **Museo de las Californias**, inside the architecturally daring **Centro Cultural Tijuana** (aka El Cubo, the Cube), offers an excellent history of the border region from prehistory to the present; there's signage in English.

A **passport** is required for the border crossing (cbp.gov/contact/ports/san-ysidro-class). Driving into Mexico is not recommended. By public transportation, the **San Diego Trolley Blue Line** runs from downtown San Diego to San Ysidro, at the border. Cross the border on foot, and walk approximately 20 minutes to La Revo; follow signs reading 'Centro Downtown.' If traveling by taxi on the Mexican side, be sure to take a taxi with a meter.

sea or fish. Just inland at **Mission Bay** (sandiego.gov), you can play beach volleyball and zip around Fiesta Island on water skis or fly a kite at Mission Bay Park. Sailing, windsurfing and kayaking dominate northwest Mission Bay, and there's delightful cycling and inline skating on miles of paved recreational paths.

THE DRIVE
Heading north of Pacific Beach on Mission Blvd, turn left onto Loring St, which curves right onto La Jolla Blvd. Winding through several traffic circles (roundabouts), the boulevard streams along the coast for 3 miles to downtown La Jolla, stretched along Pearl St east of the beach.

06 LA JOLLA
Sitting pretty and privileged on one of SoCal's loveliest sweeps of coast, La Jolla (say la-hoy-ah, if you please, similar to *joya*, the Spanish word for 'jewel') is a ritzy town of shimmering beaches, downtown fashionista boutiques and clifftop mansions.

Take advantage of the sunshine by kayaking and snorkeling at La Jolla Cove, or go scuba diving and snorkeling in **San Diego–La Jolla Underwater Park**, a protected ecological zone harboring a variety of marine life, kelp forests, reefs and canyons. Waves have carved a series of caves into the sandstone cliffs east of La Jolla Cove. From land, you can walk down 145 spooky steps to the Sunny Jim Cave, accessed via the **Cave Store** (cavestore.com).

Heading north along La Jolla Shores Dr, the oceanfront **Birch Aquarium** (aquarium.ucsd.edu) has kid-friendly tide pool displays. Another 5 miles further north, **Torrey Pines State Natural Reserve** (torreypine.org) protects the endangered Torrey pine tree and offers nature walks above a state beach, where hang gliders dramatically soar in for a landing.

THE DRIVE
Driving below the natural preserve next to Torrey Pines State Beach, panoramic ocean views open up as the coastal highway narrows and crosses over a lagoon, then climbs the sandstone cliffs toward Del Mar, just over 10 miles away.

07 DEL MAR
The ritziest of North County's seaside suburbs is home to the pink, Mediterranean-style **Del Mar Racetrack & Fairgrounds** (dmtc.comp), cofounded in 1937 by celebrities including Bing Crosby and Oliver Hardy. It's worth braving the crowds on opening day, if only to see the amazing spectacle of over-the-top hats.

Brightly colored hot-air balloons are another trademark sight in Del Mar – book ahead for a sunset flight with **California Dreamin'** (californiadreamin.com). Downtown Del Mar (sometimes called 'the village') extends for about a mile along Camino del Mar. At its hub, **Del Mar Plaza** (delmarplaza.com) shopping center has restaurants, boutiques and upper-level terraces that look out to sea. At the west end of 15th St, beachfront **Seagrove Park** has grassy lawns, perfect for picnicking.

THE DRIVE
Continue up the coast on Camino del Mar, leading onto S Coast Hwy 101 into Solana Beach, where the arts, fashion and antiques shops of Cedros Ave Design District are just one block inland. Continue north on S Coast Hwy 101 into Encinitas, about 6 miles north of Del Mar.

08 ENCINITAS
Technically part of Encinitas, the southern satellite of **Cardiff-by-the-Sea** has groovy restaurants, surf shops and new-agey businesses lined up along the coast. Known for its surfing breaks and laid-back crowds, Cardiff sits by the coastal **San Elijo Lagoon** (sdparks.org), a 979-acre ecological preserve that is popular with bird watchers and hikers. Stop by the nature center for kid-friendly educational exhibits and wide-angle views from the 2nd-floor observation deck.

MEET SOME SEALS AT THE CHILDREN'S POOL

Along the coast in La Jolla, take your kids to the **Children's Pool**. But not for swimming!

For decades, seals and sea lions have been lolling on the protected beach, and children now come to watch the pinnipeds and their pups. Animal rights groups have duked it out in court to protect the cove as a rookery, while some local swimmers and divers want the seals removed.

For now the seals remain, surrounded by a simple rope barrier during pupping season to keep humans at bay – you can also view them from the coast wall. The beach and cove are off Coast Blvd.

Carlsbad Ranch Flower Fields

Since Paramahansa Yogananda built his **Self-Realization Fellowship Retreat** (encinitastemple.org) by the sea here in 1937, Encinitas has been a magnet for healers and spiritual seekers. The fellowship's compact but lovely meditation garden has wonderful ocean vistas, a stream and koi pond.

The gold lotus domes of the hermitage mark the turn-out for Swami's, a powerful reef break surfed by territorial locals. Apart from outdoor cafes, bars, restaurants and surf shops, downtown's main attraction is the 1928 **La Paloma Theatre** (lapalomatheatre.com), an arthouse cinema screening indie, international and cult films nightly.

THE DRIVE
About 4 miles north of Encinitas, S Coast Hwy 101 becomes Carlsbad Blvd, slowly rolling north along the ocean cliffs for more than 5 miles into Carlsbad Village. If you go too far, you'll hit Oceanside, largely a commuter town for Marine Corps Base Camp Pendleton..

09 CARLSBAD
One of California's last remaining tidal wetlands, **Batiquitos Lagoon** (batiquitosfoundation.org) separates Carlsbad from Encinitas.

Go hiking here to see prickly pear cactus, coastal sage scrub and eucalyptus trees, as well as great heron and snowy egrets. Then detour inland past the springtime blooms of **Carlsbad Ranch Flower Fields** (theflowerfields.com) to **Legoland California Resort** (legoland.com/california), a fun fantasy park of rides, shows and attractions for the elementary-school set. Tots can dig for dinosaur bones, pilot helicopters and earn their driver's license, while mom and dad will probably get a kick out of Miniland USA, recreating such national landmarks as the White House, the Golden Gate Bridge and Las Vegas, all made of Lego blocks.

Back at the coast, you can go beachcombing for seashells on the long, sandy beaches, off Carlsbad Blvd. The beaches run south of Carlsbad Village Dr, where a beach **boardwalk** allows for sunset strolls and selfies.

29

SoCal Pop Culture

BEST FOR MOVIE FANS

See Burbank's behind-the-scenes studio tours.

DURATION	DISTANCE	GREAT FOR
3 days	245 miles / 395km	Nature, Families

BEST TIME TO GO	Year-round, although winter can be rainy.

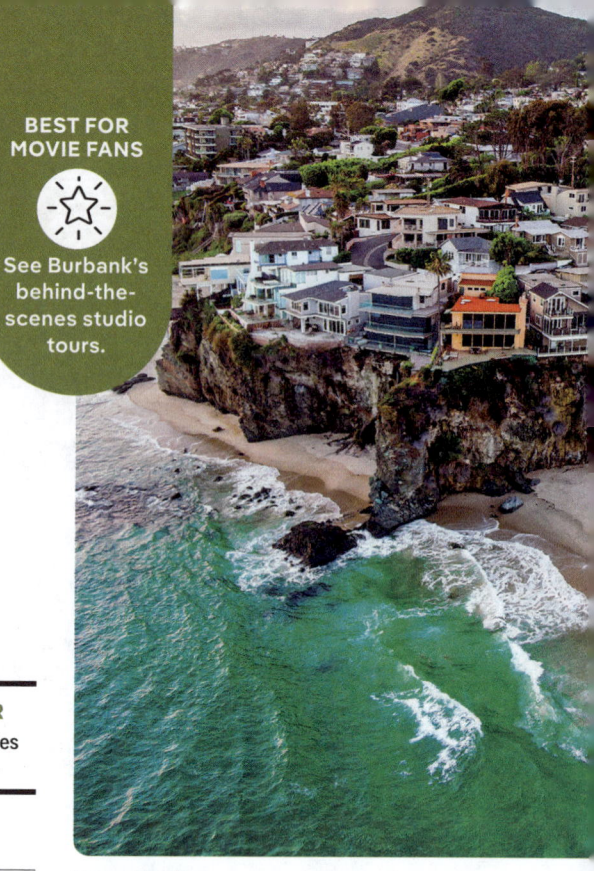

Laguna Beach

Begin on the cinematic beaches of Orange County. Then zoom northwest along the Pacific past the skater punks of Venice Beach, Hollywood moguls' mansions in Malibu and celebrity haunts in Santa Barbara. Swing back to LA's San Fernando Valley for a TV and movie studio tour, then wind up in Hollywood with a cruise down the rockin' Sunset Strip.

Link Your Trip

19 Santa Barbara Wine Country

Follow Hwy 154 up into the mountains of the Santa Ynez Valley, where *Sideways* wine country is ready for its close-up.

27 Disneyland & Orange County Beaches

If you can't get enough of the OC's sunny sands, keep cruising south on coastal Hwy 1, then hit Disneyland.

01 LAGUNA BEACH

Filled with cliffs and coves, Laguna may be the OC's most photogenic beach town, as seen in the 1954 Judy Garland classic *A Star is Born*, MTV's *Laguna Beach*, Bravo's *Real Housewives of Orange County*, and the Netflix series *Dead to Me*.

The real Laguna is more bohemian bonhomie than Hollywood hype, but visitors can shop the chic boutiques in downtown's village, then strike a pose on Main Beach in your teeny-weeny bikini. Jealously guarded by locals, **Thousand Steps Beach** (off 9th Ave) is hidden off Hwy 1 just south of Mission

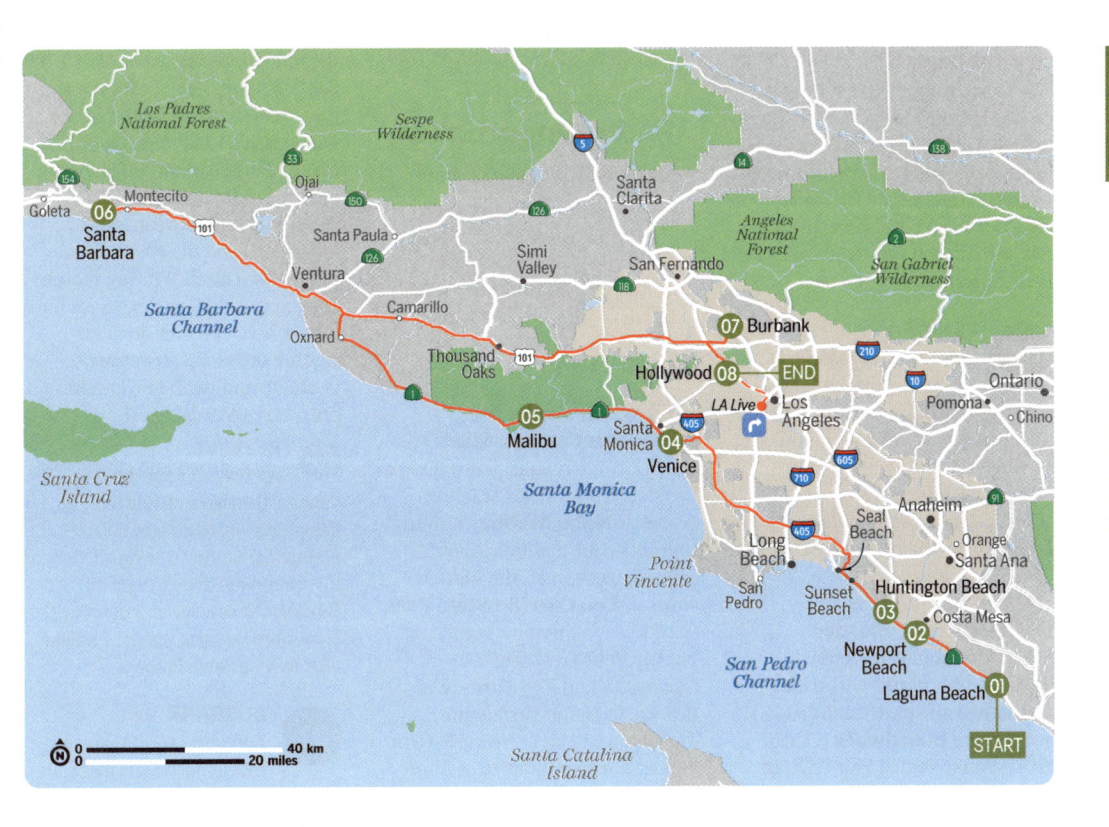

Hospital, where a stairway leads down to a rocky beach, postcard-perfect for sunbathing.

🚗 THE DRIVE
Join Hwy 1, aka PCH, for the quick 10-mile trip north to Newport Beach, passing oceanfront Crystal Cove State Park. Exit onto Newport Blvd, following it down onto the Balboa Peninsula.

02 NEWPORT BEACH
Even if you've never visited Newport Beach, if you've seen *The OC*, *Arrested Development* or the *Real Housewives* series, the local culture of yachtsmen, trophy wives, their beautiful yet angsty teens, and, yes, frozen bananas on a stick will be oh-so-familiar. The **Newport Beach Film Fest** (newportbeachfilmfest.com), headquartered in the chichi Lido Village shopping district, offers up-close-and-personal stargazing.

The 2-mile, oceanfront Balboa Peninsula connects the Balboa and Newport Piers, teeming with surfers and glamazons, and more lifestyles of the rich and famous revolve around the posh mall **Fashion Island** (shopfashionisland.com).

🚗 THE DRIVE
Keep going north up Hwy 1, often crawling with bumper-to-bumper traffic on summer weekends when everyone's heading to the beach. Relax, it's only 4 miles to Huntington Beach, at the intersection of Main St and PCH.

03 HUNTINGTON BEACH
Huntington Beach has been the SoCal surf hot spot since George Freeth first demonstrated the Hawaiian sport of wave-riding here a century ago. 'HB' has even trademarked its nickname 'Surf City USA'. Surf scenes for the reboot of *90210* were shot at Huntington State Beach, and James Corden and pals received lifeguard training here. Buyers for major retailers come to see what surfers are wearing and then market the look, while volleyballers blithely play on the golden sand and skaters whiz past the oceanfront pier.

BEST ROAD TRIPS: CALIFORNIA

🚗 **THE DRIVE**
Keep going north for 12 miles on Hwy 1 passing Sunset Beach. Then join I-405 north, driving past industrial areas of Los Angeles. Take the Hwy 90 westbound exit toward Marina del Rey, slingshot around the marina to Pacific Ave by the beach, turn right and roll north to Venice.

04 VENICE
Venice Beach has been a lure for filmmakers since its founding in 1905, so you may experience déjà vu if you've seen *Speed*, *The Doors*, *White Men Can't Jump*, *I Love You Man*, *The Big Lebowski*, *Nightcrawler*, *LA Story*, or the opening of TV's *Three's Company*.

Nowadays, new-age hippies, modern-day muscled Schwarzeneggers, cannabis seekers, goth punks and tribal drummers all share the must-see **Venice Boardwalk** (Ocean Front Walk; Venice Pier to Rose Ave). Venice is also the birthplace of SoCal skater-punk culture, as chronicled in the movies *Dogtown and Z Boys* and *Lords of Dogtown*. So board your board, strap on some in-line skates, or hop on a fluorescent beach cruiser and shake what yo' mama gave you.

🚗 **THE DRIVE**
Drive north on Ocean Ave and rejoin PCH past I-10. Cruise past Santa Monica's carnival pier with its solar-powered Ferris wheel. Keep following PCH north as it curves alongside the ocean to Malibu, just over a dozen miles away.

05 MALIBU
Mile for fabulous oceanfront mile, Malibu may have SoCal's densest celebrity quotient. Keep your eyes peeled for A-listers sipping iced lattes as they shop at the **Malibu Country Mart** (malibucountrymart.com). Down the street, spot sushi-scarfing celebs at **Nobu Malibu** (noburestaurants.com/malibu). About 15 miles further west, the hidden coves of **Leo Carrillo State Park** (parks.ca.gov) made a romantic backdrop in *Pirates of the Caribbean* and *The Karate Kid*. Beware of rough surf: John Travolta and Olivia Newton-John almost got swept out to sea here in the opening scene of Grease.

🚗 **THE DRIVE**
Hug the coast by following Hwy 1 north, which turns inland to intersect Hwy 101, a multilane freeway that swings back to the coast at Ventura, then flows past ocean cliffs and beaches northwest to Santa Barbara, about a 90-minute trip from Malibu without traffic jams.

06 SANTA BARBARA
A Mediterranean vibe and red-roofed, white-stucco streetscape give credence to Santa Barbara's nickname, the 'American Riviera.' Spanish Colonial Revival buildings clustered along downtown's **State St** have made cameos in countless movies, including *The Graduate*, *It's Complicated* and *20th Century Women*. A 45-minute drive up into the mountains via scenic Hwy 154, Santa Barbara's wine country sets the hilarious scene for the Oscar-winning 2004 film *Sideways*. Just east of Santa Barbara off Hwy 101, celeb-heavy **Montecito** is a leafy suburb tucked between the mountains and the Pacific. Heavy hitters like Oprah Winfrey, Steven Spielberg and Ellen Degeneres have homes here and occasionally venture out along downtown's boutique-and-patio-lined main drag, Coast Village Road.

🚗 **THE DRIVE**
Take Hwy 101 south back to Ventura, then head up into the mountains via the steep Conjeo (Camarillo) Grade. Leveling off, Hwy 101 zooms east through the San Fernando Valley. Veer left onto Hwy 134 toward Burbank, almost 90 miles after leaving Santa Barbara.

07 BURBANK
Long ago, the TV and movie biz (locals just call it 'the Industry') decamped from Hollywood, and the San Fernando Valley has since been the origin of countless blockbusters (and also, infamously, ground zero for SoCal's porn industry). 'The Valley' also gave the world 1980s 'Valley Girl' speak and SoCal's ubiquitous mall-rat culture.

Go behind the scenes on the **Warner Bros Studio Tour** (wbstudiotour.com), or take your screaming tweens and teens to **Universal Studios Hollywood** (universalstudioshollywood.com) theme park, where you can escape into the Wizarding World of Harry Potter, ride a tram tour past working sound stages and pick up free tickets for a live TV show taping. To buy cast-off TV and movie star fashions, visit **It's a Wrap!** (itsawraphollywood.com).

📷 **Photo Opportunity**
Your favorite star on the Hollywood Walk of Fame.

THE DRIVE

It's a quick 3-mile trip south on Hwy 101 from Universal Studios to Hollywood. Take the Highland Ave exit and drive south on Highland Ave, which intersects Hollywood Blvd.

08 HOLLYWOOD

Like an ageing starlet making a comeback, this LA neighborhood is undergoing a not-quite-ready-for-its-close-up renaissance of hip hotels, restored movie palaces and glitzy bars and nightclubs. Although you're unlikely to see any in-person celebrities, the pink-starred **Hollywood Walk of Fame** (walkoffame.com) still attracts millions of wide-eyed visitors every year. Snap a souvenir photo amid the concrete handprints and footprints outside the **TCL Chinese Theatre** (tclchinesetheatres.com), and swing by the **Dolby Theatre** (dolbytheatre.com), home to the Academy Awards ceremony, before visiting the **Hollywood Museum** (thehollywoodmuseum.com), a trove of costumes, props and memorabilia.

Cruise west along the **Sunset Strip**, packed with celeb-slumming bars and dog-eared rock venues where the Rolling Stones and the Doors once tore up the stages.

DETOUR
LA Live
Start: 08 Hollywood

Next to downtown's **Crypto.com Arena** (cryptoarena.com), the saucer-shaped sports and entertainment arena, **LA Live** (lalive.com) is a shiny corporate entertainment hub. Glimpse larger-than-life statues of Magic Johnson and Wayne Gretzky. Visitors to the **Grammy Museum** (grammymuseum.org) can get lost in sound chambers; try mixing and remixing, singing and rapping; and view icons like GnR's bass drum, Yo-Yo Ma's cello and MJ's glove enshrined like holy relics (though exhibitions do rotate). It's about 8 miles southeast of Hollywood via Hwy 101 and I-110 south (exit at 8th St).

Venice Boardwalk

30
Route 66

BEST ROAD

Find yourself on National Trails Hwy between Amboy and Ludlow.

Joshua trees along Route 66

DURATION	DISTANCE	GREAT FOR
3–4 days	350 miles / 565km	Literary Landscapes

BEST TIME TO GO	Spring and fall, for cruising with the windows down, without summer heat.

For generations of Americans, California, with its sparkling waters and sunny skies, was the promised land for road-trippers on Route 66. Follow their tracks through the gauntlet of Mojave Desert ghost towns, railway whistle-stops like Barstow and Victorville, and across the Cajon Pass. Finally, wind through the LA Basin and put your vehicle in park near the crashing ocean waves in Santa Monica.

Link Your Trip

32 Palm Springs & Joshua Tree Oases
Cut southwest on I-10 out of San Bernardino and head for a pastiche of palms, mountains, oases and whimsical Joshua trees.

03 Pacific Coast Highways
This equally classic route takes you on a cruise along California's epic coastal ribbon: Hwy 1. When you finish Route 66, follow Hwy 1 north.

01 NEEDLES

At the Arizona border, the arched 1916 **Old Trails Bridge** marked the Mother Road's entrance to California until 1948. In the movie version of John Steinbeck's novel *The Grapes of Wrath*, the Depression-era Joad family used it to cross the Colorado River. For the best vantage point of the bridge, head to the Route 66 Welcome Sign off National Trails Hwy about a quarter mile south of I-40 (exit 153).

About 14 miles north, the jewel of the dusty railroad town of Needles is the restored **El Garces train** depot. It's one of only a few remaining 'Harvey Houses', a chain of early 20th-century railway hotels and restaurants managed by the Fred Harvey Company. They were famous for employing traveling waitresses as portrayed in the 1946 MGM musical *The Harvey Girls*.

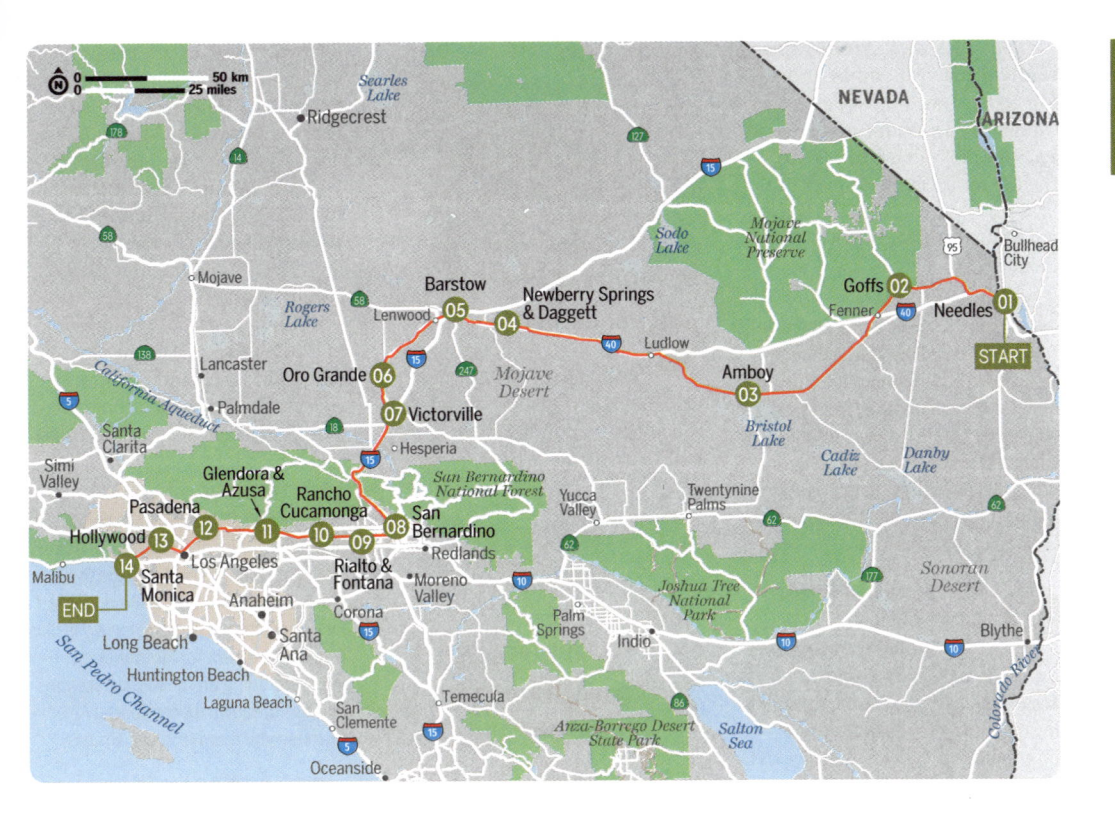

THE DRIVE
Drive west on I-40 for about 15 miles, take exit 133 and follow Hwy 95 north for 6 miles. Turn left and follow Goffs Rd (Historic Route 66) for another 15 miles. You'll inevitably be running alongside a long train – this is a primary rail shipping route to the West Coast.

02 GOFFS
The 1914 Spanish **Mission–style schoolhouse** (mdhca.org) in Goffs (population 12) is a fun stop along this sun-drenched stretch of highway. In the old classroom – complete with wooden desks and a US flag sporting 48 stars – photographs illustrate the tough life on the edge of the Mojave. Outside you're free to wander around a graveyard of gracefully rusting vintage cars, gas pumps and even a bullet-riddled yellow school bus.

THE DRIVE
Until the flood-damaged Route 66 stretch between Fenner and Amboy reopens, you need to detour 30 miles west on I-40 and cut 12 miles south on Kelbaker Rd before rejoining the National Trails Hwy. Just before reaching Amboy, keep an eye out for a pair of gleaming white, massive Chinese guardian lion sculptures incongruously perched in the sun-baked emptiness.

03 AMBOY
In the near-ghost town of Amboy, **Roy's Motel & Cafe** (visitamboy.com) has been a popular pit stop since 1938. If you believe the lore, Roy once cooked his famous Route 66 double cheeseburger on the hood of a '63 Mercury. There's no food or lodging today, but at least Roy's iconic neon sign kicked back into glimmering glory in 2019.

Two miles west, **Amboy Crater** (blm.gov/visit/amboy-crater) is a 250ft-high, almost perfectly symmetrical volcanic cinder cone. It's a 3-mile round-trip hike to the top for great views over the lava fields where NASA engineers field-tested the Mars Rover (avoid in summer).

THE DRIVE
Travel 28 miles along National Trails Hwy to Ludlow. Turn right onto Crucero Rd and pass under I-40, then follow the north frontage road west for 8 miles before it makes a sharp left and crosses under I-40 on Lavic Rd. Take the first right to get back on National Trails Hwy and travel past Lavic Lake volcanic field.

04 NEWBERRY SPRINGS & DAGGETT
Near **Newberry Springs**, Route 66 passes by the grizzled **Bagdad Cafe**, the main filming location of Percy Adlon's eponymous 1987 cult flick starring CCH Pounder and Jack Palance. The interior is chockablock with posters, movie stills and memorabilia, while outside the old water tower and Airstream trailer are slowly rusting away.

The highway passes under I-40 and 12 miles later reaches windswept **Daggett**, site of the harsh California inspection station faced by Dust Bowl refugees in *The Grapes of Wrath*. Pay your respects to such early desert adventurers as Sierra Nevada naturalist John Muir at the long-shuttered **Stone Hotel**. A fun 6-mile detour north, **Calico Ghost Town Regional Park** (calicotown.com) is a park of reconstructed pioneer-era buildings amid vestiges of a late-19th-century silver-mining operation.

THE DRIVE
Return to Daggett, then drive west to Nebo Rd, turn left and rejoin I-40. You'll drive about 4 miles before exiting at E Main St, which runs through workaday Barstow, a railroad settlement and historic crossroads, where murals adorn empty buildings downtown. Turn right on N 1st St.

05 BARSTOW
Exit I-40 onto Main St in the Barstow, a railroad settlement and historic crossroads, where murals adorn empty buildings downtown.

TOP TIP:
Navigating the Mother Road

Because Route 66 is no longer an official road, it doesn't appear on many maps, although AAA state maps show portions. Consult these sources for info:

Historic Route 66 (historic66.com) Offers turn-by-turn directions.

National Historic Route 66 Federation (national66.org) Has links to myriad attractions and resources.

EZ66 Guide for Travelers Jerry McClanahan's intricately detailed book is a must.

Follow N 1st St over a trestle bridge across the Mojave River to the beautifully restored 1911 **Harvey House**, nicknamed Casa del Desierto and designed by Western architect Mary Colter. Inside is the **Route 66 Mother Road Museum** (route66museum.org) with B&W photographs, a 1915 Ford Motel T and odds and ends from the heyday of Route 66 travel. At the depot's other end you'll find an outdoor collection of historic locomotives, a bright-red caboose and railroad relics.

THE DRIVE
Leaving Barstow via Main St, rejoin the National Trails Hwy heading west as it meanders alongside the Mojave River through Lenwood. Loved by Harley riders, this rural byway is like a scavenger hunt for Mother Road ruins, including antique filling stations and tumbledown motor courts. After 25 miles you'll arrive in Oro Grande.

06 ORO GRANDE
Colorful as a box of crayons, **Elmer's Bottle Tree Ranch** in Oro Grande is a quirky piece of roadside folk art with over 200 'bottle trees.' It's the work of Elmer Long, an artistic genius and career man at the cement factory just outside of town. Elmer, who died in 2019, used bottles in all sorts of colors, shapes and sizes to build this offbeat sculpture garden, incorporating telephone poles, railroad signs and other bric-a-brac.

THE DRIVE
Continue south on National Trails Hwy and cross over the Mojave River on a 1930s steel-truss bridge, then roll into downtown Victorville, a trip of 12 miles.

Entrance to Main St, Barstow

BARSTOW

ROUTE 66

07 VICTORVILLE

Opposite the railroad tracks in Victorville, the **California Route 66 Museum** (califrt66museum.org) is an adorably cluttered kitchen sink's worth of yesteryear's treasures. Exhibits include old signs and roadside memorabilia as well as a selfie-worthy '50s diner and a flower-power VW 'Love Bus'.

THE DRIVE
Get on I-15 south and travel over the legendary Cajon Pass, a haven for trainspotters. Descending into San Bernardino, follow I-215 and take exit 45 for Baseline St. Head east and turn left onto N 'E' St.

08 SAN BERNARDINO

Look for the golden arches outside the unofficial **First McDonald's Museum** (facebook.com/first originalmcdonaldsmuseum). Though not technically in the original building created in 1948 by Dick and Mac McDonald, it was here that salesman Ray Kroc dropped by hoping to sell the brothers a mixer. Eventually Kroc used his moxie – as portrayed by Michael Keaton in *The Founder* (2016) – to buy the rights to the McDonald's name and build an empire. Half of the museum is devoted to Route 66, with some neat photographs and maps.

Photo Opportunity

Laying on faded asphalt by a Route 66 sign.

THE DRIVE
Turn west on 5th St, leaving San Bernardino via Foothill Blvd, which continues straight into the urban sprawl of Greater Los Angeles. It's a long haul west to Pasadena (over 50 miles), with stop-and-go traffic most of the way, but there are some gems to uncover en route.

09 RIALTO & FONTANA

In **Rialto**, swing by the **Wigwam Motel**, a cluster of 32ft-tall tipis that have welcomed travelers since 1950. Cruising through **Fontana**, birthplace of the Hells Angels biker club, pause for a photo by the **Giant Orange**, a 1930s juice stand of the kind that was once a fixture alongside SoCal's citrus groves. It used to offer weary Route 66 travelers 'all the juice you could drink' for a mere 10

Colorado Blvd, Pasadena

cents. Find it in the parking lot of **Bono's Italian Restaurant** (bonositalianrestaurantgolden. com), a historic Route 66 diner that was reimagined as a pizza and pasta parlor in 2019.

🚗 **THE DRIVE**
Continue west on Foothill Blvd to Rancho Cucamonga.

10 RANCHO CUCAMONGA

Rancho Cucamonga is home to two old-school steakhouses with a Route 66 pedigree. First up is the **Magic Lamp Inn**, easily recognized by its fabulous neon Aladdin's lamp. Its interior sparkles with shiny dark woods and stained-glass windows. A bit further on, storied **Sycamore Inn** (thesycamoreinn. com) has fed its juicy steaks to generations of meat lovers, including Marilyn Monroe.

🚗 **THE DRIVE**
Continue driving west on Foothill Blvd.

11 GLENDORA & AZUSA

A key stop in **Glendora** is **The Hat**, a small local chain that's been serving its famous hot pastrami sandwiches since 1951. Route 66 continues as Huntington Dr in **Duarte**, where a boisterous Route 66 parade rolls through in September. Turn right on Magnolia Ave and rejoin Foothill Blvd in **Azusa** whose supposedly haunted **1925 Aztec Hotel** sports a striking Mayan Revival–style facade. Hollywood celebs knocked 'em back in this beloved landmark en route to the Santa Anita racetrack.

🚗 **THE DRIVE**
Continue west on Foothill Blvd, then turn left (south) on Santa Anita Ave, right (west) on Huntington Dr and right again on Colorado Pl past the

---

WHY I LOVE THIS TRIP

Andrea Schulte-Peevers, writer

The final stretch of America's most storied road trip adds a cinematic, sensory dimension to your SoCal adventure. Follow the dreams of generations of pioneers as you steer through open desert lidded by cornflower-blue skies, past mysterious ghost towns and sunbaked mountains until the LA megalopolis and the shimmering Pacific salute you with sparkling promise and glamour.

1930s Santa Anita Park horse-racing track. It's where the Marx Brothers filmed *A Day at the Races* (1937) and where legendary thoroughbred Seabiscuit once ran.

12 PASADENA

Colorado Blvd leads straight into bustling Old Pasadena, where boutiques and cafes are housed in handsomely restored historic Spanish Colonial Revival–style buildings. Follow Fair Oaks Ave south to the nostalgic 1915 **Fair Oaks Pharmacy** where so-called 'soda jerks' still dish out 'phosphates' (flavored syrup, soda water and 'secret potion'), giant banana splits and other sugary kicks.

🚗 **THE DRIVE**
Rejoin the modern world on the Pasadena Fwy (Hwy 110), which streams south into LA. One of the first freeways in the US, it's a truck-free state historic freeway. Take exit 24B and follow Sunset Blvd northwest to Santa Monica Blvd westbound.

13 HOLLYWOOD

The exact track that Route 66 ran through Tinseltown isn't possible to follow these days (it changed several times) at **Ovation Hollywood** (ovationhollywood.com) shopping, dining and entertainment complex in the center of the action. Travelers looking for a creepy-fun communion with stars of yesteryear should stroll the **Hollywood Forever Cemetery** (hollywoodforever.com) next to Paramount Pictures, which is crowded with such famous 'immortals' as Rudolph Valentino, Jayne Mansfield and Cecil B DeMille. Buy a map at the flower shop near the entrance.

🚗 **THE DRIVE**
Follow Santa Monica Blvd west for 13 miles to reach the end of the road – it meets Ocean Ave at Palisades Park. Hwy 1 is downhill from Ocean Ave heading north. The pier is a few blocks to the south.

14 SANTA MONICA

This is the end of the line: Route 66 reaches its finish, over 2400 miles from its starting point in Chicago, on an ocean bluff in **Palisades Park**, where a Will Rogers Hwy memorial plaque marks the official end of the Mother Road. Celebrate on **Santa Monica Pier** (santamonicapier.org), where you can ride a 1920s carousel featured in *The Sting* (1973) and enjoy other attractions and carnival rides. With the glittering Pacific as a backdrop, take a selfie with the 'Santa Monica 66 End of Trail' sign. Then hit the beach.

BEST ROAD TRIPS: CALIFORNIA

31

Life in Death Valley

BEST FOR HISTORY

Touch the past at Harmony Borax Works

DURATION	DISTANCE	GREAT FOR
3 days	365 miles / 585km	Families, Nature

BEST TIME TO GO	February to April for spring wildflower blooms and cooler temperatures.

Zabriskie Point (p174)

The name evokes all that is harsh, hot and hellish – a punishing, barren and lifeless place of Old Testament severity. Ghost towns and abandoned mines are proof of the human struggle to survive here. Yet a scenic drive through the park reveals that nature is spectacularly alive in Death Valley: sensuous sand dunes, water-sculpted canyons, extinct volcanic craters, palm-shaded oases, soaring mountains and plenty of endemic wildlife.

Link Your Trip

22 Eastern Sierra Scenic Byway

From Panamint Springs, it's 50 miles northwest to Lone Pine, a gateway to lofty Sierra Nevada peaks, via Hwys 190, 136 and 395.

30 Route 66

From Baker, drive south through the Mojave National Preserve and across I-40 to meet California's original road trip.

01 BAKER

Death Valley is a land of extremes – you'll find the lowest elevation in North America here, not far from Mt Whitney, the highest peak in the US outside Alaska. More infamously, Death Valley is the hottest place in the nation. Just take a look at the **World's Largest Thermometer** in Baker, right off I-15. An eye-catching tower of roadside kitsch, it stands 134ft tall to commemorate the record-breaking temperature of 134°F (57°C) measured on July 10, 1913.

THE DRIVE

From Baker, follow Hwy 127 (Death Valley Rd) north for 50 miles, crossing railroad tracks and zooming through

of Joshua trees, ending with panoramic desert views peppered with colorful cinder cones. From here it's another 38 miles back to Baker. The entire detour clocks in at 180 miles.

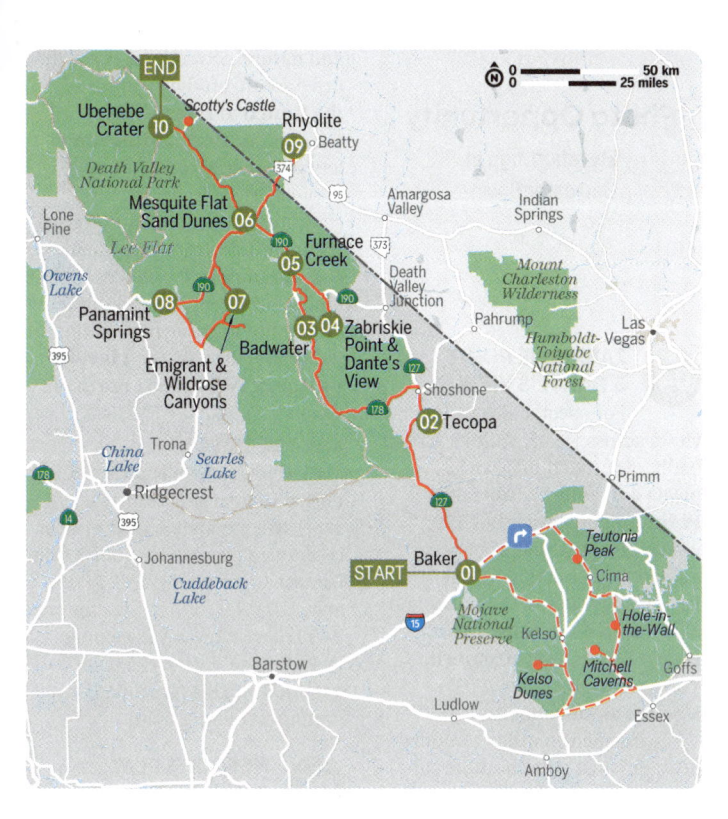

02 TECOPA

Even when the desert looks bone-dry, you can still find oases such as the dusty outpost of Tecopa. Natural hot springs used by Native Americans for centuries bubble up at three basic resorts. The best of the bunch is **Delight's Hot Springs Resort** (delightshotspringsresort.com), which has four private soaking pools adorned with endearing desert-themed murals. A fun 5-mile detour south, **China Ranch Date Farm** (chinaranch.com) is a refreshingly green refuge where you can go hiking or bird-watching, then stock up on fresh dates or try their yummy date shakes. It's well sign-posted from Tecopa. The last stretch is unpaved, steep and winding, sometimes requiring 4WD (or park and walk in). At the junction of Old Spanish Trail Hwy and Tecopa Hot Springs road, you'll drive past an old railroad tie shack housing **Death Valley Brewing** (deathvalleybrewing.com), a teensy craft brewery where non-drivers can quench their thirst with an ale or IPA.

THE DRIVE

Continue north on Tecopa Hot Springs Rd to rejoin Hwy 127. Turn right and drive 4 miles north to Shoshone, your last chance for gas, drinks and snacks (p339) until Furnace Creek, some 70 miles away. Turn left onto Hwy 178 (Jubilee Pass Rd), which wrenches right at Ashford Junction, becoming Badwater Rd and curving lazily north along the valley floor.

a serene desert landscape. Turn right onto Old Spanish Trail Hwy and drive 4 miles east toward Tecopa.

DETOUR
Mojave National Preserve
Start: 01 **Baker**

For another dose of Wild West history, point the wheels toward the lonely **Mojave National Preserve** (nps.gov/moja), southeast of Baker off I-15. Make a beeline for the Kelso Depot, a gracefully restored 1920s Spanish Mission–style railway station rebooted as the preserve's main visitor center.

Watch the 20-minute introductory movie and poke around the exhibits of local history and lore. Head south to the honey-colored Kelso Dunes that are among the tallest sand piles in the US. Hiking to the top will have you mopping your brow but also give you a chance to hear the dunes 'sing', ie emanate a low humming or booming sound caused by shifting sands.

Head south to I-40, turn east and exit on Essex Rd, then drive north to the otherworldly **Mitchell Caverns** (book ahead for a tour). A bit further north, scramble around the hole-riddled cliffs of **Hole-in-the-Wall**, once used by Native Americans to escape Western ranchers.

Drive north, then turn left on the old Mojave Rd blazed by Spanish missionaries, fur trappers and traders and, oddly enough, camels on an 1867 military expedition. Head right toward Cima, then veer left to reach the trailhead for **Teutonia Peak**, a 3-mile round-trip hike through the world's largest forest

03 BADWATER

Cresting **Jubilee Pass** (1290ft), the highway dips down into Death Valley itself. Despite its harsh name, the valley is actually a thriving wildlife habitat and has supported human life for millennia, from Shoshone tribespeople to Old West pioneers, gold seekers and borax miners.

It's the silence and solemnity of the vast expanse that inspires today. That cracked, parched-looking salt pan extending across the valley floor, which suddenly sears your retinas with its dazzling white light, is **Badwater**. At 282ft below sea level, it's the lowest point in North America.

A boardwalk hovers over the constantly evaporating bed of salty, mineralized water, almost alien in its beauty. Prehistoric Lake Manly covered the entire valley during the last ice age, and in 2005 it briefly reappeared for the first time in recorded human history when heavy rainfall could not be absorbed by the dry, compressed desert soil. This was followed by a spectacular superbloom of red poppies, yellow primroses, purple sand verbena and other desert flowers. The phenomenon reoccurred in 2015 and again in 2019.

THE DRIVE
Eight miles north of Badwater, past the Natural Bridge turnoff on your right and the bizarre salt crystals of Devils Golf Course on your left, detour along Artists Drive, a one-way 9-mile scenic loop (no vehicles with trailers or over 25ft long). Rejoining Badwater Rd, drive 5 miles north, then go right on Hwy 190 for 3.5 miles to Zabriskie Point.

Photo Opportunity
Elevation sign at Badwater Basin.

04 ZABRISKIE POINT & DANTE'S VIEW

For spectacular valley views across Death Valley's golden badlands eroded into waves, pleats and gullies, **Zabriskie Point** (ps.gov/deva; Hwy 190; p) can't be beat. The spot was named for a manager of the Pacific Coast Borax Company and also inspired the title of Michelangelo Antonio's 1970s movie. The cover of U2's *Joshua Tree* album was also shot here.

To escape the valley's midday heat, or catch a memorable sunset, continue for 20 miles uphill from Zabriskie Point to breezy **Dante's View** (nps.gov/deva). From this lofty perch you can simultaneously view the highest (Mt Whitney) and lowest (Badwater) points in the contiguous USA. Budget at least half an hour (each way) for the winding drive.

THE DRIVE
Backtrack downhill, then turn left on Hwy 190 and drive 7 miles, past the elegant Inn at Furnace Creek and the Badwater Rd turnoff, before rolling past the Ranch at Furnace Creek to the park's excellent visitor center.

05 FURNACE CREEK

At the visitor center, don't miss the gorgeously shot 20-minute movie introducing you to the park's history, geology and natural attractions. A short drive south, on the grounds of the **Ranch at Death Valley**, the outdoor **Borax Museum** lets you poke around a jumble of pioneer-era transportation equipment, including an original 'Twenty Mule Team' wagon and a steam tractor. To see where the mules kicked off their 165-mile slog to the nearest train station in Mojave, drop by the **Harmony Borax Works**, just north of Furnace Creek.

THE DRIVE
If you didn't fill up outside the park, Furnace Creek has an expensive gas station with 24-hour credit-card pumps. Head north from Furnace Creek on Hwy 190. After about 20 miles, turn left to stay on Hwy 190 west toward Stovepipe Wells Village. Just over 5 miles later, pull into the Mesquite Flat parking lot on your right.

06 MESQUITE FLAT SAND DUNES

It's time to take up a famous strand of history in Death Valley: the story of the lost forty-niners. When the California gold rush took off in 1849, a small group of pioneers chanced what they hoped would be a shortcut to the California goldfields, leaving behind the Old Spanish Trail.

Exhausted, dangerously low on food and water, and struggling with broken wagons and worn-out pack animals, the woeful group arrived near Furnace Creek on Christmas Eve. Failing to get their wagons across the Panamint Mountains, the survivors slaughtered their oxen and burned their wagons near what today is the **Mesquite Flat**. Get out of the car to hike up and down across the rolling field of sand dunes

BADWATER BASIN

282 FEET / 85.5 METERS

BELOW SEA LEVEL

that look like a mini Sahara. They are at their most photogenic at sunrise or sunset when bathed in soft light and accented by long, deep shadows. Keep an eye out for animal tracks.

🚗 THE DRIVE

You can fill up the gas tank and buy food and drinks at Stovepipe Wells Village, 2 miles further west along Hwy 190. Heading west, you'll pass the side road to Mosaic Canyon on your left before reaching Emigrant Canyon Rd after 9 miles. Turn left and start winding uphill toward Emigrant Pass

07 EMIGRANT & WILDROSE CANYONS

Faced with no other choice, the forty-niner pioneers eventually walked out of torturous Death Valley over **Emigrant Pass**. As they left, one woman reputedly looked back and fatalistically uttered the words: good-bye, death valley.

Later pioneers flooded back when gold was discovered in Death Valley, including at Skidoo, a boomtown that went bust in the early 20th century, and where the influential silent movie *Greed* was filmed in 1923. Nothing remains of the ghost-town site today. Further south, the ruined Eureka Mine is en route to vertigo-inducing **Aguereberry Point**, where you can see the Funeral Mountains and the parched valley spread out below.

Both of these side trips travel on rough, rutted dirt roads (high-clearance 4WD vehicles recommended). Turn left onto Wildrose Canyon Rd to reach the abandoned **Wildrose Charcoal Kilns**. Built in 1876, these beehive-shaped stone kilns produced the charcoal needed by the miners for smelting Death Valley's silver and lead ore. The landscape is subalpine, with forests of piñon pine and juniper; it can be covered with snow, even in spring.

Wildrose Charcoal Kilns

THE DRIVE

Backtrack downhill, turning left at the intersection with Emigrant Canyon Rd onto Wildrose Canyon Rd, which snakes through a flash-flood zone (don't attempt this road except during dry weather). After 14 miles, turn right on Panamint Valley Rd and drive north to Hwy 190, then turn left. The longer all-weather route is to backtrack down Emigrant Canyon Rd to Hwy 190, then turn left for the 22-mile drive to Panamint Springs.

08 PANAMINT SPRINGS

At the far western edge of Death Valley National Park, Panamint Springs is an off-grid camp with incredible views back at the muscular Panamint Range. In spring, you can drive the 2.5-mile graded gravel road, followed by a mile-long cross-country scramble, to **Darwin Falls**. Here, a natural-spring cascade plunges into a gorge, embraced by willows that attract migratory birds in springtime.

Continuing west on the highway for about 8 miles takes you to Father Crowley Vista, which peers deep into **Rainbow Canyon**, aka Star Wars Canyon, created by lava flows and scattered with multihued volcanic cinders. With any luck, you get to witness US Air Force and Navy fighter jets zooming through the canyon on training runs.

THE DRIVE

Turn around and drive back downhill east on Hwy 190. About 7 miles past Stovepipe Wells Village, turn left and then right onto Daylight Pass Rd for 16 miles, exiting the park and following Hwy 374 into Nevada for 9 miles to the signposted turnoff for Rhyolite on your left.

09 RHYOLITE

Just 4 miles west of Beatty, NV, Rhyolite was the queen of Death Valley's mines during its heyday. It epitomizes the hurly-burly, boom-and-bust story of Western gold-rush mining towns.

After the first nugget was discovered in 1904, the population soared to 8000 by 1908, only to plummet a couple of years later when the mines began petering out. The remaining ruins, including a school, store, bank and railway station, reflect the high standard of living created for such a short period. One much photographed curiosity is a house made of thousands of beer bottles. En route, you'll pass the surreal **Goldwell Open Air Museum**, a trippy sculpture installation rising up from the desert floor. It was conceived in 1984 by the late Belgian artist Albert Szukalski and added to over the years by fellow creatives. Standout pieces include a giant prospector incongruously accompanied by a penguin, and a ghostly plaster cast version of Da Vinci's *Last Supper*.

THE DRIVE

Backtrack down Daylight Pass Rd, turning right onto Scotty's Castle Rd, which winds for 33 miles through the valley, shadowed by the Grapevine Mountains. Turn left near the ranger station at Grapevine Junction onto the side road to arrive near Ubehebe Crater after about 5 miles.

10 UBEHEBE CRATER

One of the most impressive geological features in the northern valley, 600ft-deep Ubehebe Crater is believed to have formed some 2100 years ago in a single eruptive event by the meeting of fiery magma and cool groundwater. Its Martian beauty is easily appreciated from the parking lot, but for closer inspection and compelling views into its volcanic depth embark on the 1.5-mile trek along the rim (not recommended if vertigo-prone). For a longer walk, add a detour to **Little Hebe Crater**.

WHY I LOVE THIS TRIP

Andrea Schulte-Peevers, writer

Yes, it can get hotter than Satan's hoof, but most of the year Death Valley is a sensory immersion in nature at its most primal and soul-stirring. Feel your spirits soar and your mind clear as you steer through this pastiche of sun-blistered mountains, sensuous sand dunes, crackling salt flats and untamed canyons. Delight in the light playing otherworldly tricks on the landscape throughout the day, then look forward to being cradled by a starry canopy at night.

32

Palm Springs & Joshua Tree Oases

BEST FOR SOLITUDE

Hike to the Lost Palms Oasis for a sense of peace.

DURATION	DISTANCE	GREAT FOR
2–3 days	170 miles / 274kM	Nature

BEST TIME TO GO	February to April for spring wildflower blooms and cooler temperatures.

Ladder-backed woodpecker, Big Morongo Canyon Preserve

Just a short drive from the chic resorts of Palm Springs, the vast Mojave and Sonoran Deserts are serenely spiritual places. You may find that what at first looked like desolate sands transform on foot into perfect beauty: shady palm tree and cactus gardens, tiny wildflowers pushing up from hard-baked soil in spring, natural hot-springs pools for soaking, and uncountable stars overhead in the inky dark.

Link Your Trip

30 Route 66

Follow Hwy 62 east of Twentynine Palms, turn left onto Godwin Rd, then right onto Amboy Rd for a 50-mile journey to join America's 'Mother Road.'

33 Temecula, Julian & Anza-Borrego

From Mecca, drive along the Salton Sea's western shore, then head inland to Borrego Springs, a 50-mile trip.

01 PALM SPRINGS

Hollywood celebs have always counted on Palm Springs as a quick escape from LA. Today, this desert resort town is a showcase of retro-chic mid-century modern buildings. Stop at the **Palm Springs Visitors Center** (visitpalmsprings.com), inside a 1965 gas station by Albert Frey, to pick up a self-guided architectural tour map. Then drive uphill to be whisked from desert floor to alpine forest on the rotating **Palm Springs Aerial Tramway** (pstramway.com) in just 15 minutes. Back down, drive south on Palm Canyon Dr to get your culture kicks at the excellent **Palm Springs Art Museum** (psmuseum.org), followed by a hop between art galleries, cafes, cocktail bars, trendy restaurants and chic boutiques. Finally, head 10 miles downvalley for a saunter around the magnificent gardens of **Sunnylands** (sunnylands.org), the desert retreat where Walter and Leonore Annenberg once welcomed US presidents, royalty and celebs.

THE DRIVE
Drive north out of downtown Palm Springs along Indian Canyon Dr for 7 miles, passing over I-10. Turn right onto Dillon Rd, then after 2.5 miles cut a left onto Palm Dr, which heads north into central Desert Hot Springs.

02 DESERT HOT SPRINGS
In 1774 Spanish explorer Juan Bautista de Anza was the first European to encounter the desert Cahuilla tribe. Afterward, the Spanish name Agua Caliente came to refer to both the indigenous people and the natural hot springs that still bubble up restoratively from below the town of **Desert Hot Springs** (visit deserthotsprings.com). You can 'take the waters' in family-friendly resorts or stylish adult-only healing hideaways like the **Two Bunch Palms Resort & Spa** (twobunchpalms.com/spa) that sits atop an actual oasis. Imitate Tim Robbins who enjoyed a mud bath here in the 1992 Robert Altman's film *The Player*, then bounce between pools and sunbathing areas or enjoy a massage all the while maintaining the code of silence (actually, whispers only).

THE DRIVE
Head west on Pierson Blvd back to Indian Canyon Dr. Turn right and drive northwest through the dusty outskirts of Desert Hot Springs. Turn right onto Hwy 62 eastbound toward Yucca Valley; after about 4 miles, turn right onto East Dr and look for signs for Big Morongo Canyon Preserve.

03 BIG MORONGO CANYON PRESERVE
An oasis hidden in the high desert, **Big Morongo Canyon Preserve** (parks.sbcounty.gov) is a riparian habitat flush with cottonwood and willow trees. Attracted by the water, mule deer, bighorn sheep, coyotes and other critters pass through this wildlife corridor linking the San Gorgonio Mountains and Joshua Tree National Park.

The preserve is also an internationally recognized bird-watching hot spot; around 250 bird species have been identified here, including at least 72 that use the area as breeding grounds, such as the coral-red summer tanager and the brown-crested flycatcher.

Keep an eye out (better yet, bring binoculars) as you trek along several short trails meandering through this marshy land where hummingbirds flutter and woodpeckers attack trees.

THE DRIVE
Rejoin Hwy 62 eastbound which soon passes through Yucca Valley where you'll find some cool roadside antiques, vintage shops, art galleries and cafes. Continue east for another 16 miles to the town of Joshua Tree,

which makes a handy base for the night. If necessary, fill up your gas tank at the intersection with Park Blvd before turning right and driving 5 miles to Joshua Tree National Park's west entrance.

04 JOSHUA TREE NATIONAL PARK

It's time to jump into **Joshua Tree National Park** (nps.gov/jotr), a wonderland of bulbous boulders and jumbo rocks interspersed with sandy forests of Joshua trees. Related to agave plants, Joshua trees were named by Mormon settlers who thought the twisted, spiky arms resembled a prophet's arms stretching toward God. Revel in the scenery as you drive along the winding park road for about 8 miles to **Hidden Valley** parking area. From here, an easy 1-mile loop trail meanders between whimsical rock clusters to a hidden valley where cattle rustlers once hid their hoard. If you enjoy history and Western lore, check with the national park office for ranger-led walking tours of nearby **Keys Ranch** (nps.gov/jotr), where pioneer homesteaders tried their hand at cattle ranching, mining and desert farming here in the 19th century.

THE DRIVE
Backtrack to Park Blvd, turn left and head south again past jumbled rock formations and fields of spiky Joshua trees. Take a right turn toward Keys View. You'll pass several trailheads and roadside interpretive exhibits over the next 5.5 miles leading up to the viewpoint.

05 KEYS VIEW

Make sure you embark at least an hour before sunset for the drive up to Keys View (5185ft), where panoramic views look into the Coachella Valley and reach as far south as the shimmering Salton Sea or, on an unusually clear day, Mexico's Signal Mountain.

Also looming in the distance are Mt San Jacinto (10,834ft) and Mt San Gorgonio (11,500ft), Southern California's highest peaks that are often snow-dusted until late spring. Down below snakes a section of the San Andreas Fault.

THE DRIVE
Head back downhill to Park Blvd. Turn right and wind through the park's Wonderland of Rocks (where boulders call out to scampering kids and serious rock jocks alike), passing more campgrounds. After 10 miles, veer left to stay on Park Blvd and drive north for 8 miles toward the town of Twentynine Palms onto Utah Trail.

06 OASIS OF MARA

Drop by **Joshua Tree National Park's Oasis Visitor Center** (nps.gov/jotr) for its educational exhibits about Southern California's desert fan palms. These palms are often found growing along fault lines, where cracks in the earth's crust allow subterranean water to surface.

Outside the visitor center, a gentle half-mile nature trail leads around the Oasis of Mara with the original 29 palm trees that gave Twentynine Palms its name. They were planted by native Serranos who named the area Mara, meaning 'the place of little springs and much grass'.

Ask for directions to the trailhead off Hwy 62 for the 3-mile, round-trip hike to **49 Palms Oasis**, where a sun-exposed dirt trail marches you over a ridge, then drops you into a rocky gorge, doggedly heading down past barrel cacti toward a distant speck of green.

THE DRIVE
Drive back south on Utah Trail and re-enter the park. Follow Park Blvd south, turning left at the first major junction onto Pinto Basin Rd for a winding 30-mile drive southeast to Cottonwood Spring.

07 COTTONWOOD SPRING

On your drive to Cottonwood Spring, you'll pass from the high Mojave Desert into the lower Sonoran Desert. Stop at the **Cholla Cactus Garden**, where a quarter-mile loop winds through a dense grove of 'teddy bear' cholla cactus and ocotillo plants that look like green octopus tentacles and are adorned with flaming scarlet flowers in spring.

Turn left at the **Cottonwood Visitor Center** (nps.gov/jotr) for a short drive east past the campground to **Cottonwood Spring**. Once used by the Cahuilla, who left behind archaeological evidence such as mortars and clay pots, the springs became a hotbed for gold mining in the late 19th century. The now-dry springs are the start of the moderately strenuous 7.5-mile round-trip trek out to **Lost Palms Oasis**, a fan-palm oasis blessed with solitude and scenery.

Photo Opportunity
Catch the sunset from Keys View.

THE DRIVE

Head south from Cottonwood Springs and drive across I-10 to pick up scenic Box Canyon Rd, which burrows a hole through the desert, twisting its way toward the Salton Sea. Take 66th Ave west to Mecca, then turn right onto Hwy 111 and drive northwest toward Indio.

DETOUR
Salton Sea & Slab City
Start: 7 Cottonwood Spring

Driving along Hwy 111 southeast of Mecca, you soon hit a most unexpected sight: California's largest lake in the middle of its largest desert.

The Salton Sea was created by accident in 1905 when spring flooding breached irrigation canals built to bring water from the Colorado River to the farmland in the Imperial Valley. As a long-time stopover along the Pacific Flyway, it's a prime birding spot. Alas, the winged creatures' survival is threatened by decreasing water levels and rising salinity from decades of agricultural runoff.

About 10 miles east of the Salton Sea, near Niland, an even stranger sight is the folk-art Salvation Mountain (salvationmountaininc.org), an artificial hill slathered in paint and decorated with flowers, waterfalls and messages.

It's part of Slab City, an off-grid community set up on the remains of a former military base. It attracts society dropouts, drifters, retirees and just plain kooky folk – thousands in the winter, a few hardened souls year-round. Self-dubbed 'the last free place on earth', the Slabs is more organized than it appears, with individual 'neighborhoods' and even a library

08 COACHELLA VALLEY

The hot but fertile Coachella Valley may be world-famous for its star-studded indie music and art festival held every April in Indio, but it's also the ideal place to find the date of your dreams – the kind that grows on trees, that is. Date farms let you sample exotic-sounding varieties like halawy, deglet noor and zahidi for free. The signature taste of the valley is a rich date shake from certified-organic **Oasis Date Gardens** (oasisdate.com) in Thermal or the 1920s pioneer **Shields Date Garden** (shieldsdategarden.com) in Indio.

Coachella Valley

33

Temecula, Julian & Anza-Borrego

BEST FOR FAMILIES

Bring the gang to Julian's apple pie and gold mine tours.

DURATION	DISTANCE	GREAT FOR
3 days	300 miles / 485km	Wineries, families

BEST TIME TO GO	February to April for wildflowers and moderate temperatures.

Vineyard, Temecula Valley

In just about any season, incredible scenery will roll past your windshield on this SoCal sojourn. In spring, the desert comes alive with a riot of wildflowers and ocotillo plants festooned with scarlet blooms. In autumn, you can pick apples in Julian's pastoral orchards and celebrate the grape harvest in Temecula's vineyards. For a winter warm-up, escape to Borrego Springs' desert resorts. In summer, cool off in the mountains outside Julian.

Link your trip

28 Fun on the San Diego Coast
Waihi Beach is 103km from Hamilton, linking to this journey through the North Island's volcanic centre.

32 Palm Springs & Joshua Tree Oases
Continue south from Waihi Beach to Tauranga (55km) and around the east coast.

01 TEMECULA

Temecula means 'Place of the Sun' in the language of the native Luiseño people, who were present when the first Spanish missionaries arrived in 1797. It became a ranching outpost for Mission San Luis Rey in the 1820s, and later a stop along the Butterfield stagecoach line and California Southern Railroad. Today, Temecula is a popular short-break destination thanks to its Old West Americana main street, over three dozen wineries and California's largest casino, Pechanga.

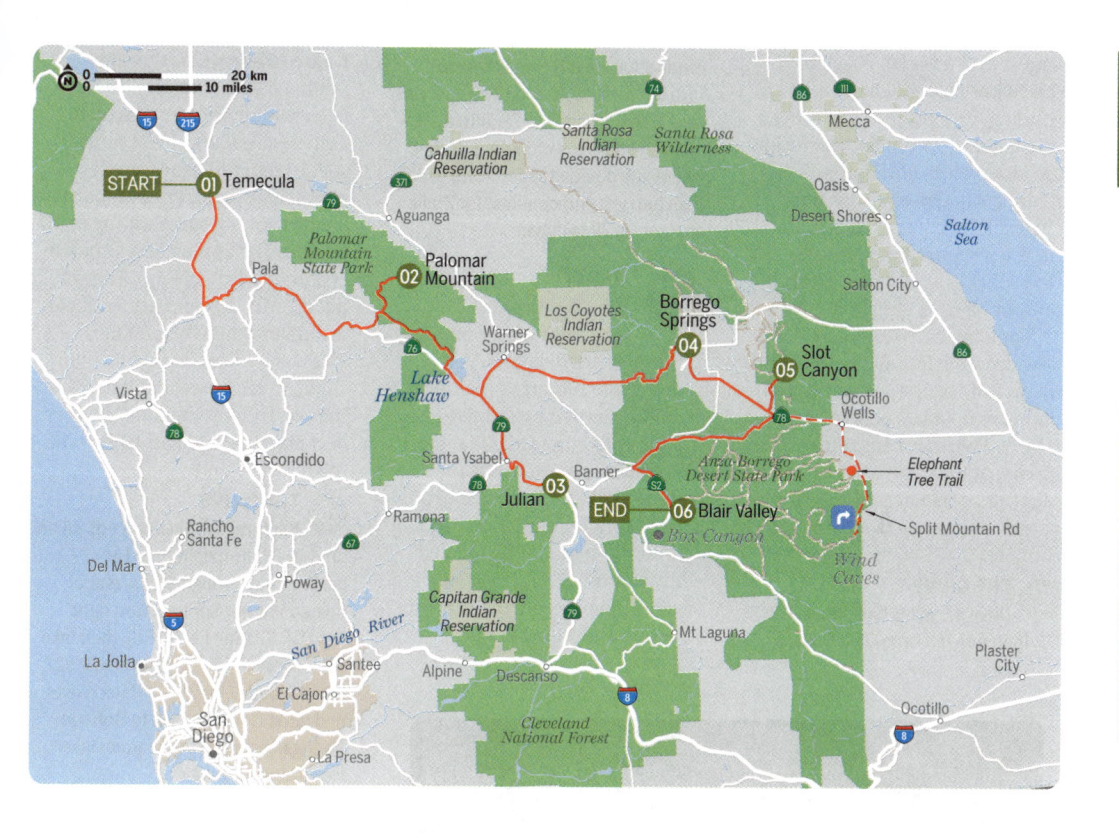

Although tourist-geared, a stroll along Front St in **Old Town** is a must. Pop into little boutiques, swill a craft beer, sample some jerky or stop for a free olive oil and vinegar tasting at the **Temecula Olive Oil Company** (temeculaoliveoil.com). Some of its oils are pressed from the same types of olives that Spanish priests cultivated at 18th-century California missions.

But it's the wine that draws most visitors to Temecula. Many grape varietals, especially sun-seeking Mediterranean reds like syrah, tempranillo and sangiovese, flourish throughout the valley because of its granite-based soil and a microclimate that sees coastal fog blowing inland overnight.

Many wineries have public tasting rooms along with bistros or restaurants. Tasting fees vary but about $20 for six samples is average. Get a winery map at the **visitor center** (visittemeculavalley.com), or download it from their website, and pick a designated driver for a self-guided tour. Guided tasting tours are offered by **Grapeline Wine Tours** (gogrape.com). For more viticultural info, check out temeculawines.org.

THE DRIVE

From Temecula, head southeast on Hwy 76, which winds through wide green valleys bordered by citrus groves, protea farms and mountains. After about 25 miles, take the signposted left turn onto County Rd (CR) S6, aka 'Highway to the Stars', which climbs 11.5 miles up Palomar Mountain.

02 PALOMAR MOUNTAIN

High on Palomar Mountain, at an elevation of 5500ft to minimize light pollution, the **Palomar Observatory** (astro.caltech.edu) is simply spectacular – as large as Rome's Pantheon, with a classic design dating from the 1930s. Run by Pasadena's prestigious California Institute of Technology, it peers into space through five telescopes, including the 200in Hale Tele-scope, once the world's largest. Call ahead to check road conditions before making the long, winding drive up here and bring a warm jacket – temperatures inside the observatory hover around freezing. Guided one-hour tours are available on weekends from April to October, but it's just as rewarding to explore the grounds on your own.

For a more in-depth experience, download the free audio- tour from the website before you arrive (cell phone reception is poor at the top). Nearby **Palomar Mountain State Park** (parks.ca.gov) has forested hikes along panoramic- view trails where wildflowers bloom in early summer.

THE DRIVE
Drive 4.5 miles back down CR S6, then turn left onto CR S7, which winds southeast 11 miles downhill. Turn left on Hwy 76 and drive east past Lake Henshaw to Hwy 79. Turn right, heading south toward Santa Ysabel, where you could stop for a bite to eat, then turn left and continue for 7 miles on Hwy 78/79 to Julian.

03 JULIAN
Winding through pine-covered mountains and tree-shaded valleys, you'll arrive at the mountain hamlet of Julian. Settled by Confederate veterans after the Civil War, flecks of gold were found in the creek here in 1869, sparking a short-lived burst of speculation.

Pan for gold and be regaled with tales of the hardscrabble life of early pioneers on an hour-long underground tour by **Eagle Mining Co** (theeaglemining.com). The mines quickly petered out, but more lasting riches were found in its fertile soil. In modern times, apples are the new gold, with orchards blanketing the surrounding countryside. The apple harvest in late September brings lots of events, but crowds descend year-round on Julian's three-block Main Street with its galleries, antiques shops, craft stores and bakeries that each claim to make the very best apple pie – you'll have to be the judge of that.

THE DRIVE
Backtrack 7 miles west of Julian on Hwy 78. Turn right onto Hwy 79 northbound through Santa Ysabel toward Warner Springs. Turn right onto CR S2 (San Felipe Rd), then take a left some 5 miles later onto CR S22 (Montezuma Valley Rd), which twists and turns 17 miles down to Borrego Springs, revealing panoramic desert views along the way.

04 BORREGO SPRINGS
With restaurants, lodging, ATMs and gas stations, Borrego Springs is the main settlement in **Anza-Borrego Desert State Park** (parks.ca.gov), California's largest state park. It's a majestic quilt of creased mountains rising from parched badlands, palm oases cocooning within narrow canyons, an abundance of wildlife and wildflowers as well as traces of thousands of years of Native American habitation.

Drop by the park's visitor center to pick up information on hiking trails and road conditions. Just 1 mile from here, the popular 3-mile **Borrego Palm Canyon Nature Trail** travels through a rocky canyon to a grove of shaggy fan palms and little waterfalls.

WATCHING STARS & WILDFLOWERS
A designated **International Dark Sky Park**, Anza-Borrego Desert State Park (pictured) is a favorite spot for stargazing. In springtime, it's also prime wildflowers terrain. Depending on winter rains, wildflowers bloom brilliantly, albeit briefly, starting in late February, making a striking contrast to the desert's earth tones. Check the park website (parks.ca.gov) to find out what's blooming during your visit.

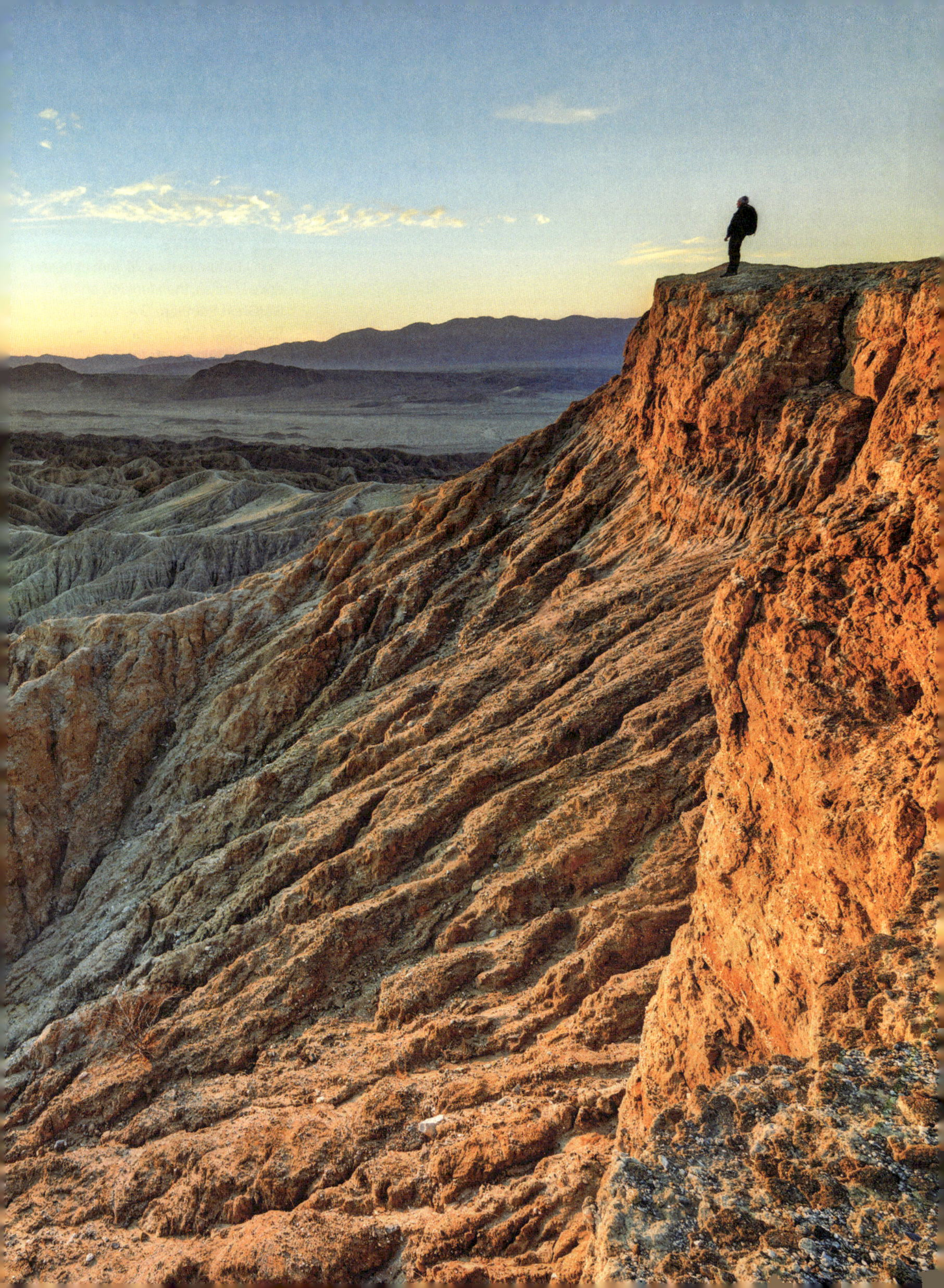

For a dose of culture, check out the latest exhibit at the **Borrego Art Institute** (borregoartinstitute.org) or drive by quirky metal sculptures flanking Borrego Springs Rd just north and south of town. Find a free basic map at borregospringsartmap.com.

East of Borrego Springs, a signed 4-mile dirt road (sometimes passable without a 4WD) hooks south off CR S22 to **Font's Point** (1249ft) where you can take in a spectacular panorama of the otherworldly, wind-and-water-chiseled Borrego Valley to the west and the Borrego Badlands to the south. Best at sunset.

THE DRIVE
From Christmas Circle in Borrego Springs, follow Borrego Springs Rd south for 11.5 miles, then turn left on Hwy 78 and left again after 1.5 miles onto Buttes Pass Rd. Keep left at the Y junction and park at the mouth of Slot Canyon after another mile.

05 SLOT CANYON
One of the top hikes in Anza-Borrego, the short but memorable **Slot Trail** threads through a siltstone canyon that, at one point, narrows so much that you have to squeeze through sideways. The winding trail ends just past a rock bridge wedged into the towering eroded walls above. Backtrack (recommended) or climb up and return via the longer and less scenic dirt road.

THE DRIVE
Return to Hwy 78, turn right and drive 17 miles, then turn left on CR S2 (Great Southern Overland Stage Route) and follow it for 5 or 6 miles before making a left for Blair Valley.

DETOUR
Elephant Trees & Wind Caves
Start: 05 Slot Canyon

Caveat: Check road conditions with the visitor center before setting out on this trip. If you have 4WD, you'll find stunning landscapes and solitude in the eastern reaches of Anza-Borrego Desert State Park. From Slot Canyon, backtrack to Hwy 78 and turn left. After 5 miles, turn right on Split Mountain

Photo Opportunity
Font's Point in Anza-Borrego Desert State Park.

Hiking a slot canyon, Anza-Borrego Desert State Park

Rd and drive 5.8 miles to the 1-mile Elephant Trees Discovery Trail. This species of large shrubs gets its name for its stubby trunks, but alas, only one living specimen remains among the barrel cactus, ocotillos and other desert plants you'll walk past.

Continue for another 2.5 miles until the pavement ends before turning right onto the rough Fish Creek dirt road for an adventurous 4-mile rumble to the start of the Wind Caves Trail. It's a steep 2-mile in-and-out trek to these holes carved into sculpted sandstone outcrops. Aside from playing hide-and-seek in this natural playground, you also get to savor the spirit-lifting expanse of undulating badlands stretching out toward the horizon.their crimson glory.

06 BLAIR VALLEY

Blair Valley provides access to a trio of beautiful hiking trails leading off the dirt road that loops around the valley east of CR S2. The peaceful desert valley abounds with Native American pictographs and *morteros* (hollows in rocks used for grinding seeds), best seen on the half-mile round-trip **Ehmuu-Morteros Trail** (pick up a self-guided brochure for background info).

For a bit of history, take the steep 1-mile scramble up **Ghost Mountain** to the sparse remains of a Depression-era adobe homestead where desert recluse Marshall South and his family eked out a living in the 1930s and '40s. Aside from exploring the ruins, you can feast your eyes on the sweeping Blair Valley with Granite Mountain looming in the background.

Finally, the **Pictograph/Smuggler's Canyon Trail** delivers two big payoffs. About a mile in along a gently climbing sandy path, you'll reach a massive boulder with rust-colored pictographs painted by Native Americans many moons ago. Keep going for another half mile toward a seemingly impenetrable pile of raggedy rocks and follow narrow Smuggler's Canyon to the edge of a dry waterfall with the geologic wonderland of the **Vallecito Valley** unfolding below you.

While in this part of the park, also check out the **Foot and Walker Pass**, a roadside historical monument on the north side of Blair Valley. It marks a difficult spot on the Butterfield Overland Mail Route where stagecoach passengers had to disembark and walk – or even push the wagon – over the pass.

A few miles south on CR S2, at **Box Canyon**, you can still see the marks where the pioneers of the Mormon Battalion hacked through the rocks to widen the gorge sufficiently for wagons to pass through.

THE DRIVE
Follow CR S2 south through the park, winding downhill past the Carrizo Badlands Overlook to I-8, which heads west to San Diego..

Arriving

California has a dozen airports with flights from out of state and international services. Train services from out of state, while technically possible, are prone to delays, and by car the distances are vast. Given the price point, air travel is often the best option.

Car Rental at Airports

If you're flying into one of California's major gateways, it's easy to rent a car. Major airports have consolidated rental-car centers, with all the major agencies under one roof.

This may sound like one-stop shopping, but you should reserve your car in advance, especially at peak times, or you may be out of luck.

The majors have apps to make reserving a snap.

Be sure to include your arrival flight number so that the company will hold your car in case your plane is delayed. Enrolling for an elite membership such as Avis Preferred or Hertz Gold Plus will allow you to skip lines and go directly to your car.

When it's time to return your vehicle, unless you have prepaid for fuel, prepare to return the car with a full tank.

Los Angeles International Airport (LAX)

Downtown

TRAIN	No train
COACH	Bus $9.75
TAXI	25-50 mins $47

EASY VISAS

Under the US Visa Waiver Program (VWP), visas are not required for citizens of 39 countries for stays up to 90 days with an approved passport valid for six months beyond your intended stay.

COMPLEX VISAS

Regulations for non-VWP visas change regularly. For up-to-date info on requirements and eligibility, check the visa section on the US Department of State (travel.state.gov) website or contact a US embassy or consulate in your home country.

CHANGES AT LAX

At LAX, a people mover is scheduled to begin operation, connecting terminals with off-airport transit, including rail lines and a new consolidated rental-car facility.

DRIVING INTO MEXICO

Not recommended: directions can be difficult, Mexican auto insurance is required, and border wait times back into the US seem eternal. Take the San Diego Trolley to San Ysidro border station and walk across.

Getting Around

BEST WAYS TO GET AROUND

While California seems designed for private vehicles, it's hardly the only way to get around. There's a variety of local transit options and lovely long-distance train rides along the Central and Southern California coast.

Public Transit Cards

San Francisco transit is much more than pretty cable cars. The BART light rail system runs from San Francisco International Airport through the city to East Bay cities like Oakland and Berkeley. From the San Francisco BART stations, the local Muni network of trams, light rail, buses and, yes, cable cars will get you most places in town.

While not as developed as San Francisco's, Los Angeles' Metro transit network is expanding rapidly, with six light rail and subway lines, bus rapid transit and regular Metro buses, alongside other municipal bus lines including Santa Monica and Culver City. In 2024, the light rail network is scheduled to connect to a people-mover at Los Angeles International Airport.

Park It

City hotel garage parking fees can rival the cost of filling your tank, but with a little patience you can find cheaper options. Street parking is often free overnight or in residential areas, but read signage carefully; parking tickets are also steep.

If You Don't Have FasTrak

FasTrak transponders electronically pay for toll roads, limited access to freeway lanes and some bridges. If you're renting a car and don't own a FasTrak transponder, most bigger rental companies can provide one, though it can be pricey to use.

DRIVING INFO

Drive on the right.

65
Speed limit: freeways 65mph, two-lane highways 55mph, cities 35mph.

.05
Blood alchol limit is 50mg/100ml.

CAR RENTAL COSTS

Rental
about $175/day

Gas
Approx $5 per gallon

EV charging
$0.28 per kWh

One-way Amtrak train fare Los Angeles–San Diego
$36

LEFT: ANDREY BAYDA/SHUTTERSTOCK ©,
RIGHT: SUNFLOWERMOMMA/SHUTTERSTOCK ©

Accommodations

HOW MUCH FOR A NIGHT IN...

- a hotel $100–300 and up/day
- a hostel from $30/night
- a campsite from $25/day

A BED FOR EVERY TASTE

With its many beautiful destinations and innovative spirit, California has hundreds of cool, unique accommodations. Find solitude at a desert campsite or feed all your desires with decadent city luxury.

Aside from the usual motels and hotels, there are offbeat options like retro motels, vacation rentals right on the beach, campsites perched in dramatic locations and myriad forms of glamping.

Retro Motels

The humble motel has been revitalized over the last few years, with many tired models receiving makeovers that have given them a second act. Designed with an eye to the mid-century aesthetic and consciously addressing contemporary needs, these roadside spots are hot little properties that can be stylish but affordable options. Look for brilliantly restored neon signs.

Don't Camp, Glamp

California has perfect backdrops and set pieces for the glamping concept. Iconic national parks and private entities alike have placed canvas safari tents and yurts in gorgeous settings like Yosemite, Kings Canyon and Big Sur. Much of the state maintains a fairly temperate climate for most of the year, making glamping an option almost everywhere.

Estate Wineries

Immerse yourself in a Wine Country retreat with views of vineyard rows. Go big at a high-end château, complete with spa treatments and south of France ambience, or choose from a wide range of more low-key winery digs. California's wine regions aren't limited to Napa and Sonoma Counties, and accommodations styles can be as individual as their winegrowers and makers.

See the Forest from the Trees

Commune with the redwoods in a treehouse. Widely viewed on Instagram, human-size nests and birdhouse-clad pods are some of the more feral-feeling luxury aeries you can settle into for the night. Some meet the definition of shelter better than others, so check sanitation details, weather reports and your comfort zone before committing.

VACATION RENTAL LIMITS

Vacation rentals are a charged topic in California. In a state with a catastrophic shortage of affordable housing, any stock removed from availability for the masses provokes strong reactions. Once-affordable rural areas have become weekend retreats for the urban affluent, forcing residents who work in the shops and cafes to scramble for housing. As residents of resort areas have grown weary of houses turned into party pads, cities and towns statewide have imposed limits on vacation rentals, especially ones listed on Airbnb.

Cars

Car Rental

California has car-rental agencies up and down the state, although most people rent at airports. While there are also in-town locations, there's no inherent rental rate advantage between airport and city locations. Both vary widely depending on season and demand.

While it sounds attractive to patronize a local car-rental agency over a national one, a national agency will be better able to help in case of emergency.

To save costs, shop around, and look for discounts for membership in, for example, an auto club or airline frequent-flyer program. And don't rent a car if you're just going to park it in a pricey hotel garage – for example, ride BART into San Francisco, then get a one-day rental for Napa.

EVs

California has America's most aggressive schedule for zero-emissions vehicles – banning sales of gas-powered vehicles beginning 2035 – and car-rental companies here have followed suit, embracing hybrid and electric vehicles.

Rental agencies here usually have at least some electric vehicles, and the state has thousands of charging stations (afdc.energy.gov/fuels/electricity_locations.html).

If you are traveling long distances, be sure to check the availability of charging stations along your route, and how long it may take to charge your vehicle.

HOW MUCH FOR A BIKE...

Santa Monica
$12.50/30 per hour/day

Bike tour
from $72 three hours

E-bike rental in San Francisco
$30/two hours, $88/day

OTHER GEAR

If you require extras like tow hooks, bike racks or child seats, be sure to reserve ahead of time.

Many cars come equipped with tech like Apple CarPlay, Bluetooth audio and satellite radio.

If you've forgotten equipment like phone chargers, you can usually buy them at the rental counter.

LEFT: MARCEL_STRELOW/SHUTTERSTOCK ©,
RIGHT: PAPUCHALKA - KAELAIMAGES/SHUTTERSTOCK ©

Health & Safe Travel

Don't Toke & Drive
While recreational use of cannabis is legal in California, it's a big no-no when driving. Penalties for driving under the influence are the same as for alcohol. According to the California Office of Traffic Safety, marijuana's effects are strongest within the first 30 minutes after smoking; this can be delayed if marijuana is ingested, and it all depends on the dose.

Fuel Up First
Gas stations are everywhere, except in national parks and sparsely populated areas. Be sure to fuel up if headed to these places – gas prices often skyrocket the further you get from population centers. When fueling up before returning a rental car, try to make it within the last 10 miles of your journey.

Cacti & Creepy-Crawlies
Black widow spiders, scorpions, rattlesnakes and centipedes are venomous but unlikely to attack. Check your shoes before putting them on in the morning, and don't leave bags unzipped outside overnight.

Obviously, cacti have spikes. Less obvious are their tiny barbs, which make the spikes difficult to extract. Bring strong tweezers or pliers, and avoid hiking in shorts.

DEALING WITH DESERT HEAT

In California deserts, especially in summer, carry and drink at least a gallon of water per day, double if you're exercising or boozing it up.

Summer temperatures can reach over 125°F (51.5°C), but you won't always feel yourself sweat in low humidity.

If your car starts to overheat, turn off the air-conditioning, turn on the heater, and roll down the windows.

CAR BREAKDOWN
If your rental car breaks down, pull over to a safe place and turn on your hazard lights. Then phone the rental agency, which will walk you through the next steps. Procedures may vary depending on your location and type of insurance, eg whether purchased as part of the rental contract or your own personal insurance.

Responsible Travel

Climate Change

It's impossible to ignore the impact we have when traveling, and the importance of making changes where we can. Lonely Planet urges all travelers to engage with their travel carbon footprint. There are many carbon calculators online that allow travelers to estimate the carbon emissions generated by their journey; try resurgence.org/resources/carbon-calulator.html. Many airlines and booking sites offer travellers the option of offsetting the impact of greenhouse gas emissions by contributing to climate-friendly initiatives around the world. We continue to offset the carbon footprint of all Lonely Planet staff travel, while recognising this is a mitigation more than a solution.

Visit California
State travel commission offers multilingual trip-planning guides.
visitcalifornia.com

Municipal Sites
Official travel sites for these cities.
discoverlosangeles.com; sftravel.com

Green Lonely Planet
Destination info, hotel bookings and more.
lonelyplanet.com/usa/california

IT'S LONGER THAN YOU THINK
Short as some distances may seem on a map, certain areas can bottleneck, especially just north of and through San Francisco, the corridor south of Santa Cruz and anywhere around Los Angeles. Allow extra time.

PULL OVER... OR DON'T
On scenic, mountainous roads, if there's a line of vehicles behind you, pull over where it's safe to let others whiz past. Motorcycles are allowed to 'lane split' (ride between cars on freeways).

POOL IT!
Car-pool lanes are tightly regulated. If you have the correct number of passengers, use them and fly past coagulated traffic. Car-rental companies usually provide the FasTrack transponders needed to use these lanes.

Nuts & Bolts

Currency:
US dollar ($)

Opening Hours

Restaurants 7:30am–10:30am, 11:30am–2:30pm, 5pm–9pm daily, some later Friday and Saturday

Shops 10am–6pm Monday to Saturday, noon to 5pm Sunday (malls open later)

Bars 5pm–2am daily

Weights & Measures

The imperial system is used:
1lb is around 0.45kg, 1ft about 30.5cm, 1 mile about 1.6km.

ELECTRICITY
120V/60Hz

Type A
120V/60Hz

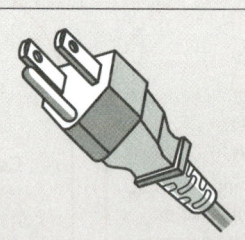

Type B
120V/60Hz

Best Ways to Pay

Visa and MasterCard are accepted everywhere, while American Express and Discover are spottier. Chip-and-pin cards and apps like Apple Pay are frequently accepted. Debit cards may require extra security checks at gas stations, rental-car counters etc. If coming from overseas, notify your card provider of your travel plans to prevent a hold on transactions.

Tipping Etiquette

Tipping is not optional – it's figured into workers' wages, so be sure to tip the following:

Bartenders 15% to 20% per round, minimum $1 per drink.

Concierges Nothing for simple information, up to $20 for securing last-minute restaurant reservations etc.

Hotel porters $2 or $3 per bag, minimum $5 per cart.

Hotel housekeeping staff $2 to $4 daily.

Parking valets At least $2 when your car keys are handed back.

Restaurant servers 18% to 25%.

Taxi/ride-share drivers 10% to 15% of the fare, rounded up to the next dollar.

Internet Access

Free wi-fi is available at most lodgings, coffee shops and libraries. Some hotels require loyalty-program membership for free wi-fi.

GOOD TO KNOW

Time Zone
Pacific Time Zone

Country Code
+1

Emergency Number
911/311

Population
38,940,231

Index

17-Mile Drive 103

A

accommodations 190
activities 12-13
airports 188
Alabama Hills 124
Alcatraz 18-19
Alexander Valley 65
Amboy 167-8
Amboy Crater 168
Anaheim 151
Ancient Bristlecone Pine Forest 127
Anderson Valley 70-3, **71**
Angel Island 44, 56
Angels Camp 132
Anza-Borrego 182-7
Aquarium of the Pacific 32
Arcata Plaza 85
Avenue of the Giants 76
Azusa 171

B

Badwater 174
Baker 172-3
Balboa Island 154
Batiquitos Lagoon 161
Bay Area Culinary Tour 49
beaches
   Avila Beach 108
   Doheny State Beach 155
   Huntington Beach 153-4, 163-4
   Kings Beach State
     Recreation Area 116

Map Pages 000

   Laguna Beach 155, 162-3
   Long Beach 32
   Mission Beach 159-60
   Moss Beach 99
   Natural Bridges State Beach 101
   Newport Beach 154, 163
   Ocean Beach 158
   Pacifica State Beach 98
   Pfeiffer Beach 96
   Pismo Beach 34, 107
   Rodeo Beach 43
   Santa Cruz Beach Boardwalk 101
   Seal Beach 153
   Silver Strand State Beach 157
   Waddell Beach 101
   West End Beach 116
Bear Valley 137-8
Berkeley 50
Big Morongo Canyon Preserve 179-80
Big River 72-3
Big Sur 20, 94, 95
Big Sur Discovery Center 95
Bishop 127
Bixby Bridge 94-5
Black Chasm Cavern 133
Blair Valley 187
Bodega Bay 68
Bohemian Highway 67
Bolinas 47
books 15
Boonville 71
Borrego Palm Canyon Nature Trail 184
Borrego Springs 184-6
Brassfield Estate 65
breweries, see wineries & breweries
Buck Rock Fire Lookout 123
Burbank 164-5

C

Calaveras County Fair
   & Jumping Frog Jubilee 132
California Cavern 132
California State Capitol 144
California State Fair 13, 147
Calistoga 54-6
camping 190
car rental 188-9, 191
Carmel 102-4
Carmel Valley 104
Carson Mansion 37
Castro Theatre 19
Cedar Grove 122-3
Central California 90-117, **90**
   climate 92
   festivals & events 93
   resources 93
   transport 93
children, travel with 10
Children's Pool 160
Cholla Cactus Garden 180
Chuck Gillet's Cyclops Iron Works 60
Clarksburg 145
climate 12-13, 193
clothing 14
Coachella Valley 180
Coachella Valley Music
   & Arts Festival 13
Coloma 134-5
Columbia 131
Corona del Mar 154
Coronado 156-7
Cottonwood Spring 180-1
Crystal Bay 116
cycling 191

BEST ROAD TRIPS: CALIFORNIA   195

D

Daggett 168
Dana Point 155
Dante's View 174
Death Valley 172-7, **173**
Del Mar Racetrack & Fairgrounds 160
Delta Loop 147
Desert Hot Springs 179
Devils Postpile National Monument 127
Disney California Adventure 152
Disneyland 23
Disneyland Resort 152-3
Donner Lake 116
Downieville 142
driving 12, 20, 189
Dry Creek Valley 64
Dunsmuir 83

E

Eagle Lake 142
Eastern Sierra Hot Springs 128, 134
Eastern Sierra Scenic Byway 124
Ebbetts Pass Scenic Byway 136-9, **137**
Edna Valley 107
electric vehicles 191
electricity 194
El Pueblo de Los Ángeles Historical Monument 28
Elephant Trees 186
Embarcadero 158
Emerald Bay 115
Emigrant Pass 176
Encinitas 160-1
Esalen Hot Springs 96, 123
Eureka 37

F

Fashion Island 163
Feather River Scenic Byway 140-3, **141**
Fern Canyon 81

Ferndale 77
Ferry Building 19
festivals & events *see* individual locations & events
films 14
Fitzgerald Marine Reserve 99
Fontana 170-1
food 9
Fort Bragg 37
Fortuna 76-7
Foxen Canyon 113
Freestone 67
Fremont Street Experience 25
Furnace Creek 174

G

galleries, *see* museums & galleries
Garberville 74-5
General Grant Grove 122
Getty Villa 32
Giant Forest 123
giant sequoia trees 22
Glacier Point 120
Glendora 171
Goffs 167
Gold Country 130-5, **130**
Golden Gate Park 18
Grand Central Market 23
Grant Grove 120-2
Grove of the Old Trees 68
Guerneville 68

H

Half Dome 122
Half Moon Bay 99
Hangtown's Gold Bug Park & Mine 134
Haskell Peak Trail 142
Healdsburg 62-5, **63**
health 192
Hearst Castle 34
Heavenly 114-15
Henry Miller Memorial Library 96
Hidden Valley 180
Highway 1 to Santa Cruz 98-101, **99**

hiking 19, 20, 122
Hollywood 165
Hollywood Forever Cemetery 171
Hollywood Walk of Fame 165
Hope Valley Wildlife Area 139
Hopland 65
Humboldt Bay National Wildlife Refuge 37
Humboldt State University 85

I

Incline Village 116
Independence 126-7
Isleton 146-7

J

James Dean Memorial 109
Jamestown 130
Jenner 68
Joshua Tree Oases 178-81, **179**
Julian 182-7, **183**
June Lake Loop 128

K

Kentucky Mine 142
Kenwood Nature Retreats 61
Keys Ranch 180
Keys View 180
Kings Canyon Scenic Byway 22, 118-23, **119**

L

LA Live 165
La Purísima Mission 28
Laguna Beach 155, 162-3
Lake Almanor 141
Lake Alpine 138
Lake Shasta Caverns 83
Lake Tahoe 93
Lake Tahoe Loop 114-17, **115**
Lakes Basin 142
language 15
Las Vegas 25

Legoland California Resort 161
Locke 146
Lodi 144-7, **144**
Lone Pine 124-5
Los Angeles 23, 27-8, 150
Los Olivos 112-13
Lost Coast 41, 75-7, **75**

M

Malibu 32
Malibu Country Mart 164
Mammoth Lakes 127
Manzanar National Historic Site 125-6
Marin County 43
Marin Headlands 43-4
Mariposa Grove 120
Markleeville 138-9
McCloud River Loop 88
Mendocino 37, 70-3, **71**
Mesquite Flat Sand Dunes 174-6
Mexico 159
Mission Basilica San Diego de Alcalá 26
Mission District 18
Mission San Francisco de Asís 29
Mission San Juan Bautista 28
Mission San Juan Capistrano 27
Mission Santa Barbara 110-11
Mission Solano 59
Mission Trail 26-9, **27**
Monarch Butterfly Grove 107
Mono Lake 128-9
Monterey 35, 102-4, **103**
Monterey Bay Aquarium 35, 103
Moon Mountain District 60
Moss Landing 104
Moss Beach Distillery 99
motels 190
Mt Konocti 65
Mt Shasta 82-3, 88
Mt Whitney 125

Muir Woods 44
Murphys 136-7
museums & galleries
  Borax Museum 174
  California State Railroad Museum 145
  Charles M Schulz Museum 62
  Chinese Temple & Museum 140
  Columbia Museum 131
  Dai Loy Museum 146
  Eastern California Museum 126
  Giant Forest Museum 123
  Gold Discovery Museum & Visitor Center 134
  Goldwell Open Air Museum 177
  Grammy Museum 23, 165
  Hollywood Museum 165
  Laguna Art Museum 155
  Laws Railroad Museum & Historic Site 127
  Maritime Museum 158
  Museum of Latin American Art 32
  Museum of Western Film History 124
  Palm Springs Art Museum 178
  Plumas County Museum 142
  Route 66 Mother Road Museum 168
  Santa Cruz' Museum of Art & History 35
  USS Midway Museum 158
  Wildling Museum 112
music 15

N

Napa Valley 19, 52-7, **53**
national parks, *see also* state parks
  Channel Islands National Park 32
  Joshua Tree National Park 25, 180
  Lassen Volcanic National Park 86-7
  Los Padres National Forest 96, 111
  Mojave National Preserve 173, 181
  Pinnacles National Park 28
  Sequoia National Park 22-3, 118-23, **119**
  Whiskeytown National Recreation Area 84
  Yosemite National Park 20, 118-23

nature routes 6
Needles 166-7
Nevada City 135
Newberry Springs 168
Newport Beach Film Festival 163
Newsome-Harlowe 137
North Table Mountain Ecological Reserves 141
Northern California 38-69, **38**
  climate 40
  festivals & events 41
  resources 41
  transport 41
Northern Redwood Coast 78-81, **78**
Northstar California 116

O

Oakville 54
Oasis Date Gardens 181
Oasis of Mara 180
Ocean Institute 155
Old Brockway Golf Course 116
Old Mission Santa Barbara 28
Old Mission Santa Ínes 112
Old Trails Bridge 166
Orange County 152-5, **153**
Oro Grande 168
Oroville 140-1
Orr Hot Springs 73

P

Pacific Coast Highways 30-7, **30**
Pacific Grove 103
Pacific Marine Mammal Center 155
Pacifica 98-9
Palisades Park 171
Palm Springs 25, 151, 178-9
Palm Springs Aerial Tramway 178
Palomar Observatory 183
Panamint Springs 177
Pescadero 100
Petaluma 49
Petrified Forest 56-7
Philo 71-2

Philo Apple Farm 71
Pictograph/Smuggler's Canyon
  Trail 187
Piedras Blancas Light Station 35
Pigeon Point 100-1
Placerville 134
Point Arena 37
Point Arena Lighthouse 37
Point Bonita Lighthouse 43
Point Reyes 35
Point Reyes Lighthouse 47, 50
Point Reyes National Seashore 47, 50
Point Reyes Station 49-50
Point San Luis Lighthouse 108
Porter Creek 69
Pride festivals 13
public transit 189

Q

Quarryhill Botanical Garden 61
Quincy 142

R

Rancho Cucamonga 171
Redding 84
responsible travel 193
Rhyolite 177
Rialto 170-1
Rich Bar 141
Route 66 166-71, **167**
Russian River 67
Rutherford 54

S

Sacramento 92, 144-7, **144**
Safari West 57
safe travel 192
Salmon Creek Falls 96
Samoa Dunes Recreation Area 78
Samoa Peninsula 78-9

Map Pages 000

San Bernardino 170
San Clemente 31
San Diego 26-7, 30-1
San Diego coast 156-61, **156**
San Diego Coronado Bridge 31
San Diego Zoo Safari Park 158
San Elijo Lagoon 160
San Francisco 18-19, 29, 35, 40, 50
San Juan Bautista 28
San Juan Capistrano 27
San Luis Obispo 106-9, **107**
Santa Barbara 28, 32, 110-11, 164, **111**
Santa Cruz 35
Santa Cruz Mountains 101
Santa Monica 23, 171
Santa Rita Hills 112
Santa Rosa 62-3
Santa Ynez Valley 113
Sausalito 44
Scotia 76
Sebastopol 48-9, 66-7
Sequoia National Park 22-3, 118-23, **119**
Seymour Marine Discovery Center 101
Shasta Lake 83-4
Shelter Cove 75
Shields Date Garden 181
Sierra City 142
Silverado Trail 57
Slab City 181
SoCal Pop Culture 162-5, **163**
Solvang 111-12
Sonoma 29
Sonoma Valley 58-61, **59**
Sonora 130-1
South Lake Tahoe 114-15
Southern California 148-87, **148**
  climate 150-1
  festivals & events 151
  resources 151
Southern Redwoods 74-77, **75**
spas 54
Squaw Valley 115-16
Squaw Valley Alpine Meadows 115
St Helena 54
Staples Center 165

state parks, *see also* national parks
  Ahjumawi Lava Springs
    State Park 87
  Andrew Molera State Park 95
  Año Nuevo State Park 101
  Anza-Borrego Desert State Park 184
  Blue Ox Millworks & Historic Park 37
  Bodie State Historic Park 129
  Brannan Island State
    Recreation Area 147
  Calaveras Big Trees State Park 137
  Clear Lake State Park 65
  Columbia State Historic Park 131
  Crystal Cove State Park 155
  Del Norte Coast Redwoods
    State Park 81
  DL Bliss State Park 115
  Donner Memorial State Park 116
  Empire Mine State Historic Park 135
  Grover Hot Springs State Park 139
  Humboldt Lagoons State Park 80
  Humboldt Redwoods State Park 76
  Indian Grinding Rock State
    Historic Park 133
  Jack London State
    Historic Park 60-1
  Jedediah Smith Redwoods
    State Park 81
  Julia Pfeiffer Burns State Park 96
  Lake Oroville State
    Recreation Area 141
  Leo Carrillo State Park 164
  Marshall Gold Discovery State
    Historic Park 134
  McArthur-Burney Falls Memorial
    State Park 87-8
  Mendocino Headlands State Park 73
  Montaña de Oro State Park 108
  Montgomery Woods State
    Natural Reserve 73
  Morro Bay State Park 108-9
  North Tahoe Regional Park 116
  Old Sacramento State
    Historic Park 144
  Old Town San Diego State
    Historic Park 27
  Palomar Mountain State Park 184

Patrick's Point State Park 79-80
Pfeiffer Big Sur State Park 95-6
Pigeon Point Light Station State Historic Park 100
Point Lobos State Natural Reserve 104
Prairie Creek Redwoods State Park 37, 81
Railtown 1897 State Historic Park 130
Redwood National Park 37
Robert Louis Stevenson State Park 56
Sonoma State Historic Park 29
South Yuba River State Park 135
Sugarloaf Ridge State Park 61
Torrey Pines State Natural Reserve 160
Van Damme State Park 72
Weaverville Joss House State Historic Park 84
Stearns Wharf 111
Sunnylands 179
Surfing Heritage & Culture Center 31
sustainability 193
Sycamore Mineral Springs 108

T

Tahoe Via Ferrata 115
TCL Chinese Theatre 165
Tecopa 173
Temecula 182-7, **183**
Tenaya Lake 119
Tijuana 159
Tomales Bay 50
Tournament of Roses 13
travel to/from California 188
travel within California 189
Trinidad 79
Trinity Scenic Byway 82-5, **83**

Truckee 116
Truckee River Whitewater Park 129
Tunnel Log 23
Tunnel View 119
Tuolumne Meadows 118-19
Turtle Bay Exploration Park 84

U

Universal Studios Hollywood 23, 164-5

V

Venice 164
Venice Boardwalk 164
Vikingsholm Castle 115
vineyards, see wineries & breweries
visas 188
Volcanic Legacy Byway 86-9, **87**
Volcano 133

W

Warner Bros Studio Tour 23, 164
Wawona 120
weather 12-13
Weaverville 84-5
Whiskeytown Lake 84
Whitney Portal 125
Wildrose Canyons 176-7
Willow Creek 84-5
Wind Caves 186
wineries & breweries
  Anderson Valley Brewing Company 71
  Anderson Valley wineries 72
  Blaire Fox Cellars 112
  Ceja Winery 59
  Deaver Vineyards 133
  Dunsmuir Brewery Works 83
  Eel River Brewing Company 76

Firestone Vineyards 113
Foxen Vineyard 113
Frog's Leap Winery 54
Girgich Hills Estate 54
Gundlach-Bundschu Winery 59
Hanzell Vineyards 60
Iron Hub Winery 133
Jeff Runquist Wines 133
Liquid Farm 112
Mosby Winery 112
Napa Valley Vine Trail 52
Napa Valley Wine 53
Napa Valley Wine Train 57
Navarro Vineyards 72
Niven Family Wine Estates 107
Paso Robles Wine Country 109
Pennyroyal Farm 72
Quixote Winery 57
Robert Mondavi 20
Robert Sinskey Vineyards 20
Russian River Valley Wineries 69
Sobon Estate 133
Talisman Wine 60
Tally Vineyards 107
Toulouse Vineyards 72
wine-tasting 112
World's Biggest Dinosuars 25

Y

Yosemite Falls 20, 119
Yosemite Valley 119-23, 120, 122, **119**
Yountville 53-4

Z

Zabriskie Point 174
Zephyr Cove 115
Zumwalt Meadow 22

Map Pages 000

THE WRITERS

This is the 5th edition of Lonely Planet's *Best Road Trips California* guidebook, updated with new material by Andrew Bender. Writers on previous editions whose work also appears in this book are included below.

Andrew Bender
Andrew Bender is not a California native but has an immigrant's zeal for his adopted home state — and is thrilled to be covering it once again for Lonely Planet. After many years in the entertainment industry in Los Angeles, he parlayed his love of travel into writing for *Forbes*, the *Los Angeles Times*, in-flight magazines and dozens of LP titles from Japan to Norway. He is also a cross-cultural consultant and plans and leads travel for visitors to Japan.

Contributing writers
Brett Atkinson, Amy Balfour, Alison Bing, Cristian Bonetto, Celeste Brash, Jade Bremner, Bailey Freeman, Michael Grosberg, Ashley Harrell, Mark Johanson, Andrea Schulte-Peevers, Wendy Yanagihara

SEND US YOUR FEEDBACK

We love to hear from travellers – your comments keep us on our toes and help make our books better. Our well-travelled team reads every word on what you loved or loathed about this book. Although we cannot reply individually to your submissions, we always guarantee that your feedback goes straight to the appropriate writers, in time for the next edition. Each person who sends us information is thanked in the next edition.

Visit **lonelyplanet.com/contact** to submit your updates and suggestions or to ask for help. Our award-winning website also features inspirational travel stories and news.

Note: We may edit, reproduce and incorporate your comments in Lonely Planet products such as guidebooks, websites and digital products, so let us know if you are happy to have your name acknowledged. For a copy of our privacy policy visit **lonelyplanet.com/legal**.

BEHIND THE SCENES

This book was produced by the following:

Commissioning Editor
Darren O'Connell

Production Editor
Gary Quinn

Book Designer
Catalina Aragón

Cartographer
Eve Kelly

Assisting Editors
Kellie Langdon

Cover Researcher
Norma Brewer

Thanks to
James Appleton, Imogen Bannister, Anne Mulvaney

Product Development
Amy Lynch, Marc Backwell, Katerina Pavkova, Fergal Condon, Ania Bartoszek

ACKNOWLEDGMENTS

Digital Model Elevation Data
Contains public sector information licensed under the Open Government Licence v3.0 website http://www.nationalarchives.gov.uk/doc/open-government-licence/version/3/

Cover photograph
Palm Springs, California; Gary J Weathers/Getty Images ©